GOING*south*

An Inside Look at Corruption and Greed, and the
Power of the HealthSouth Message Board

WILLIAM CAST, MD

Dearborn™
Trade Publishing
A **Kaplan Professional** Company

This publication is designed to provide accurate and authoritative information in regard to the subject matter covered. It is sold with the understanding that the publisher is not engaged in rendering legal, accounting, or other professional service. If legal advice or other expert assistance is required, the services of a competent professional should be sought.

President, Dearborn Publishing: Roy Lipner
Vice President and Publisher: Cynthia A. Zigmund
Senior Acquisitions Editor: Michael Cunningham
Development Editor: Karen Murphy
Senior Project Editor: Trey Thoelcke
Interior Design: Lucy Jenkins
Typesetting: Caitlin Ostrow

Published by Dearborn Trade Publishing
A Kaplan Professional Company

Printed in the United States of America

05 06 07 10 9 8 7 6 5 4 3 2 1

Library of Congress Cataloging-in-Publication Data

Cast, William.
   Going south : an inside look at corruption and greed, and the power of the HealthSouth message board / William Cast.
      p. cm.
   Includes bibliographical references and index.
   ISBN-13: 978-1-4195-2017-4
   1. Corporations–Corrupt practices–United States–Case studies.
2. Business ethics–United States–Case studies. 3. Accounting fraud
–United States. 4. HealthSouth (Firm)–Accounting.   I. Title.
   HV6769.C37 2005
   364.16'3–dc22
                                   2005022373

Dearborn Trade books are available at special quantity discounts to use for sales promotions, employee premiums, or educational purposes. Please call our Special Sales Department to order or for more information at 800-621-9621 ext. 4444, e-mail trade@dearborn.com, or write to Dearborn Trade Publishing, 30 South Wacker Drive, Suite 2500, Chicago, IL 60606-7481.

Contents

Introduction

This is the story of a crime of the Internet age. Its heroes are a complex community of individuals scattered over 2,000 locations in 50 states. Its villains are a group of corporate executives, under the command of a powerful leader, Richard Scrushy, who perpetrated a $2.7 billion fraud. The story takes place in Birmingham, Alabama—and in Indiana, Pennsylvania, Washington, D.C., and towns and cities across the nation. And it also takes place in a virtual community, which gathered and communicated through the World Wide Web using a simple Yahoo! message board.

I'm not the first person to write about Richard Scrushy and the corporate scandal surrounding HealthSouth, the company he created and built into his personal empire. Scrushy has occupied the media spotlight for some time now, appearing on national television and in articles written by talented journalists at major publications such as the *New York Times*, the *Wall Street Journal*, and *Forbes* and *Fortune* magazines.

When he became the first corporate executive to be tried under the Sarbanes-Oxley Act, business writers and bloggers around the world began detailing the daily events of Scrushy's indictment, federal trial, and eventual acquittal. But I have written this book also to tell the story of a group of HealthSouth's employees and investors who banded together to save their jobs, pensions, and investments—and much of it is told in their own voices. I'm one of those people, too—a surgeon who lives and works in Indiana, and who, for a brief and painful time, was part of the HealthSouth story.

>>> OUR HEALTHSOUTH STORY BEGINS

I knew nothing of Richard Scrushy until 1998, when my surgical center suddenly became a HealthSouth partner. Our happiness over the partnership didn't last long, however, as we were introduced quickly to the "rules" of the HealthSouth family. Scrushy's organization dictated every facet of our operation, from replacing our waiting room artwork with approved company posters and a portrait of Richard Scrushy, to mandating that Coca-Cola would be the only beverage allowed in our facility. More disturbingly, all of our accounting records and financial activities were moved to company headquarters in Birmingham, Alabama. Soon after the buyout, our center's revenues and our own salaries began to drop steeply. Financial reports were late in arriving, and none of us could understand where our center's earnings had gone.

Within the year, we surgeons parted company with Health-South. As we fought through months of legal wrangling, I had ample time to become curious about this bizarre chain of events. Top Wall Street analysts praised HealthSouth's financial strength and unbroken successes, but how could this picture be true? Nothing in the mainstream media reports about Scrushy and HealthSouth could explain to me how our experience with his company could have been so uniquely unprofitable. So I began digging a little deeper for information.

Through Internet searches under the company name, I stumbled across the Yahoo! HealthSouth finance message board. Reading the messages of posters such as **Bopper63, going_to_niceville, rodeo46, I_AM_DIRK_DIGGLER, HealthBizz,** and **rehab1KL**—all people who worked for or with HealthSouth—I realized that my center's experience with the company was far from unique. Many of the posters on the message board were not happy with their experiences with HealthSouth and Richard Scrushy. I remained a member of the message board even after my own center's split from HealthSouth was finalized, and through years of posting and reading messages, I began to form a much clearer picture of the HealthSouth organization and its leadership.

In 2002, outside sources joined in the chorus of complaints and questions I'd been reading on the message board. Headlines in the popular press finally began to raise questions about insider trading and operational excesses that the message board's posters had discussed for years. When HealthSouth announced that the Securities and Exchange Commission (SEC) had launched an investigation into whether the company had delayed disclosing to the public the expected financial impact of new Medicaid and Medicare billing regulations, many of us began to speculate as to the fate of HealthSouth and its leaders.[1] Then, on March 19, 2003, after the SEC filed formal charges,[2] the FBI raided HealthSouth's corporate headquarters, the board of directors put Scrushy on leave, top officers pled guilty to fraud, and the stock plummeted. Thousands of employees were threatened with the loss of both their jobs and their pensions.

HealthSouth's employees and small investors might have been ruined by this turn of events, as sinking company stock values drained away their retirement plans and pension funds. Analysts predicted bankruptcy for HealthSouth, and the stock was delisted and devalued. As the first waves of panic set in among investors on the Yahoo! HRC (the stock symbol for HealthSouth) message board, none of us could have predicted that the crash would create the investment opportunity of a lifetime—a chance for those who had lost everything to recoup those losses and much more. And none of us guessed that our fellow participants on the message board would lead the way toward that financial opportunity. In those fast-moving days that followed the raid and the stock delisting, I studied the message board and was swept along with the wave of traders and bottom feeders that rushed in to profit from the remains of the wrecked corporation. I followed federal indictments and congressional hearings wondering who was behind the fraud, who would be found guilty, and who would escape punishment. And I decided to risk an investment in a dime stock no longer listed on an exchange—something I would never have dreamed of doing before. And, though I didn't realize it at the time, I had begun to write this book.

In this book, I've outlined the story of the events that led up to the exposure of the fraud at HealthSouth, the convictions of some of those involved in the fraud, and the sensational trial and acquittal of the company's founder and leader during the time of the fraud, Richard Scrushy. But I didn't set out just to tell that story. I've written this book to tell about the people I met through my own experiences with HealthSouth. I wanted to explore the implications of the online information sharing and collaboration that we participated in through the Yahoo! HRC finance message board, and its implications for other investors. The Internet made it possible, for example, for former HealthSouth employees, such as **Scooterpass,** to talk with **The Dow Bum,** an engineer and risk analyst, and for them to share and distill information for the entire message board community. Also thanks to the Internet, most on the message board could buy and sell stocks online and participate in one of the wildest months of trading in this history of the stock market.

I also wanted to show the changing nature of information, by exploring yet another instance of the pervasive changes introduced through online communication. During the month that followed the FBI raid and HealthSouth "meltdown," analysts and Wall Street pundits were universal in their predictions of gloom for the company—repeating the same bits of "news" using the same stock phrases. The message board and several blogs, however, offered employees and investors real information. Their insights and varied perspectives represented the best information available anywhere on the changing fortunes of this giant corporation. I wanted my book to help explain how to use and evaluate this kind of message board information, so others could learn to supplement their understanding of current events with data that isn't always available in the mainstream press.

Although I've turned to published accounts in the mainstream media for some of the information contained in this book, my research also included personal contacts with other message board participants through phone and e-mail communications. The people I met on my Internet journey were engineers, business leaders, stock traders, accountants, physical therapists, physicians, secretaries, lawyers, and retirees. Though the group came from a variety of backgrounds and experiences, they had in common their investment in Health-South and an interest in reporting the truth about the company's arrogant culture from the very first day.

I am indebted to the dozens of HealthSouth employees who stuck with the company and the message board through terrible times. I thank many who became friends and who allowed me to quote their messages. I am also grateful to blogger Phil Smith, who attended Richard Scrushy's trial each day, and who reported what he saw there on his Web log. And, of course, I am also incredibly grateful to my wife, Anita, who saw me too often during the course of the past many months only in the glow of a computer screen.

CHAPTER *one*

Entering the Kingdom

I was in surgery when the circulating nurse stuck a pink note, reading "Call your office," to the door. Pink sticky-notes are rarely good news. Between cases, I dialed my office manager, Mary, expecting to be called to the emergency room and hoping that it was not a family call. This time, however, my fears were unfounded; the news seemed good, or so I thought at the time. Mary told me that American Surgical Centers, Inc. (ASCI)—the national company my surgical group had partnered with—was no more. After September 1997, I would be partnered officially with HealthSouth, Inc.

Before joining ASCI, my company had been an independent center. Founded in 1972 in Fort Wayne, Indiana, it was the second free-standing ambulatory surgical center in the country. Because of the growth of outpatient services and the increasing financial pressures of managed health care, we had formed a joint venture with ASCI. We knew that partnering with such a group would give us the purchasing and contract advantages of a large company. So, after considering a number of suitors, and visiting in Pasadena with ASCI's CEO David Hall, we had decided to become part of the company.

We signed the agreements and the transition to ASCI could not have been smoother. According to the agreement we'd negotiated, we surgeons would retain majority interest in the property. As general partners, ASCI would lease from us and own the majority of operations, a clean new operating company with no baggage and no cumbersome properties to depreciate. ASCI, of course, was merely preparing their company for sale, merger, or stock offering (the nation was in its heyday of roll-ups and public offerings). The agreement made a clean sale and increased the return on investment and equity.

While we were with them, ASCI was a perfect partner— David Hall ran a good operation, and Mike Kincaid, the midwestern territorial manager, worked hard to help us grow. And we wanted to grow; in fact, we thought our survival depended on it. Managed care was sweeping the U.S. health care industry, and it took no genius to see that insurers, preferred provider organizations (PPOs), and health maintenance organizations (HMOs) preferred to deal with big health care groups that could offer lower rates and tighter cost controls than could smaller operations. Insurance companies always mention quality in their advertisements, but cutting costs was the order of the day; bigger was better in the eyes of major insurers. Our center took in new surgical groups and soon had our six operating rooms filled with general surgeons, urologists, gynecological surgeons, and gastroenterologists, in addition to my own ENT (Ear, Nose, and Throat) group.

Then, in 1997, I got the call from Kincaid, telling me that HealthSouth had swallowed our group whole in what, it seemed, would result in little more than a name change for us. At the time, I didn't know much about HealthSouth except that it had facilities in Indiana and Ohio. HealthSouth was huge in the realm of outpatient health care, however, and some of the other doctors in my group were familiar with the company. HealthSouth was a rehabilitation company expanding rapidly into imaging and ambulatory surgery. The company's clinical reputation was good, by all reports. Richard Scrushy, the company's CEO, was already known for his aggressive growth strategy, and he had developed one of the hottest names in health care. We looked at HealthSouth's stock price and saw a pot of gold—HealthSouth shares had increased in value steadily since 1986. We had joined a winning health care group! We celebrated our good fortune.

HealthSouth flew me to Atlanta to shake hands with company officers and meet other doctors who had recently joined their family. I met with Pat Foster, then vice president in charge of our operations, and a room full of HealthSouth executives. Along with other partners-to-be, I saw a slide show about HealthSouth and its near-miraculous success. The HealthSouth representatives assured me that the company was going to be the biggest provider of surgery in the world, and they wanted us to be a part of the team. Everyone was pleasant and seemed eager to meet me and listen to details about our small surgical facility. I returned with a catalogue of HealthSouth logo-emblazoned goods—coffee cups, T-shirts, key chains—that I could buy for my employees, and the unmistakable impression that the HealthSouth guys never stopped selling.

Still, I was pleased when Foster and his accountant flew to Indiana to meet with us. They toured our facility and we went for a long lunch, over which I told the two men a bit of my center's history. We were early into ambulatory surgery and had learned from beginner's errors. Our facility had been designed like a hospital operating suite—in essence, like Henry Ford's assembly line. Patients entered at one end and came out the other, though later experience taught us to design our flow in a circle so that a smaller staff of nurses could see both incoming and outgoing patients. We knew a lot about ambulatory surgery and about the most important feature of all: communicating with patients at home pre-op and post-op.

As I told him about our group's evolution and the systems we'd developed, Foster nodded politely and his accountant ate his lunch in silence. I was mildly worried. It was obvious that our new partners weren't keenly interested in what we knew about ambulatory surgery, and they didn't seem to have an extensive knowledge of the topic themselves. Foster and the accountant then left, not to return. Scrushy had reorganized HealthSouth into East and West outpatient divisions, and he had assigned Foster to the West. In Indiana, we found ourselves under the direction of HealthSouth's East Vice President, P. Daryl Brown.

By all evidence, Foster hadn't passed on much background information about our operation to Brown; it seemed all past communication between our company and HealthSouth was lost to record. Brown's training and experience were in physical therapy, but he exhibited no doubt or hesitation about overseeing the operations of a surgical facility. The company had plans for us that did not bear the imprint of our opinions, and Brown and other corporate representatives soon focused their attention on bringing us into compliance with the HealthSouth model.

HealthSouth posters arrived, several bearing an inexplicable rendering of stickmen pulling a wagon. Our office manager, Mary, was told to take down our current office artwork and hang the company posters. A large photograph of HealthSouth CEO Richard Scrushy also arrived at our offices, and Mary was instructed to hang it in a prominent place in our waiting area. She also was required to spread the word: "Everyone will learn to spell Mr. Scrushy's name correctly." Within a short period, my small surgical group had been transported into some sort of parallel universe, where HealthSouth ruled supreme.

Under ASCI, Mary's duties had focused on coordinating patients' needs with those of our staff, equipment safety, employee training, and financial flow. Under HealthSouth's management, Mary's responsibility was to tend to a 50-item Pristine Audit checklist, every day: Is the bathroom clean? Is there a paper cup littering the parking lot? Is Mr. Scrushy's photograph hanging straight and in a prominent position? Mary also was subject to unannounced audits by Ernst & Young, financial accountants whose firm Scrushy paid $1.3 million or more annually to conduct "Pristine Audit" inspections. The Ernst & Young auditors would report transgressions, such as a disorderly janitor's closet, to Birmingham directly. If reported, Mary would be called from Birmingham and told to correct irregularities immediately.

HealthSouth's intrusion was not limited to meddling in the waiting room and our office manager's routine. With no notice, surgeon partners were told HealthSouth preferred to justify records on a quarterly basis, and therefore, financial statements would no longer be issued monthly. Employees would be paid twice monthly, but surgeons would receive their checks after each quarter closed. HealthSouth's Birmingham operation took over records, purchases, and as best I could determine, all other decisions for our Fort Wayne facility. Mary sent every invoice, every bill, all account information, and our payroll to headquarters; we had no checkbook.

Communications were abysmal. We dealt with a merry-go-round of accountants in Birmingham, and seldom were we able to talk to the same person twice. It was obvious that the Health-South accountants were busy with something other than paying our bills. Our surgeons' checks were late, our creditors—the banks—received our mortgage check late, and our suppliers called us frequently to inquire about unpaid bills. We surgeons received calls at home from friends in supply and services businesses, who wanted to know why—after several years of steady and reliable business—we were no longer paying our bills. In addition to the sheer embarrassment of the situation, as doctors, our credit ratings and reputations were at risk. The surgeons complained vigorously, both to Mary in our local office, and to HealthSouth directly. But, Mr. P. Daryl Brown would not hear of any change to HealthSouth's system. Those in our office were astounded at the oppressive atmosphere that Health-South was imposing upon us, but Birmingham quickly let us know that the legal contracts required our compliance.

Then, HealthSouth's bizarre intrusion began to cross the grain of our intrinsic organizational culture, as the company began meddling in our surgical routines. Surgeons tend to be mavericks, accustomed to chaos and schedules that frequently are interrupted by random emergencies. But when it comes to a surgical case and the performance of each task within the surgical procedure, surgeons are creatures of habit; they like a certain suture, a particular needle, a specific retractor. Health-South was proud of its ability to buy supplies centrally and cheaply. To make the business brutally lean, Scrushy demanded conformity in all matters, including surgical supplies. Without warning, new supplies and equipment were supplied to our surgical suites.

When surgeons are equipped with unfamiliar surgical equipment and supplies, a delicate surgery can become much more difficult and unpredictable. To make unnecessary adjustments or to be distracted by minor changes in equipment and supplies reduces the surgeon's protection of experience and promotes error. A middle ear being suctioned under the tenfold magnification of a microscope, offering a sixteenth of an inch leeway for access, is best done using suction tubing that does not torque, twist, or pull away from the surgeon. Cheap tubing is often stiffer, and though it might be adequate for some surgeries, it isn't good enough for others, and only the surgeon performing the operation knows which type of tubing is necessary for each procedure. Multiply this problem by dozens of suture types—nylon, Dacron, silk, gut, etc.—and hundreds of instruments, lenses, telescopes, and devices, and you quickly grasp the scope of potential problems that can evolve.

Surgeons will, when prodded by peers, agree on basics, and they are quite capable of making do until corrections are made or shortages remedied, but for all the reasons I've stated, they change routine only after long trial, testing, and general concensus. Never do they want new supplies dumped in the ER on orders from the front office. Many of our surgeons had come to our facility to avoid the bureaucratic dictates of hospitals and large clinics. Having HealthSouth mandating even our smallest surgical procedures from its Birmingham headquarters was worse than working with a local hospital, where at least the administrator was at hand for negotiations. Complaints to HealthSouth's Birmingham headquarters went unanswered. Among our surgical group, the demand that "we must do something" grew louder.

Oddly, the tipping point—in the form of a seemingly unimportant HealthSouth directive—involved the break room. Orders came from Birmingham that all 2,000 HealthSouth facilities would comply with new rules for what type of sodas and snacks would be offered or consumed within the premises. Coca-Cola would be the official beverage of HealthSouth, which meant no Snapple or Pepsi products would be allowed in its refrigerators or vending machines. And with that intrusive demand from Birmingham, our willingness to remain loyal subjects in the HealthSouth land of Oz ended. We told Mary, "No deal. Just tell them no. And take down those stupid posters."

The ripple effect was painful; this proved to be the final straw for Mary. Trapped between directives from her new boss in Alabama and the growing anger of the surgeons she worked with every day, she fled. When offered the director's job at a competing surgical center, she left along with our chief surgical nurse and a couple of good OR techs. HealthSouth responded by assigning a regional manager, Becky, from Toledo to manage our center. Her territory included Indiana and parts of Ohio and Kentucky, so she traveled a lot. But when she was on site, she was quick to see our problems; and because she knew people in Birmingham, she was better at promoting our interests and issues to them.

Through all of this, our center's numbers had declined and profits were down significantly. None of the revenue-producing factors had changed at our facility. The case loads, margins, costs, and collection rates should have produced the same cash flows as in the past. Only the people running the ledgers had changed. We didn't understand their accounting, and we couldn't understand why reporting continued to fall farther and farther behind; we had not had a clear financial statement in six months. Most of all, we wondered where the money went.

We asked Becky about our numbers. She felt that we needed special accounting help at headquarters and arranged for us to contact "the right person" in Birmingham. She had noticed trouble with numbers before; sometimes, she said, she would turn in numbers from her district only to see them changed at headquarters. If we'd been listening closer, we might have heard the first rumblings of the storm clouds that were gathering over HealthSouth even then.

P. Daryl Brown flew into town for a quarterly meeting to soothe the restless surgeons. He brought me a case of Pepsi, and we had long conversations about a smoother transition. He was new, he said, getting his arms around the job, the territory, but he liked our facility. "Let's give it time," he advised. We met at the Summit Club for a dinner discussion of HealthSouth's accounting, but he had little new information for us. A number of surgeons had taken our new financial statements to their personal accountants, and came back with targeted complaints. Now, a representative of each surgical group was at the table, and they peppered Brown with questions: "Where are our checks?" "Why are profits down, when business is steady?" "What's the purpose of this account called 'Reserves'?" "Where did these new costs come from?" "Why doesn't this sheet agree with our last report?" Brown summed up, replying, "Don't worry; we'll fix it real soon." But none of the problems were "fixed." Thinking back, I wonder if he could have fixed them if he'd tried.

We issued an ultimatum: "Fix it by next meeting, or we are out of here." Becky, our new HealthSouth manager, was not hopeful. She said, "They do something with the numbers when they get them. When I complained, 'Boss, those aren't my numbers on that sheet,' he replied, 'That's none of your business.'"

The final meeting was again at the Summit Club, in the 25th-floor dining room. The surgeons sat around the table at the appointed hour, but Brown did not appear. We sat, growing angrier as we waited, until Brown and his entourage walked in having just finished a nice meal at a local jazz club. "Good steaks!" he reported. Financial reports were handed out and everyone turned straight to the bottom line—and it was not satisfactory. The room was silent for more than 20 minutes. We did not speak. Brown did not speak. Finally, one of our surgeons, Jeff, said the only words possible for our group: "Not good enough." We left the room, and I never again saw P. Daryl Brown.

We began the process of our separation from Health-South, and soon realized our debt to David Hall of ASCI. HealthSouth had done its due diligence poorly; the company had bought so many centers and in such big clusters that it had glossed over the fine details of our deal. HealthSouth seemed unaware that it held sole fiscal responsibility for our Fort Wayne facility lease—even if our surgeons left the center to work at other clinics or hospitals. Our surgeons refused to bring their usual work to HealthSouth, and month-by-month the red ink flowed from Fort Wayne to Birmingham. Lawyers paraded through the halls and lingered for many billable hours over coffee and dusty documents. Eventually, we reached an agreement and bought out HealthSouth's interest in our operation. I suspect they were glad to leave, and the feeling was returned.

Business returned to its previous levels and we became, once again, an autonomous, freestanding surgical center with no national partner. Scrushy's initial advantage, namely better pricing for outpatient physical therapy, already was being eroded. We hired Becky away from HealthSouth; she was good (Pat Foster had been right about that much) and she ran the facility with great ease. We fine-tuned our acquisitions of supplies, so we had complete approval over the equipment we worked with and were still able to save money on its purchase. Becky expanded our direct marketing and recruited a pain practice to join our center. By the time we had installed our own electronic medical records, we were in our best condition ever.

But our separation from HealthSouth, like any divorce, had been grinding. While the process of negotiations and legal drafting was time-consuming and expensive, it still left me with plenty of time to try to figure out exactly what had happened to us. I began doing more digging, more reading into HealthSouth's business record. Nothing seemed to explain our experience. HealthSouth had sterling Securities and Exchange Commission (SEC) reports. Year after year, every quarter HealthSouth met analysts' projections, solved industry problems, borrowed more money, and gobbled up more competitors—each deal bigger than the last. But this unbroken chain of financial success simply didn't align with my group's unprofitable experience with Richard Scrushy and his health care empire.

In hindsight, it became apparent that HealthSouth had grown too fast to properly integrate with its new centers or to know the details of its acquisitions. HealthSouth's accounting systems were chaotic and personnel turnover in the lower levels of accounting too great to comply with the simplest request for change or review. The company's management culture was arrogant, unwelcoming to suggestions, and was based on experience obtained almost exclusively in physical therapy. Centralization of all functions was fatal, given the Birmingham office's inability to digest critical observations from their own people. Even HealthSouth vice presidents seemed to lack options for change. I called friends in Indianapolis and Evansville, Indiana, and yes, they were very aware of the craziness at HealthSouth; that was the way the company operated.

Still needing answers, I turned to the Internet and conducted searches under the terms "HealthSouth" and "Richard Scrushy." I found thousands of hits, because of the extensive industry coverage of HealthSouth's amazing growth and Scrushy's personal notoriety. Scrushy was a regular in the Alabama press, both for founding HealthSouth and because many of his charitable contributions resulted in roads, buildings, and college campuses that carried his name. The man's appetite for recognition seemed limitless.

I checked Edgar, the official site of the SEC, which carries all official reports for traded companies. There, I had access to all of HealthSouth's quarterly and year-end reports, all of which matched the information I'd already learned from other published sources. But for inside news, nothing could touch the message boards, and Yahoo! had the corner on messages regarding HealthSouth. To reach HealthSouth's message board, I merely went to http://www.yahoo.com and typed the HealthSouth trading symbol (HRC) in the symbols box. That produced a screen showing a grid of the company's financial values, alongside a list of related information pages maintained by Yahoo!. One of these was a hyperlink named Message Board. I clicked the link, and was taken to a page filled with messages written by posters with aliases such as **bopper63, scooterpass, JRM30655, sharecropper,** and **figpooh.** Many message topic lines featured comments and questions that alluded to Scrushy's reputation and behavior, as well as to HealthSouth's bizarre corporate culture.

Reading the messages, I soon learned that the message board was populated by stock traders, disgruntled employees, and health care workers—those who lauded the company and those whose only purpose was to bash their supervisors, HealthSouth in general, or Scrushy himself. The company had enjoyed a slow but steady increase in stock price since 1986, but by the late 1990s explosive growth had taken company shares from $5 to $10, then to $20, and then $30. With such success, investors and traders on the message board were looking upward; they didn't welcome the criticism of HealthSouth employees, and chose to focus instead on new acquisitions.

Not everyone on the message board was looking at growth, and many unhappy employees who posted to the board made a good case for themselves. Some, like me, had become partners through merger. Other posters were local doctors, therapists, and nurses. Not everyone was critical, but too many were. No one denied Scrushy's ability or autonomy; still, most agreed that he dominated his board of directors and intimidated his own company officers. I noted with interest, for example, message #52 by **ezmd,** which was written early in 1998 and later removed from the message board: ". . . it seems that the company has grown too big for it's britches. LT Debt is stifling and managed care contracts are becoming unmanageable . . . this company manages to spend money like it's water. If more Wall Street "gurus" knew what was really going on inside this company I think there would be a blood bath in this company's stock. If you thought yesterday's 5 percent drop was scary wait until earnings come out—talk about a sacrifial lamb!! Richard Scrushy, the CEO, boasts that the company has "never missed it's earnings." Mr. Scrushy, NEVER SAY NEVER."[1]

I also took note of message #82, by **LocalMD,** which was written on February 16, 1998: "I am an MD with some rather unfortunate dealings with HRC operations. It seems to me that they are great with acquisitions, but that their management in operations leaves a lot to be desired. I bailed out of the stock a month ago at 24½ and I am still waiting for their earnings report. When is it coming?"[2]

After that first day in 1998, reading the Yahoo! board became one of my daily rituals. I read messages from **Blackie** and **Swirlingturd; rehab1KL** and **HealthBizz; Mansion House** and **SisterSavant; Jeff_Sux** and **I_AM_DIRK_DIGGLER.** Nearly all would respond to my posts, and many would correspond directly with me by e-mail. I had a list including **bopper63, scooterpass, JRM30655, inman, The_Dow_Bum, fAt, Bhambamalady, BernieBildeman,** and **Corstrat** with whom I could chat by cell phone. Getting updates from these message board posters was like being at another HealthSouth clinic, at a trading room, or even on the executive floor of company headquarters, just below Scrushy's penthouse offices. And four years later, when a series of small lawsuits and litigations erupted into a full-blown SEC investigation and Scrushy's ouster from the company he'd built, when the mainstream media was filled with stories of Scrushy, his bizarre leadership style, and the shaky practices of his tottering behemoth, I had to ask myself the same question that had drawn me to the message board in the first place: How could any of this have happened?

What didn't make sense, even considering the growth and stock market profits that masked fraud at Scrushy's operation, was the perplexing lack of critical thinking and reporting by media and analysts who covered HealthSouth and its leader. Scrushy certainly hadn't maintained a low profile, and the message board contained messages from hundreds of people who were talking openly of serious problems the mainstream media failed to mention. Wall Street's analysts also remained uninterested and seemingly unaware of the information on the Yahoo! message board, even after Scrushy sued to have some messages removed, bringing national attention to critical posts. Long before the March 2003 raid on HealthSouth's gleaming headquarters in Birmingham, Alabama, I knew something was wrong at the company; my experience and those of many participants in the Yahoo! message board confirmed it. But none of us could have guessed the extent of the scandal that was brewing.

As I think back to my early experiences with HealthSouth, a comment made at that long-ago, get-acquainted lunch with Pat Foster lingers in my mind. I had asked him to consider an immediate change in surgical center structure, and asked if he would consider discussing the change with Scrushy. Foster, his face drawn in something less than a smile, had said, "Many times I don't get to go into Mr. Scrushy's office. Mr. Martin and Mr. Scrushy go into his office and huddle there alone, while I sit in the waiting room." With that comment, I had learned that this vice president wasn't a HealthSouth insider. And though I didn't understand this situation at the time, remembering it did help me later understand why Foster wasn't indicted along with Scrushy, Martin, and other HealthSouth officers.

Following the raid, the mainstream media had jumped on the investigative bandwagon, and many journalists explored the man *Fortune* magazine dubbed the "the insatiable King Richard."[3] Not surprisingly, common sense had been the best guide for my small surgical group in Fort Wayne, Indiana, when we escaped from the HealthSouth kingdom. There was no parallel universe; HealthSouth wasn't a financial dynamo. It was a company whose corporate officers—some of those officers, at least—were hiding the financial realities of its indulgence in unmanaged growth, corporate excess, and flawed oversight. Analysts were asleep, and no one was looking beneath Richard Scrushy's overblown hype to try to discover the real story of the man and the company he created and controlled.

CHAPTER two

The Legend of HealthSouth

By now, many sources have told the story of Richard Scrushy and HealthSouth. Scrushy can and does lay claim to modest beginnings and uses his history effectively on his Web site and in personal radio and television talk shows. His post-indictment "News Service" Web site (subtitled "Setting the Record Straight") offered an online biography that opened with the statement: "Born in 1952 in Selma, Alabama—a town known as the birthplace of the civil rights movement—Richard Scrushy is now fighting for his own rights and freedoms in the face of false allegations." The biography goes on to state that Scrushy is "clearly the visionary who created HealthSouth from the ground up, listing the company on the New York Stock Exchange, consolidating the industry into an efficient operation, aligning the company with excellent physicians across the country, and overseeing approximately $6.5 billion in strategic acquisitions." About his federal trial for money laundering, conspiracy, and securities fraud, Scrushy's bio said only that "Richard is working diligently to clear his good name of the false accusations being made against him in connection with the alleged fraudulent activities of HealthSouth. He also focuses on the real-estate development business, Marin, Inc., and assists his wife Leslie with her company, uppseedaisees."[1]

To document his rise to fame, Scrushy has helped to create a more permanent record of sorts. In 2001, as HealthSouth CEO, Richard Scrushy sought the services of Write Stuff Enterprises and writer Jeffrey Rodengan to craft a book about his company—a book that would tell the world of his struggles and accomplishments in building a Fortune 500 health care company from a tiny group of physical therapy clinics. *The Story of HealthSouth* remains essentially a flattering and expensive promotional piece about Scrushy's adventures as an entrepreneur—a sanitized chronicle of the company's less well-known early years and the series of successful ventures that culminated in the creation of one of the world's leading health care companies.

Another version of Scrushy's personal history was told to the jury in Birmingham Federal Court in January of 2005, by his defense attorney, Jim Parkman. Parkman portrays himself as an authentic southern "character," whose down-home approach prompted one writer from the *Wall Street Journal* to observe: "With his good-ole-boy manner and deep southern drawl, Mr. Parkman is more accustomed to representing defendants accused of driving drunk than executives facing 58 counts of corporate corruption."[2] In his opening statement, Parkman described how Scrushy elevated himself above humble beginnings and eventually went on to form the fledgling business that would become HealthSouth with four trusted associates, a one-room office, a folding table, and four chairs. Parkman proudly told the jurors: "Did you know in the beginning that because they only had four chairs, one of the founding members of HealthSouth had to stay at home and do the work there because he couldn't sit down? They didn't have enough chairs to do it."[3]

But there is much more to Scrushy's bootstraps story than Scrushy, Parkman, or *The Story of HealthSouth* have revealed. Of all the accounts of Scrushy's early years, one of the most detailed and interesting comes from a July 2003 article in *Fortune* magazine, written by John Helyar, titled "The Insatiable King Richard."[4] That article is worth reading in full, but here, I'll offer just a brief overview of the profile of Scrushy's early years that is presented in Helyar's story.

>>> SCRUSHY'S EARLY YEARS

Richard Marin Scrushy was born in 1952 in Selma, Alabama. Scrushy's father, Gerald, sold cash registers; his mother, Grace, was a nurse. Scrushy attended Selma's Parrish High school, where he went by his middle name, Marin.[5] By all indications, his high school experience was unremarkable. He participated in few school activities (none were listed under his name in his school yearbooks), but was deeply interested in playing in local garage bands. He wasn't good enough to lead the bands, but he was able to limp along with such local musical talent as The Born Losers. When Scrushy's high school sweetheart, Debbie Cody, became pregnant with his child, Scrushy's world changed. He married Debbie, dropped out of school, and took a job pumping gas. When a second child was born, Scrushy went to work as a bricklayer to support his family.[6]

In spite of these discouraging realities, Scrushy's mother knew that he was smart enough to do better things with his life. According to Helyar, she told her son that hospitals had a growing need for respiratory therapists, and at her urging, Scrushy finally returned to school and got an education the way many who must struggle upward do, through local community colleges. After getting his GED, Scrushy attended

Wallace State Community College, then went on to study for one year at Jefferson State Community College in Birmingham. After another year of clinical training at the University of Alabama, Scrushy graduated in 1974. Over the next five years, he worked in relatively low-level jobs, teaching or managing respiratory therapy programs. He divorced his first wife, and was married again, this time to Karen Brooks.

Then, in 1979, Scrushy was hired by Lifemark, a Houston-based hospital chain that was hungry for the abundance of Medicare money available at the time. This was the event that would lead to Scrushy's later great fortune in the health care industry. Scrushy had an abundance of energy and chutzpah and, in 1983, he also had a great idea. The key to his success was a single prediction—that government regulation in the form of payment changes would hurt hospital inpatient reimbursement and help boost outpatient profits. Scrushy was well aware of profits to be made in outpatient therapy, especially so long as government programs continued to exclude physical therapy from prospective payment programs. So, when Lifemark was acquired in 1983, Scrushy decided to leave the company, along with four of his colleagues, to start his own physical therapy business. Scrushy, Aaron Beam Jr., Anthony Tanner, and Eugene Smith incorporated their business in Birmingham on January 23, 1984.[7] Scrushy was on his way to becoming a full-blown entrepreneur and corporate success.

Richard Scrushy was in the forefront of care for injured workers, at least temporarily. He recognized the commercial value to employers when physical rehabilitation returned injured workers more quickly to their jobs, saving everyone money. Because he had begun his career as a physical therapist, Scrushy knew clinical physical therapy and understood its economics. By 1986, HealthSouth had made it to the big time. The company had gone public and reported over $20 million in annual revenues.[8]

Growth was steady until the early 1990s. The balance sheets of other companies were hurting after market turmoil in 1987, but Scrushy cleverly had the foresight to raise an additional $22 million with a secondary stock offering, so he was poised with cash for acquisitions. He began to buy hospitals and clinics, such as Pine Island Sports Medicine Clinic. He also acquired Neurologic Rehabilitation Systems of Detroit and the Columbia, South Carolina, Rehabilitation Hospital, and hospitals in Largo, Florida, and Charlotte, North Carolina. As his small company grew larger, Scrushy took pride in being involved in every aspect of the operation, and it was reported that he read and responded to every letter sent to the company.[9]

It was in 1990 that *Forbes* magazine took notice of HealthSouth's growth and pointed out the company's prominence in health care. It reported that Scrushy owned 8 percent of the company's 10 million shares, a market capitalization of $224 million. In its glowing account, *Forbes* also speculated that HealthSouth's only problem was living up to Wall Street's expectations. But to anyone following the news, that was no problem at all. HealthSouth's earnings were up 50 percent that year, causing Scrushy to comment: "Operations are off to a very good start."[10]

At that time, HealthSouth ran 14 inpatient rehabilitation centers and 31 outpatient centers in 21 states. Scrushy was credited with bravado, street smarts, and almost prescient business acumen by an industry publication. In a May 1991 interview in *Rehabilitation Today*, Scrushy revealed one of the keys to his company's success: ". . . lack of executive perks, cars . . . country club memberships . . . We were lean and mean when we started and we want to keep it that way."[11] Were that ever true, his style began to change as the company grew into the 1990s. As Scrushy's company—and personal wealth—grew, Scrushy took time to enjoy one of his original loves—he organized his own country band, and named it "Proxy." Bill Owens, now HealthSouth controller, joined the band as a drummer. When Proxy landed a gig at a local venue, Scrushy would let HealthSouth vendors know where and when the band was performing, just in case they wanted to turn up and show their enthusiasm for Richard Scrushy and his music.[12]

Scrushy had been among the first to see that the era of venture capital roll-ups and public offerings in health care favored growth for his company. Small companies, he knew, could not deal with either increased competition or large capital needs; they could not survive the onslaught of managed care by HMOs and PPOs. In fragmented industries such as the optical business and physical therapy, venture capitalists purchased "ma and pa" businesses for somewhere around twice their annual earnings, bundled them into a larger company, claiming (or so their numbers showed) synergies of size, then issued a public stock offering and sold the companies at six or more times their rate of earnings. Aware of the benefits of this strategy, Scrushy began what would become a decade-long strategy of growth fueled by acquisition. Scrushy rolled up the rehabilitation business and then he rolled up ambulatory surgery into his operations. He financed those acquisitions by selling more of his popular, high-profits-to-earnings-ratio stock and issuing bonds. Wall Street was eager to lend him money: HealthSouth margins were the highest in the industry, and each year showed more growth.

In 1992, Scrushy created three divisions: Medical Centers headed by Larry House; Rehabilitation Hospitals headed by James Bennett; and Outpatient Centers headed by P. Daryl Brown. HealthSouth was named to 1992's *Forbes* list of 200 Best Small Companies, an honor that required a five-year annual return on equity (ROE) of over 9.5 percent and sales and earnings growth of 8 percent.[13]

In December of 1993, Scrushy expanded on his strategy of buying a few units at a time and began to acquire whole companies; he boldly doubled the company's size by acquiring 28 rehabilitation units and 45 outpatient centers from National Medical Enterprise for $350 million. HealthSouth was now the nation's biggest rehabilitation enterprise. The year 1994 ended with revenues of $500 million and total assets of $1.5 billion. HealthSouth had 18,000 employees in 33 states. Scrushy also bought a new corporate jet that year, which he piloted.[14]

For 1995, Scrushy planned even more acquisitions. He began by acquiring Surgical Health Corporation (SHC) in Atlanta and then NovaCare in King of Prussia, Pennsylvania. In August, he bought California-based Sutter Surgery Centers' 12 facilities for $37 million. The buying spree continued: Caremark International sold HealthSouth its 120 outpatient rehabilitation centers located in 13 states; and Scrushy's last acquisition that year was Advantage Health Corporation in Boston, adding two more states with 156 facilities. HealthSouth now operated in 42 states and only Columbia HCA was a bigger health care company. The board of directors rewarded Scrushy with a $5 million bonus.[15] This bonus effectively doubled what he had been paid in 1994.[16]

Scrushy wisely tapped into the glitzy image of sports medicine both for public relations hype and to add younger patients to his company's rehabilitation roles (a move calculated to decrease HealthSouth's dependence on older patients and low reimbursement from Medicare). He instituted a sports medicine program and recruited sports stars to promote the company's image in that growing field.[17] Orthopedics, neurology, and neurosurgery became profitable sources of referrals to Scrushy's physical therapy business, and they provided high-profile, marketable services. Scrushy missed no opportunity to entertain reporters and politicians with demonstrations of lasers, MRI machines, and such advances as the radiation Gamma Knife.

Staff members of that period now say that much of the vaunted corporate culture portrayed by the company and praised by reporters was fiction, and everyone in management knew it. Scrushy ruled over his workers with an iron fist, as many would later attest to on the Yahoo! financial HRC message board. As HealthSouth gobbled up health care facilities across the country, managers of those facilities learned to fear the "Pristine Audits" conducted for Scrushy by the accounting firm of Ernst & Young. The accountants would monitor such small details as the cleanliness of a facility's parking lots to the "attitudes of the receptionists and the taste of the food."[18] Any problems were reported to Birmingham and brought swift reprisals from HealthSouth headquarters.

Scrushy devoted increasing time and corporate assets to his musical hobby, too. He formed a commercial band named Dallas County Line, and recruited professional musicians from Nashville who were experienced in playing for such bands as The Oak Ridge Boys. He was the band's composer, promoter, lead vocalist, and lead guitarist. A video of Dallas County Line was featured at HealthSouth meetings. Scrushy often flew the band members to Nashville for practice, and he even flew them to Australia as part of the band's much-vaunted "Down Under Tour."[19] The band had the use of a HealthSouth building that was equipped with expensive, modern recording gear. Members of the band also held executive positions at HealthSouth. Bill Owens was among them as was Ken Livesay, who also had been an accountant at Ernst & Young.

Scrushy often filled upper-level positions with people who hadn't previously held such substantial—or high-paying—positions.[20] The stock options that he offered his executives gave them ample reason to tolerate Scrushy's demanding form of micromanagement. And, as Helyar notes in his account for *Fortune,* "Scrushy cared less about what people in the trenches thought than about what people on Wall Street did. His pay was closely tied to the stock price, and HealthSouth's shares rose 60% in 1995 alone."[21]

>>> HEALTHSOUTH CROSSES THE LINE

But, while Scrushy may have had the money and influence to "buy" success for his musical group, he wasn't able to bluff his way around the corporate stage he now occupied. As Scrushy strayed into hospital management, physician practice management, diagnostic imaging, and ambulatory surgery, his judgments became less acute, and HealthSouth's profits suffered. Slowly and for a long time unnoticed by analysts, the company's errors began to multiply. And by 1997, the news from Washington was bad: Congress's Medicare overhaul bill, passed that year and set to go into effect in 2002, was going to seriously diminish payments to medical service providers. Medicare was responsible for a sizeable portion of HealthSouth's revenues. In spite of this bad news, however, Scrushy never faltered in his public assurances that the change wouldn't impact HealthSouth's profits.

Even before the Medicaid announcement, however, the financial situation at HealthSouth had prompted its leaders to look for some way to mask the company's fiscal realities. The company's rapid acquisition of health care facilities had helped mask profit shortfalls in previous years, but by the second quarter of 1996, HealthSouth CFO Aaron Beam knew that the company's revenues were not going to meet analyst predictions. In the past, the company had made use of a number of "aggressive accounting" maneuvers to make financial reports look their best. But this time, as Beam would later testify in court, those solutions wouldn't solve the problem. Beam told the court that when he delivered the news to Scrushy and explained to him that there were no legal means for adequately adjusting the financial report, Scrushy simply said, "Fix it."[22]

Beam went on to testify that Bill Owens did just that, inflating the company's reported profits by approximately $7 million. Although this sum wasn't staggering for a company the size of HealthSouth, it set off a series of fraudulent reports that would escalate quickly in scale. In its federal indictment, the government asserted that over the next five years, Health-South would inflate its earnings statements by approximately $2.7 billion.[23] In his own court testimony, Owens would say about that first "fix": "Unfortunately, it's a line once you cross it, it is difficult to cross back."[24]

Scrushy, apparently unfazed, continued to indulge in his entertainment interests, buying more planes for the company's growing fleet (and for the use of his new band). Scrushy also completed construction of HealthSouth's $50 million, 150,000-square-foot headquarters on 74 acres south of Alabama Interstate 459. He approached the property from a private road reserved for his use. Inside, Scrushy had builders install (in addition to his private elevator) a grand wrought-iron curving staircase that ascended to his penthouse aerie and was used only by those who had the clearance of his radio-equipped guards. The top floor featured a personal trophy room, complete with a replica of his first office and desk (much as Thomas Edison's laboratories are preserved in Fort Meyers and Menlo Park). He commissioned special statuary of his own design for outside the building entrance: a group of oversized stainless steel stick-men pulling a wagon.[25] "Pulling the Wagon" became his mantra for the company, and he placed the image on posters in HealthSouth facilities. If employees saw irony in the stainless steel message of teamwork decorating a building so royally equipped for executive privilege, they wisely remained silent.

Scrushy was also beginning to exhibit grandiose and seemingly paranoid behavior that would alternately alarm and annoy many who worked at headquarters. By now, he had an armored BMW, and bodyguards accompanied him to the Monday morning meetings. And some around the office began whispering that he could listen in on the phone lines of HealthSouth officers.[26] Scrushy continued to elevate his style:

more and bigger jet airplanes, increasingly splashy show business ventures, and grand vacation mansions in Palm Beach, Florida, and Lake Martin, Alabama. His Lake Martin mansion was a vanity extreme even for the "King," as Scrushy was coming to be known among some employees. Local comment had it that Lake Martin was Scrushy's revenge for being denied membership in the Birmingham Country Club. The lake palace was home to his seaplane and huge cigar boats, in which he frequently roared around the lake, much to the annoyance of the more sedate lakefront property owners.[27]

Scrushy launched HealthSouth show business in a big way by starting a road show for children called "Go for It!" featuring sports stars who gave lectures on fitness in a highly charged, MTV-like atmosphere. It featured laser lights, dancing girls in costumes, and games that Scrushy said combined entertainment with a healthful message. The early shows were successful and HealthSouth hired buses to fill arenas with school children.[28] Not all parents approved of the show-girl atmosphere, however, especially as the dances and the costumes became increasingly titillating. As Helyar's article in *Fortune* notes: "Teachers who'd brought their classes for inspirational messages instead found 3rd Faze shaking their booty. Some marched their kids right out."[29] Scrushy brushed aside criticism, however, and broadened his stage show into a television program. Meanwhile, the company's financial problems were multiplying with each false quarterly report.

If any single event could serve as metaphor for Health-South's corporate culture in the late 1990s, it would be the company's annual meeting. Employees called it The Prom. Becky, a district manager, recalled the 1996 meeting in a phone conversation with me: "I believed back then," she said. "They told me that it was none of my business when I pointed out to my boss that our numbers were reported wrong. Things didn't make sense to me, but I believed in the company, and The Prom was a blast. Mr. Scrushy flew employees and spouses to Orlando and put us up in a fine hotel. The Prom was a black tie affair and HealthSouth provided tuxedos for the men. The boss came onstage in a huge BMW; he got out with music playing and laser lights and took the microphone to give us a pep talk: Things were great and going to be better. I remember him dressed in black leading his band, The Dallas County Line. He played really good, for a CEO. Looking back, I can't believe that I fell for all of that."[30]

Another ex-employee, **Scooterpass,** who became a regular message board visitor and who carefully disguised his identity by posting as a young woman, became suspicious and disillusioned by The Prom and sold his HealthSouth stock: "It was confusing. A hospital manager who had been reprimanded a month or so before because he missed his numbers, was called up on the stage to receive a plaque for financial achievement."[31]

>>> AFTER THE DANCE

Away from the scrutiny of HealthSouth's Birmingham headquarters and outside the din of HealthSouth's 1997 "Prom," a seemingly insignificant event had passed without notice. That year, a financial message board opened on Yahoo! devoted to the discussion of HealthSouth and its stock. As the stock, traded under the symbol HRC, topped out near $30 and began to decline, the message board was joined by a gaggle of pumpers and bashers, who engaged in debates regarding the pros and cons of the stock, the company, and its leaders. The message board also provided an open forum for anyone with an urge to talk about the man and his empire. A host of anonymous critics on the board also began to tell anyone who would listen to look behind the curtain at HealthSouth to find out what Richard Scrushy and his company were *really* like. The information on the message board would later confound Richard Scrushy and enrich some of his employees.

CHAPTER three

The HealthSouth Yahoo! Message Board

When I began using the Yahoo! HealthSouth message board in November 1997, I became part of a growing movement in electronic communication. As a society, we have seen the importance of this movement but have yet to realize the consequences of changes to come from the electronic public forums of message boards, blogs (Web logs), and instant messaging. In 2004, a blogger investigated and corrected a report by Dan Rather about President Bush in a much-publicized event that embarrassed Rather and may have nudged him toward early retirement. Howard Dean's presidential campaign success on the Internet may have forever changed the pattern of national politics.

Jonathan Carson and James Felton, writing for *International Corporate Governance,* opened their paper on how Internet message boards affect corporations by saying: "The flow of unauthorized corporate information has changed dramatically in the past few years as Internet message boards have moved from the fringe to the mainstream."[1] Carson and Felton noted the impact of message boards on corporate governance by citing whistle-blowers on the Yahoo! Enron board. They relate that two years before the Enron fraud became public, "the one place that investors could have received indications about the mounting crisis was Enron's Yahoo! stock board." Such information included postings like the one from Enron message board poster **arthur86plz,** which said: "Dig deep . . . you'll see a growing mountain of off-balance sheet debt which will eventually swallow this company. There's a reason they layer so many subsidiaries and affiliates. Be careful."[2] The HealthSouth board carried many similar messages.

>>> THE MESSAGE BOARD EVOLVES

The HealthSouth message board began as a quiet place in November 1997. That month, only a dozen or more messages appeared per day, most containing such common cheerleader content as "This is a great company." But the character of the message board evolved rapidly, for a number of reasons. First, as more investors and employees became aware of the HealthSouth message board, more of them read and posted to it. HealthSouth stock had just peaked in price, and its investors were excited about the company's progress. Further, health care was in the nation's political bombsights, and changes proposed during the Clinton administration were frightening investors in that sector. Quickly the stock prices of all health care companies dropped sharply, and the board heated up with messages about HealthSouth's operations and stock values.

Although the Yahoo! HealthSouth (HRC) board had posters from every continent—**Platina** was from Norway, **kffman** was from Korea, and **Q**, an Asian, posted from Amsterdam—

FIGURE 3.1

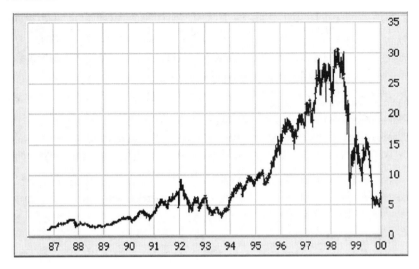

the majority of posters were from the United States, and most of those from Alabama, the corporate home of HealthSouth. Although even local factors, including events within the city of Birmingham and the ongoing developments in Richard Scrushy's life, influenced both the mainstream press and the Yahoo! message board, HealthSouth's stock price and the tone of the stock market in general probably exercised the most influence over the character and content of the messages I read during 1997 and 1998. As can be seen in Figure 3.1, the first sharp downward jolt came at the beginning of 1998 following a volatile but steady advance in price from $5 in 1994.

This was a critical time for Scrushy's fortunes. He held millions of stock options, and both investors and employees knew that one day he would need to sell them. Talk on the message board began to include grumblings about Scrushy's stock sales, controlling management style, and excessive spending, as well as rumors of investigations into HealthSouth's accounting practices.

I noticed the first ugly employee message in March of 1998, posted by a person who identified himself by the alias **swirlingturd,** and who said he was an ex-employee: "Wont be long . . . ," he posted, ". . . until we have another Columbia situation with HRC. What a shady bunch. If you knew how they really are, you wouldn't put a dime in these guys. You are all fools, chasing a rainbow with a pot of crap at the end in Birmingham."[3] I knew that this poster was referring to the massive 1997 fraud investigation into the Columbia/HCA health care corporation, which eventually forced the company to pay out over $1.7 billion in civil and criminal settlements. I just didn't understand how that incident offered any parallels to HealthSouth.

Other message board posters also wanted to know exactly what this poster was talking about. Most had heard this kind of accusation before, and so their replies asked the original poster to give specific information; some accused him of being a lazy doctor who didn't want to keep up with the workload in one of HealthSouth's growing facilities: "Don't blame the company for becoming more efficient," read one posted reply. Another poster reminded **swirlingturd** of HealthSouth's 45 quarters of earnings success and asked him: "How can you bet against Scrushy?"

In response to the message board posters' demands for specifics, **swirlingturd** laid his story on the line: "I'll make it short and sweet," he wrote. His posting went on to say that he had been recruited for a job as facility administrator, charged with overseeing the opening of a new wing—a job that required him to sell his home and relocate to a city 500 miles away. **Swirlingturd** took the job and successfully managed the facility expansion, but he was then fired soon after the new wing opened. Because he was still in his probationary period, HealthSouth simply released him without citing a cause. He wrote: "I picked up my roots, bought another home, and now a few months later, I'm starting over." **Swirlingturd** said he'd heard similar stories from other people who had worked for the company, and that the company couldn't survive if it didn't learn to treat its employees better: "Think what you may, but I'm warning you that HRC is headed for a fall," he warned on the message board.[4]

He was answered by a new poster who said he, too, was fired after a merger. You can't believe how it is, he said, "until you work for this company." This poster went on to make the observation that "any company that needs bodyguards for the CEO must have problems."[5] Another message was equivocal. It was titled "CEO selling stock" and in it **hi_there_63146** said: "I heard from a large shareholder that there has been a great deal of insider trading . . . I got nervous last week and sold a majority of my holdings in the company . . . I think that the CEO with the recent enormous wealth, divorce, new wife, MDM (MedPartners) crash, has a lot of distractions going on . . . so I can't quite get a handle on what's what."[6]

I read these posts with reservation. I asked myself the same questions any reasonable person would: Are these stories credible or embellished? Are the posters honest or deceitful? Are they merely spiteful people who are taking advantage of the message board to smear a past employer? Certainly, my experiences with HealthSouth had shown me glimpses of the dark side of its corporate culture. And today, many of these posters' claims have been verified by federal indictments and subsequent court testimony. But as I read the messages back in the summer and fall of 1998, I decided to look for agreement among other posters and corroborating information from sources outside the message board. The message board had shouted a warning, which is all that I could know without further digging.

As I became more experienced with message boards, I began to look for aids in judging the honesty and accuracy of message content. I learned, for example, to look for and read the biographies some posters made available on Yahoo!. I also learned to check the date the poster registered under a given alias. If an author had joined the message board only recently, I learned that he or she might be a single-issue poster, who joined the board simply to yell "fire" then exit. I also learned to call up the past messages of any poster, so I could search and review past postings for consistency and accuracy. Naturally, an alias who has a long history of credible observations is more believable. And, I learned to look for the date and time of a message posting, to see whether it was posted during stock market hours, or on the weekend or other after-hours periods when most schools and businesses are closed. Prank posts and off-topic chatting are more common off hours.

Of course, I also read **swirlingturd**'s messages through the filter of my own experience with HealthSouth. His posts and others like them described just the kind of management arrogance I had encountered in my dealings with the company. And while I was able to see a pattern emerging among the comments from other HealthSouth employees, I had to admit that the message boards of nearly all big companies contain reports damning management. Some are valid complaints, some are posted by short sellers (those who bet on and want the price to go down), and some are merely pranks. I realized that I would need to learn to evaluate hundreds of messages to form a valid picture of the health, character, and culture of HealthSouth—or any given company—based on the information posted on such boards. As I evaluated the information on the HealthSouth message board, I was satisfied that complainers had legitimate gripes. **Swirlingturd,** unlike many employees who had an axe to grind, did not linger over his problems; he placed his message, answered questions, and moved on—all things I learned to view as favoring the reliability of a poster's information.

In April, another poster asked why HealthSouth wasn't paying any dividends, particularly in light of the company's many unbroken quarters of sterling financial performance. By July, yet another poster called HealthSouth a "pyramid scheme calling itself a company," and speculated that the only thing keeping the company afloat was Scrushy's "bullshit." The poster warned, ". . . just hope the Feds knock before they kick open the door on this billing scam."[7] Throughout August of 1998, I watched for more posts and quickly saw many that characterized HealthSouth using terms that described a rigid, authoritarian, and inbred culture of a type certain to create stress among employees. This message, in particular, rang true to me:

> **LocalMD: HRC   #363   8/07/98**
>
> "I am an MD with some extensive past and present dealings with HRC and I am previous shareholder. This is a house of cards. Earnings are driven by acquisition, a pyramid scam . . ."

In the same month, poster **tpaulson** wrote: ". . . this stock will tank because it pays too much for the businesses it purchases, then does nothing to increase earnings. You can't buy something at a 10.5 multiple and still give your stockholders a good return. This is true especially when you don't know how to run your new businesses or treat your employees (as mentioned by earlier messages) and therefore do nothing to increase the profits of the facilities you just paid too much for."[8]

In September, HealthSouth announced that its profits would decline because of pricing pressures from managed-care clients. As a result, HealthSouth stock tanked, falling to around $8 from a preannouncement rate of $28. Poster **jr_111** agreed with earlier posters who had predicted a fall for the company: "You may not be far wrong. I have heard rumors of a federal lawsuit for several weeks now . . . Only passing along a rumor I heard. Take it for what it is worth."[9] **BLACKIE_071998** rose to the company's defense: ". . . the HRC management has made it very clear that anyone screwing the system or regulatory process will get fired and HRC will stand behind the feds to prosecute to the fullest extend. Management has a big stake in this company . . . The market is down 180 points in 2 days."[10]

But the later-to-be-infamous **I_AM_DIRK_DIGGLER** agreed with other posters that the company had internal problems: "**. . .** For the record . . . I worked for HRC and hated it . . . my own accord. I think that their leadership is totally self-serving, and out of touch with reality. I also think their billing practices may in time become subjected to rigorous scrutiny."[11]

Then, in October of 1998, I encountered the messages from **Rodeo49;** this poster was a clinic owner and administrator in the northwest who, like me, had sold his clinics to a company that was then acquired by HealthSouth. He wrote: ". . . I sold my clinics to another company, who was acquired by another . . . that company was then gobbled up by HS . . . the northwest is a mess, lots of resignations, revenue down, morale . . . not so good . . . as for screwshy . . . the guy has an ego as big as Montana and a mouth to match . . . I just didn't fit in with the good ole . . . Alabama boys . . ."[12] His experience sounded so much like that of my own organization, that I was certain this poster was telling the truth.

Another person, who posted under the alias **HealthBizz,** admitted to being a competitor, but only as a consultant. He wrote: "Not everyone on this board that blasts Healthsouth's upper management is a former employee . . . I work in the healthcare field with many companies. I can tell you that the distrust and dislike of Healthsouth and Mr. Skrushy is practically universal." When another poster accused **HealthBizz** of having a grudge against HealthSouth management, he replied: "I do have a grudge against this company and it's senior managers. I think it's the largest mis-managed company in the nation . . . Healthsouth is a house of cards in much the same way Columbia/HCA was . . ."[13]

HealthBizz went on to post a list of the things that he hated about HealthSouth and its culture. He cited secret questionnaires sent to employees' homes asking if coworkers used the copier for personal use or had Internet access at work. **HealthBizz** listed other such incidents: a Pristine Audit in which secretaries were written up for using Post-it notes wastefully; employees being required to know the spelling of Scrushy's name (I'd had personal experience with this demand); new employees being led through Scrushy's personal museum to see Scrushy's first desk; the ten corporate jets HealthSouth kept for executives; and a good-ole-boy network that rewarded a follower mentality and squelched independent thinking. After reading his complaints, others joined in. For example, there were posts from female clinicians pointing to a culture of male dominance and a glass-ceiling for female employees in general. In agreement with many of the posters, including **Rodeo49** and **HealthBizz,** I posted: "Better your company be overrun by Huns or attacked by Vikings from the sea than be acquired by HealthSouth."

>>> POSTERS FROM WITHIN HEALTHSOUTH

No company wants its employees to air their grievances in a public forum. Many will agree that it seems basically unfair for one side to post anonymously; giving the other side no opportunity for response. Management in most organizations discourages employees from posting messages while on the job, and in many companies it is grounds for dismissal. But when critical institutional information or trade secrets are made public in message boards, grounds exist for legal action. As I read the HealthSouth message board in late 1998, I realized that **CrazyCPA** was teetering on the borderline.

I assumed that **CrazyCPA** posted from inside Health-South; his knowledge of accounting and specific references to HealthSouth's methods suggested to me that he worked in the HealthSouth accounting department. **CrazyCPA** spoke well and listed facts with precision in his posted messages. He indicted HealthSouth's board of directors for lack of oversight, and he criticized insiders—and Scrushy in particular—for exercising stock options and immediately selling all of those optioned shares. Specifically, he targeted HealthSouth's accounting, pointing out clearly that the acquisition accounting used by HealthSouth conveniently obscured a true picture of operating results and finances.

Yahoo! later removed **CrazyCPA**'s messages, but responses to his messages are still posted. These responses reflect that as early as October of 1998 many of the posters to the Yahoo! message board were in agreement with **CrazyCPA** in questioning HealthSouth and its operations.

Poster **Jeopardy11,** for example, joined in a thread discussing the general character of HealthSouth and its management. While **CrazyCPA** was quite direct in accusing HealthSouth of accounting irregularities, **Jeopardy11** more gently suggested that HealthSouth's accounting distorted a true picture of its earnings. While **CrazyCPA**'s messages alluded to practices that might be fraudulent, **Jeopardy11** cited practices that seemed unethical, though technically legal, as in this long message he wrote in October of 1998:

Jeopardy11: Wagon Pullers #1224   10/21/98

". . . What I have found lacking with most of the managers at HS is a lack of courage and a lack of business experience. Most of the mid-level operational managers come 'up through the ranks' and with no outside experience and no particular demonstrated ability to drive a successful operation. They do however, rise based on their ability to toe

---

the line or 'pull the wagon' as it were. This is essential behavior within the HS culture because of the . . . arrogance
of upper management. Richard Screwshy has stated directly to 'his team' of managers that many of them could
be replaced by green college students . . . What was left
was a group of hard working or sycophantic (or possibly
both) people, scared by the reality that they were in over
their heads . . . Since HS is a relatively young and heretofore
growing organization, the juggernaut has masked over
these essential weaknesses in the culture which projects
the thinking and ideals of the leaders of the enterprise . . .
Any consultant worth anything would predict that this is a
formula for disaster . . ."

In subsequent messages, **Jeopardy11** catalogued Health-
South warning signals: the fleet of jets, Scrushy's massive
ego, and a push within the facilities toward commodity
health care. He asked if being the Holiday Inn or Wal-Mart of
medical services—a point of comparison frequently used
when describing HealthSouth—was really what customers
wanted in health care.[14] He said that when acquisitions
stopped, the fog that surrounded HealthSouth's results
would be lifted and then operations must change: "There
needs to be a housecleaning of the Alabama boys," he said.
Jeopardy11 criticized HealthSouth's Wall Street partners,
saying: "I have never understood why the venture capitalists
poured so much cash into an inbred BOD [board of directors]
and inexperienced management." He observed that if Health-
South were such a good idea, a revolution in the operations
of health care, he found it hard to understand why no insurance companies—institutions who knew the economics of
health care—had invested in the company. **Jeopardy11** saw a
great similarity between the financial messes at Columbia/
HCA and HealthSouth.[15]

A retired doctor, using the alias **fdzllc** (some on the message board who claimed to know him called him Dr. Gabe), answered **Jeopardy11** in an extended conversation. The doctor had posted on the message board almost since its inception, and he had been a loyal supporter of the company and often a defender of Scrushy. He challenged **Jeopardy11** and **CrazyCPA**: "You . . . continue dishing out non facts and lies," and he defended the July insider sales (when share prices were much higher) as a necessity: ". . . Being an accountant you do not comment on the IRS aspect of those shares sold and the need to pay taxes at the time of the sale arising from options sales."[16] He pointed out that HealthSouth was growing and therefore needed to use acquisition accounting. The doctor complained that **Jeopardy11** didn't know what he was talking about when he accused the board of directors of being crooked and inept, and of hiding things. He called **Jeopardy11** a vituperous snake, just another creep, and said he'd fire him if he were his boss. And **Jeopardy11** answered in his usual calm manner:

Jeopardy11: "Quality Cancer" #1267 10/24/98

". . . I will use a medical metaphor. A patient can have essentially strong and healthy parts and suffer from a systemic desease or cancer . . . Simillarly, I believe that relatively drastic measures may have to be taken to excise or, at least, retard the growth of that which I consider a cancer to a potentially vital organization . . . I see HS as suferring from a form of brain tumor which causes the patient to behave inappropriately and even self-destructively . . ."

But both **CrazyCPA** and **Jeopardy11** found support for their views among other posters. **HealthBizz** had been among the first to agree: "Here here for CRZYCPA: I don't know where you came from but you're totally correct. I got the same impression of these people when I was flying with them one of their corporate jets this spring. They have learned nothing at all from Rick Scott and the Columbia mess."[17] There were somewhat fewer posts in opposition, saying such things as "Of course HealthSouth fires people. What are they supposed to do, become bloated and inefficient?" and, "Of course Scrushy sold his options; is he supposed to have all of his wealth tied up in one stock?"

>>> A TESTAMENT TO "WISDOM OF CROWDS"

Scanning the Yahoo! HRC message board, based on the ideas and information I read there, I gained a new perspective on the company. Within only a few months, I also had learned a great deal about message boards. I was—and I remain to be—convinced that message boards provide valuable access to investment information available nowhere else. The advice and information I learned on the HRC message board helped me reach a decision to sell my stock, long before headquarters was raided by the FBI and stock prices dropped to just pennies a share. As for future investments, I will pause before buying if I discover cogently discouraging posts on public message boards, such as those I encountered about HealthSouth during the years preceding the 2003 raid.

James Surowiecki, who writes the financial column for *The New Yorker*, explored the value of small group behavior, much like that demonstrated on the HRC message board, in his book *The Wisdom of Crowds*. In his book, Surowiecki draws a careful distinction between an opinion derived from a small group and a consensus, sought perhaps by compromises among committee members. Surowiecki goes on to document how the wisdom of a group has often proved greater than that of any single member. For example, in a jelly-beans-in-a-jar guessing contest, the average of the groups' guesses is repeatedly accurate to within 2 to 3 percent.

The subtitle of his book, "Why the Many Are Smarter Than the Few and How Collective Wisdom Shapes Business, Economies, Societies, and Nations," suggests that the principle underlying the process has remarkably broad application. In a chaotic market with little information, a small, diverse group with reasonable expertise and information can submit opinions that, like a scattergram, aggregate around a correct answer. As Surowiecki explains: "The problem starts when people's decisions are not made all at once but rather in a sequence."[18] To gain the most precision from the opinions of a group, according to Surowiecki, three conditions are necessary: diversity, independence, and decentralization. While the message board was not an ideal example of this model—because the problem was not precisely defined and because there was no simple way to aggregate the opinions—it did provide independent opinion from about ten traders. And, importantly, the group did not initially discourage "shorts," or negative opinions, regarding valuation of HealthSouth. Instead, it worked within the entire "bell curve" of opinion. And, because the group's opinions regarding price were posted publicly, one could see the range of their computations and bracket the midpoint. The message board group fit Surowiecki's conclusion that "the idea of the wisdom of crowds is not that a group will always give you the right answer, but that on average it will always come up with a better answer than any individual could provide."[19]

I later would discover that, along with a large dose of speculation, profanity, and gossip, the Yahoo! HealthSouth message board did, indeed, contain a great deal of wisdom during the years preceding Scrushy's ouster.

In a 2005 telephone conversation with Bryan Marsal, crisis manager for Alvarez and Marsal, I learned just how accurate the long messages of **Jeopardy11** and **CrazyCPA** had been in their assessment of the culture at HealthSouth. Marsal was involved with the crisis management of both Republic Health and Arthur Andersen, and his company was brought in to operate HealthSouth after the FBI raid. I asked Marsal if he had found anything different at HealthSouth that he had not seen dozens of times before. After a thoughtful pause, he replied that there was a pattern at HealthSouth in which employees were overpaid in relation to the general employment market.

A recent college or even high school graduate might be hired in at, for example, $35,000 and soon be making $60,000; the next year or so he or she might be paid over $100,000. The salaries are merely examples; the key is that people were earning salaries they knew they couldn't make anywhere else. "They got hooked on the money," Marsal said. "I don't know whether it was an intentional way to keep employees quiet or if it was just an accident. But it worked that way."[20] This was the very information **Jeopardy11** had been trying to tell the message board in his October 1998 posting titled "Wagon Pullers."[21]

>>> SCRUSHY QUIETS THE MESSAGE BOARD

An investor always should be suspicious when management tries to bury an issue, or when management prevents free conversation among individuals about its operations. As the postings on the Yahoo! message board grew increasingly critical of HealthSouth throughout 1998, they eventually came to the attention of Richard Scrushy, and he began to take action to silence the message board. Predictably, when Scrushy sued Yahoo! for release of the names of posters, his action had the effect of temporarily quieting some of the negative message board content. It was also a move against short-selling and a damper against negative publicity. Although this seemed good for the company, it may have been an illusion. While it is a fact that conversation on the message board helped hundreds of HealthSouth employees recover losses caused by the financial crash, the message board's broader contribution, however, may come from whatever role it played in shaping new laws regarding free speech on the Internet. Scrushy's lawsuit and other attempts to intimidate the message board posters, therefore, had far-reaching consequences.

CHAPTER four

Free Speech versus Richard Scrushy

"Anonymity is a shield from the tyranny of the majority . . . It thus exemplifies the purpose behind the Bill of Rights and of the First Amendment in particular: to protect unpopular individuals from retaliation–and their ideas from suppression– at the hand of an intolerant society."
SUPREME COURT JUSTICE JOHN PAUL STEVENS

As 1998 began, Richard Scrushy was enjoying a hero's role among America's most powerful CEOs. As a poor boy who had bootstrapped himself to great success, Scrushy drew the admiration of even the cynical press. His personal triumph added to the financial success of HealthSouth, and its importance to Birmingham continued to shield him from broad criticism. During the previous year, HealthSouth's stock value had risen by more than 40 percent, and even though many assumed 1997's Medicare overhaul bill would threaten the company's profits, HealthSouth's claims to the contrary seemed to stave off investor fear.[1] Investors had no way of knowing, of course, that the company's financial claims had been untrue for some time. A March 19, 2003, Securities and Exchange Commission (SEC) complaint would later charge that when the Medicare overhaul bill went into effect, Scrushy and HealthSouth senior officers had been skewing the company's financial reports for nearly a decade, convening meetings in which they "fixed" the company's earnings reports to match Wall Street analysts' projections. "By 1997," the complaint stated, "the attendees referred to these meetings as 'family meetings' and referred to themselves as 'family members.'"[2] HealthSouth paid its top officers enormous salaries, which helped strengthen this 'family's' bonds of loyalty—for a while.

Though these alleged activities were carefully hidden from the public, HealthSouth's employees, business partners, and other Scrushy associates were beginning to grumble about the company's rigid management culture and Scrushy's flamboyant excesses. A June 1999 *Fortune* magazine article would compare HealthSouth to Graceland, saying that Scrushy's headquarters was "a place positively reeking of self-worship and control."[3] Scrushy's princely compensation package, over $111 million in 1997 (including stock sales), drew public attention, as did his lavish lifestyle; that same year, Scrushy flew 150 guests to Jamaica to help celebrate his marriage to his third wife, Leslie. On occasion, Scrushy's behavior drew the scorn of the people of Birmingham. His plans to build a big-league sports stadium there were quashed, after he was quoted in a Birmingham paper as saying that his plan had the backing of "the little people."[4] And certainly employees at HealthSouth's headquarters were heard to grumble about the atmosphere there. They chaffed at having to endure the rush-hour crush of traffic at the entrance to HealthSouth's campus while Scrushy enjoyed his own private roadway and entrance. They resented his use of a private elevator, which they suspected was a means of avoiding direct interaction with "staff."

Scrushy's staff meetings, called Monday Morning Beatings, were known for intimidation.[5] Many on the message board believed the rumors that powerful microphones in his penthouse trophy room captured any unfavorable remarks whispered by visitors.[6] He has denied that his fifth-floor telephone system allowed him to listen in on his executives' phone calls, but the 2003 Federal Indictment, Sec. 37., states: "Richard Scrushy would and did seek to control his co-conspirators, HealthSouth employees and Board of Directors by (a) threats, (b) intimidation, and (c) taking various steps to monitor the activity of said persons, including obtaining and reading their emails, placing them under surveillance, and installing equipment that permitted him to eavesdrop on electronic and telephonic communications . . ."[7]

Abelson and Freudenheim, in their *New York Times* article, "The Scrushy Mix: Strict and So Lenient," wrote: "The company has taken other steps to quiet employees, largely through its security force, some former HealthSouth executives say. Security officers appeared to closely monitor the activities of employees and others, they said."[8] And, while his eavesdropping and bullying tactics may have helped to stifle any negative commentary within HealthSouth's headquarters, they only added to the chorus of complaints and questions about his management style and HealthSouth's performance that was growing louder outside the corporate walls. And the most vocal of Scrushy's critics were posting messages on the Yahoo! HRC message board.

Although HealthSouth still appeared to be a financial dynamo during early 1998, by the end of the third quarter, adjusted earnings announcements helped drive the company's stock down dramatically. At the same time, this activity drew more visitors and participants to the HRC message board, where the talk was becoming louder and uglier. HealthSouth's corporate culture made it a magnet for gossip, and the message board was a tabloid free-for-all, fueled by the observations and accusations of HealthSouth employees, investors, and associates who were familiar with Scrushy and his organization. The group traded stories of the executives' personal misbehavior, the company's failing corporate strategy, weird management practices and demands, and speculations about the company's finances. Newcomers to the message board were surprised to read stories of high-rolling executives and their testosterone-driven, womanizing culture.

Like Hyde Park's Speakers' Corner, message boards exist as a tribute to freedom of expression. But Scrushy wasn't accustomed to bearing graciously the criticism that accompanies such freedom. According to a *Wall Street Journal* article, Scrushy first became aware of the Yahoo! message board in late 1998, when business associates began asking him what he thought of the postings. When Scrushy learned that he was being bashed on the Yahoo! message board, he moved quickly to silence his detractors. Scrushy's aides say that, after reading some of the postings, he immediately assigned staff to follow the board and report to him on what was being said. Regular participants on the board also believed that corporate staff, under aliases that masked their in-house identities, was assigned to the board to defend company policy and to refute allegations (perhaps a more common corporate practice than generally admitted to).

HealthSouth attorneys subpoenaed Yahoo! for the release of names and demographic data related to a long list of message board participant aliases. Scrushy clearly intended to track down and sue—or at least intimidate—those who posted unfavorable remarks. Though Scrushy subpoenaed for information on approximately 300 message board participants, Yahoo! released information identifying only those who its legal department agreed might be guilty of libel or slander—in all, fewer than 10 percent of the aliases on Scrushy's list. The individuals and messages Scrushy targeted with his lawsuits and threats accurately bracket multiple issues of free speech: **I_AM_DIRK_DIGGLER** (**DIRK**) was vulgar, insulting, untruthful, and even threatening. He admitted to being an ex-employee of the company, and he falsely claimed to have been secretly inside the Scrushy home. Some participants on the message board could have been posting messages from work, using company time and equipment. **HealthBizz,** a health care consultant, was a competitor with an admitted grudge against the company, but one who posted with extensive industry and company knowledge. Kim Landry, **rehab1KL,** was a Health-South employee who had a grievance, but who has consistently contended that her posts were accurate. **Bopper63** was an investor in HealthSouth by way of a merger; his wife worked at a HealthSouth surgery center.

As I read the postings of these individuals, I had a hard time separating fact from fantasy. One surprised newcomer to the board echoed my own astonishment at the bitterness, lack of civility, and adolescent rage expressed in some of the messages. Even those who were amused by **DIRK**'s fantasies, for example, didn't believe them, but most seemed to agree that he was out of bounds with his sexual comments. Then, there was the silly, "notes-in-school," feigned romance between **HealthBizz** and **rehab1KL** that was doubly irritating to those who felt that their romantic posts cast doubt on the credence of the opinions about HealthSouth contained in their other messages. Several company loyalists, such as **fdzllc** and **John_Wayne,** a poster likely to have been planted by the home office, felt compelled to rush vehemently to the aid of both Scrushy and HealthSouth. It was soap opera online: Will **rehab1KL** meet **HealthBizz** in New Orleans? Will they have an affair? Will the good doctor, **fdzllc,** have a stroke? Is **CrazyCPA** a spy, and will he be caught? Will **Jeopardy11** finish his thesis before Scrushy nails him? One message said: "This is the best thing on any screen," and many posters must have shared that sentiment.

For all the entertainment it offered, however, the board had its dark side. Many posts were filled with insults and obscenities, directed at Scrushy and his company, as well as other posters. It is impossible to chronicle all of such messages, because Yahoo! removed critical passages after the subpoena and settlement. All of **CrazyCPA**'s messages are missing from the board records, although the posts of those who responded to him are still on record, some partially edited by Yahoo!. Also gone are the **"I_AM_DIRK_DIGGLER"** posts that falsely suggested that he was stalking Scrushy and having sexual contact with Leslie Scrushy. As such, the **"I_AM_DIRK_DIGGLER"** messages may have been the message board's least defensible content under claims of First Amendment freedoms. Peter Krum had taken his Yahoo! alias from the name of a young porno star character in the movie *Boogie Nights*. True to his namesake, **DIRK** often laced his messages with references to his sexual prowess and experiences. Though many of **DIRK**'s later postings contained little more than fantasy and crude lies, he also wrote often about HealthSouth itself and his negative experiences with the company.

In August of 1998, **I_AM_DIRK_DIGGLER** wrote: "I worked for HRC and hated it. I left under my own accord. I think that their leadership is totally self-serving, and out of touch with reality. I also think their billing practices may in time become subjected to rigorous scrutiny. There is a reason why they are at 23 and change even with their glowing financials."[9]

And, in another message, titled "HRC is Deceptive," he wrote: ". . . when I was hired, I was told how it was possible to get up to a 9% raise, IF you worked hard and got a level 5. What a joke. I put my blood and guts in, got a level 4 for 2 years in a row. When I asked what I had to do to get a 5, I was told that you would have to 'walk on water.' NO ONE GETS A 5!! . . . The 401K is a joke . . . Unbelievable how stingy this company is . . . I want my piece of the pie now. Instead, Richard is out buying islands and real estate with employee bonuses.[10]

Although some posters accused **DIRK** of lying about his experience with HealthSouth, other message board participants responded and spurred him on. Landry, posting under her alias **rehab1KL,** for example, echoed the sentiments of most who were dragged through Scrushy's Pristine Audits when she wrote: "Choking: Wish I could get rid of the Albatross around my neck!!!!! Instead of Pristine Audits they should be auditing the manner in which employees are treated which is not very good. Wish my full time job was being one of the idiotic auditors . . ."[11] **DIRK** had agreed: "The pristine audit crap is a joke foisted on HealthSouth workers by the bunch of hillbillies that run the place. I am glad to be out of there and glad to get that monkey off my back."[12]

While **rehab1KL** and **DIRK** wrote messages attacking Scrushy, HealthSouth, and its officers, they were answered by a number of company loyalists, some of whom appeared to be stock-holding doctors and managers. One such supporter was **fdzllc.** He said, with considerable support from the rest of the board, that while **rehab1KL** and **DIRK** were entertaining, most on the board were sick of their tiresome crap: "Get a shovel and bury yourselves in a hole full of the bullshit you two constantly spout . . ."[13] he said. In a message written on October 7, 1998, Landry replied:

---

rehab1KL: HeatlhBiTzz   #924

". . . Everyone keeps talking about 3Q reports and how the stocks are going to rebound. HA, like a bad check! Mr. Screwshe is crumbling underneath his crooked empire. I see it coming and the picture is very clear. 7 mil[lion dollar] Islands, extravagant corporate office with a private elevator for Screwshe and his cromies. Megalomaniacs . . . Their own private subdivision that is gated . . . Uses corporate jets to fly his band around and has his own team of managers that take care of his instruments and that is all they do full time.

He has 3 or 4 corporate pilots and all they do is fly him and his cronies around the country. I would continue but I have to go to a real job now. One where I am respected along with the other employees. HealthSouth believes that Motivation comes from Intimidation . . . See ya . . ."[14]

FIGURE 4.1

* * *

DIRK's salacious insults couldn't have been the only thing worrying Scrushy at this time. As Figure 4.1 shows, HRC had dropped by 50 percent following HealthSouth's September 1998 announcement that it would not meet analyst estimates for 1998 and 1999. Suddenly, HRC was listed among those stocks suffering a sudden fall to new lows, and **DIRK** was a cheerleader for the bears.

I_AM_DIRK_DIGGLER: Attention All HRC Addicts #963

"For those of you who seem to think that HRC is going to rebound to it's old levels, you are all FUC_ING IDIOTS. Just for shits and giggles, name a few high fliers that too the dive this year and have rebounded . . . and when this loser pops 10, bail."[15]

Dropping stock prices, when added to the bad news of lawsuits filed against HealthSouth for insider trading, improper Medicare billing, and fraud allegations associated with a Scrushy family business, gave the message board plenty of fodder for conversations and debate.[16] A storm of stock volatility brought more traders to the message board, and discussions of trading became intermixed with those of the company's fundamentals.

Still, many who now were in the red were ready to get on with business. A poster named **cjo10** complained: "Really people, can we talk facts here?"[17] And **Trade_naked** said: "Give us a break. Enough of the child like behavior . . . Will HRC make it and why?"[18] Landry responded, ". . . The only recovery may be when Screwshe and his cronies go to prison . . . HA! It is going to happen, guys."[19] Multiple posters reminded **rehab1KL, HealthBizz, DIRK,** and others who complained of Scrushy's management that they didn't care how the company treated its employees. These investors held HealthSouth stock strictly to make a profit, and saw no connection between the company's management style and its potential for future profitability. Look at the big picture, some posters advised. **Jeopardy11** posted this message in reply:

Jeopardy11: Bigg's Picture #1285

". . . I haven't met all the CEO's in this world but I've met a few and Richard Scrushy and many of his cohorts are unique. Just take a look at the HS website and review this monument to the house built by Big Dick. I defy you to show me a more self-aggrandizing site dedicated to a corporation. This is his public persona. To imagine how he is one-on-one, read through this site and count the number of favorable things said about him. Personally, I find his level of narcissism bordering on pathological. And if you don't think his personality reflects on the big picture then you are due for some more reflection."[20]

HealthBizz weighed in with disgust at those who didn't care about management; they were in it "for the money." He said: "The people that stand up for this company either don't know enough about what goes on and how they do business, or they just care . . . about price. They believe that ethics have no place in business . . . since they stick up for Healthsouth until the dying end, they will be left, with shit."[21]

>>> DIRK GETS SCRUSHY'S ATTENTION

In the midst of these heated exchanges, Peter Krum began a series of unwise personal posts under his **I_AM_DIRK_DIGGLER** alias. His false claims that he had been inside the Scrushy home and had several sexual encounters with Leslie Scrushy may have been the messages that finally brought King Richard's attention to the message board. Although other posters protested the crudeness of his over-the-top claims, Peter Krum and Kim Landry were exchanging supportive messages on the board the day Richard Scrushy made a "John Doe" filing in Dade County, Florida, that would eventually enable him to subpoena Yahoo!'s records and track down Krum at his place of business[22]:

I__AM__DIRK__DIGGLER: Rehab   #1096

". . . Thanks for your flattering comments. I think it is pretty funny that some of our readers take such offense to me. Anyone who takes these boards so seriously is an even bigger jackass than I am. By the way, what did you think of HRC's 'no tape' policy? EVEN IN YOUR OWN OFFICE! Talk about a group of yo-yos with nothing better to do than enforce petty and or demeaning policies. By the way, I love your spunk. Keep posting and take care of your ass . . . etc."[23]

According to Michael Moss, writing for the *Wall Street Journal*, within four days of receiving the subpoena, Yahoo! released Krum's name, and Scrushy's hired detectives had tracked down the formerly anonymous poster to his job at Pennsylvania State University. Scrushy and his wife sued Krum, and filed criminal charges that claimed harassment and stalking.[24] As word got out about the lawsuit, the message board posters reacted:

---

watosh1: HealthSouth vs Dirk #1495 10/31/98

"It seems to me that any huge organization that spends its time sleazing around the net, attempting to sue an individual for speaking his mind, must be an organization backed into a corner and running on fear. This lawsuit against Dirk is ludicrous, in my opinion. Most probably a scare tactic employed by HS to 'keep the lid' on anything negative . . . this ploy has been used many times in the past. It works for a while, but then overwhelming evidence usually nails the organization to the wall. Unfortunately, however, the initial whistle-blowers suffer the most . . ."[25]

---

bopper63: Funereal atmosphere #1514 11/02/98

"Been out of town since last Tues and what a difference 6 days makes. Although I have been insulted by Dirk on a number of occasions as I have by HealthBizz, the effect of the lawsuit has certainly stifled the posts from them. I agree, that although Dirk's posts were outrageous, the net effect of the lawsuit is to stifle this board. Did anyone really believe him? . . ."[26]

There had been rumors at HRC headquarters that Scrushy was planning to bring suit against more of the message board posters. Some, who worked at HealthSouth headquarters, left warnings on the message board: "Be careful what you say," was the watchword. **Jeopardy11** seemed to feel it was already too late to save his own job:

> **Jeopardy11: Thanks for your comments   #1418**
>
> "You are right in that I cannot share with you my background or credentials. If you know anything . . . about the arrogance, fortress mentality and paranoia that pervades the executive offices, you know that, in the least, my career is in jeopardy for many of the things that I have said here."[27]

Jeopardy11 was heard from briefly, on November 1, 1998, in a message that carried a computer link for a local newspaper article titled, "HealthSouth Sues Local Man Over Internet Messages."[28] In his message, he wrote:

> **Jeopardy11: B'ham Bullies   #1503**
>
> ". . . I went back through the entire message board to review just what had been said. The worst of them are flippant locker jabs that anyone would discount on their face and I believe could not muster the credibility to actually constitute libel.
>
> . . . It is clear that this is some form of legal intimidation. In my opinion, I don't believe Scrushy or HS would risk exposure of their peccadilloes in a forum much more public than this message board. I only hope that Dirk can enlist the support of the ACLU in this obvious attempt to use the legal system to intimidate not only Dirk but anyone else who chooses to exercise their constitutional right to express their opinion freely in a forum whose sole purpose is to accommodate such uncensored ravings."[29]

Jeopardy11's posts had made it obvious that he expected a visit from Scrushy's attorneys, and when he disappeared from the message board, the other participants assumed that **Jeopardy11** was fired. He signed off, adding: "If any Health-South attorneys feel that what I say here . . . may cause customers to 'lose faith', I look forward to hearing from you soon."

>>> A WIN FOR SCRUSHY

As part of his court settlement, Krum agreed to post an apology and confession on the HRC message board. Below is the (abbreviated) post, which appeared in February of 1999:

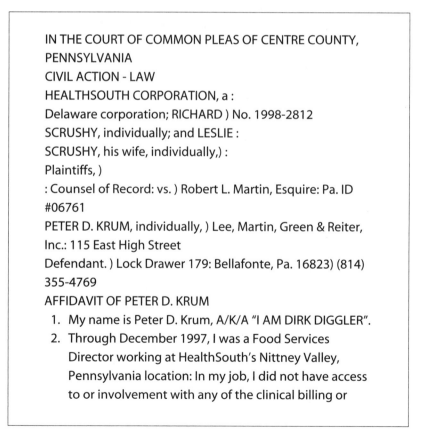

IN THE COURT OF COMMON PLEAS OF CENTRE COUNTY, PENNSYLVANIA
CIVIL ACTION - LAW
HEALTHSOUTH CORPORATION, a :
Delaware corporation; RICHARD) No. 1998-2812
SCRUSHY, individually; and LESLIE :
SCRUSHY, his wife, individually,) :
Plaintiffs,)
: Counsel of Record: vs.) Robert L. Martin, Esquire: Pa. ID #06761
PETER D. KRUM, individually,) Lee, Martin, Green & Reiter,
Inc.: 115 East High Street
Defendant.) Lock Drawer 179: Bellafonte, Pa. 16823) (814) 355-4769
AFFIDAVIT OF PETER D. KRUM

1. My name is Peter D. Krum, A/K/A "I AM DIRK DIGGLER".
2. Through December 1997, I was a Food Services Director working at HealthSouth's Nittney Valley, Pennsylvania location: In my job, I did not have access to or involvement with any of the clinical billing or

business affairs of HealthSouth. I loved my job at HealthSouth and I enjoyed the people I worked with. I left HealthSouth only to advance my responsibilities and obtain a pay increase and not because of any dissatisfaction with HealthSouth.

3. I went to work for the Pennsylvania State University as a Food and Beverage Controller. At Penn State, I had access to a computer and to the Yahoo! Finance Bulletin Board on the Internet. This is where my extremely poor judgment began.

4. When I left HealthSouth, I owned a small amount of HealthSouth stock. I sold it at that time and made a profit.

5. I assumed an anonymous screen name in order to spur the other posters on the Board to respond to me. The name was "I AM DIRK DIGGLER", a character from the movie Boggie Nights and one associated with the pornography industry and explicit sex.

6. I targeted Richard Scrushy, his wife Leslie and HealthSouth, not because I had anything against any of them, but only to satisfy my irresponsible and childish desire to be recognized as important by the other posters on the Bulletin Board. This was a grievous mistake which has hurt everyone involved.

7. I do not know Richard Scrushy or his wife and have never even met them. I now have learned that Mr. Scrushy's wife was pregnant while I was posting my sexually explicit lies about her.

8. I have never been to Birmingham.

9. I was never in contact with any HealthSouth management other than my supervisors at my location in Pennsylvania . . .

10. So, obviously one can see that my postings on the Yahoo! Finance Message Board were thoughtless lies about people and facts which I did not have access to.

11. I, Peter Krum, admit that I published false and defamatory statements of and concerning Richard Scrushy, Leslie Scrushy and HealthSouth Corporation on the Yahoo! Finance Message Board. . .

12. I, Peter Krum, admit that these messages contained explicit sexual content and lies which served to defame, humiliate, disparage, degrade, belittle and otherwise blacken the reputation of Richard Scrushy, Leslie Scrushy and HealthSouth Corporation.

13. As a result of my lies, immoral and sexually explicit behavior, I was arrested and charged with a crime. I lost my job at Penn State and a judgment was entered against me in a civil action for money damages, injunctive relief and requiring me to perform community service as a punishment for my offenses. The payments under the judgment will go to charity as requested by Mr. and Mrs. Scrushy.

14. I have been obtaining counseling from a minister in order to gain back some sense of self-worth and dignity.

15. I, Peter Krum, personally apologize to Richard Scrushy, Leslie Scrushy and all of the officers, directors and employees of HealthSouth Corporation for my senseless lies and for the pain I have caused you.

16. I hereby publicly denounce my own actions and consent to the publication of this Affidavit by the Scrushy's and HealthSouth in whatever manner they feel necessary.

17. I would also like to warn others that hiding behind a fake identity and shield of anonymity does not give one poetic license and the right to embarrass others.

18. The words contained in this Affidavit are my own and I have not been compelled to execute this document. I am signing it of my own free will because it is the truth.

VERIFICATION

Peter D. Krum hereby states that he is a party in this action and verifies that the statements made in the foregoing Affidavit are true and correct based on his personal knowledge, information and belief. The undersigned understands that the statements herein are made subject to penalties for perjury.

PETER D. KRUM[30]

The day following Krum's posted "confession," the message board talk was bland and the board had been scrubbed of many messages. Although **DIRK**'s postings raised more obvious issues than the others, most on the board saw his messages as vulgar and unbelievable parody; to these posters, charges that Krum had damaged HealthSouth's reputation seemed overblown. Was he being persecuted for mere name calling, or painful criticism, or because he sometimes delivered truth in street language? As Krum testified, "It was a really stupid game. I did not intend to harm anyone, but this was a game."[31]

As Scrushy may have hoped, his lawsuits against the message board participants served, temporarily, both to silence critics and to divert attention from his company's poor performance. Over the next week, many aliases went missing, and several were never heard from again, including **HealthBizz, Jeopardy11, swirlingturd,** and **CrazyCPA.** Even **rehab1KL,** Kim Landry, was quiet for a while. But this temporary quiet on the board didn't last for long.

Landry was a clinical employee who acted also as a physical therapy manager and marketer for HealthSouth. She began her life on the message board as a very happy employee who took pride in her work and was enthusiastic about her employer:

> **rehab1KL   New User!!!   #336 8/04/98**
>
> "I have been checking the messages on this board for ap-
> proximately six months and now I feel the need to speak
> out! . . . People are writing crap on this board and I am pret-
> ty sick of it! I have been with HealthSouth for 6 years and
> have really enjoyed my job. I sell the programs for the in-
> patient division and have been very successful in increas-
> ing volume and getting satisfaction from this job. No job is
> perfect no matter where one chooses to work but this stu-
> pid gossiping is pretty childish."

Within only a few weeks after this posting, Landry had met with the new manager of her facility. As a result of that meeting, she soon began sulking publicly. In a later posting, Landry related that she had pursued a promotion but, in spite of flawless personnel evaluations, was held back by her supervisors. According to Landry's message, her new supervisor and the facility's new CEO said they couldn't recommend her for a promotion, because they had only two months of experience working with her, in spite of her six-year tenure at the company. Landry believed they wanted to keep her in her current position because she brought in a substantial percentage of the facility's clientele. Her quick shift in opinion about Health-South caught the message board's attention:

> **employeenot: change of heart?   #513 8/24/98**
>
> "If I recall correctly, back on Aug 4 you were the happy
> healthsouthy of 6 years? Have you stopped pulling the
> wagon with the yoke around your neck? Beware!! Hope
> they dont detect your change in attitude. This is when they
> make it so difficult for you they force you out. I know this
> for a fact . . ."

Other posters weren't so sympathetic to Landry's complaints:

> **lowen5: Please discuss stock not personalities #544 9/02/98**
>
> "Please focus on the purpose of this site . . . to exchange ideas or information which may help you or others in deciding to hold, buy or sell . . . this site . . . has numerous postings attacking the lifestyle of the ceo, the working environment or corporate lifestyle . . . Please try to focus on the purpose of this site."[32]

Not all posters thought the information shared by Landry and other disgruntled employees (or ex-employees) was irrelevant. In defense of his own negative postings, **dcm555** wrote: ". . . In my opinion the CEO is a flake and a crook. By discussing his egotistical extravagances with shareholder money, I hope to convince some unknowing investor not to be a part of this scam. It is precisely the personality of the corporate leader that will be the downfall of this house-of-cards. IMHO."[33] Landry's response to critics was less measured:

> **rehab1KL: Sharecropper D*ckhead #562 9/09/98**
>
> "You are a mindless stupid,idiotic,retardo for your posting!!!!!You must work at Corporate!!!!"

In late September, Landry informed the HRC message board that she had resigned her position as Rehabilitation Liaison with HealthSouth, and would be moving to another company, as Director of Business Development. Though she left the company, however, Landry didn't stop exchanging messages with the board:

---

rehab1KL: Screwshe's Mom   #912 10/06/98

"I accidentally discovered that screwshe's parents own the company that all computers are purchased for all Healthsouth facilities. A requisition is sent to Corporate and the computers can only be purchased through this company . . . Richard is a sly SOB. Taking advantage of everyone to make millions of bucks."

At about the same time, another message board participant was raising the same issues. A poster using the name of **wiretuner** wrote: "Healthsouth facilities have to buy computer equipment from mom at inflated prices . . . a barebone lap top 7-8 grand . . . This is called cost shifting i guess? It also raises your costs . . . to enhance your medicare reimbursments."[34]

This exchange brought a response from alias **John_Wayne**, regarded by many to be a company man looking after management interests. "Poison: Your actions have evil intent, so much that I'm sure the Devil himself is very proud of you. You are the exact type of virus in today's society that penicillin was invented to eliminate. I know for a fact the company saved over 180 million dollars over the past five years through the company it used to purchase computers. It was not Richard's mother, it was his father and his father has retired." he wrote.[35]

This was not a good period for business or stock trading at HealthSouth, and the message board carried an increasing number of messages complaining about HealthSouth's operations and management. In addition to such pointed criticisms as those regarding the company's computer purchases, it was common to see messages groaning about working conditions in outlying clinics. Managers were discussed online and often by name. HealthSouth had acquired hundreds of clinics and the struggle to integrate them under central management was evident on the board. And there were foreshadowings of the coming financial disaster for HealthSouth employees, many of whom, as it turned out, had over half of their retirement money invested in company stock. As Landry and **HealthBizz** engaged in mild flirtations and planned fantasy getaways, others on the message board voiced their hopes and anxieties:

---

bopper63: Q3 Earnings forecast #1027

"... here is the bopper's prediction for Q3. The scheduled date to announce is 10/27. Look for the announcement on 10/23, no later than 10/26 to make up for past failures to communicate ... Consensus target is .28, look for .29 or possibly .30. What everyone is forgetting is the 70 new surgery centers that are doing great. When you two losers return, move your version of the dating game to the THC or UHS message board. Regards."[36]

---

bah35 forced2quit #1072

"... things are bad in Texas Our rehab. hospital got bought and the pressure began. We have had resignations from (seven) managers. This is an awful place to work ... Outpatient revenue is down 70% but we got a 100% on the pristine audit. I'm out of here."[37]

Brushing aside the criticisms of other posters, Landry continued to express her disgust with Richard Scrushy and HealthSouth's management practices. Landry said that she was not surprised by HealthSouth layoffs and that she felt terrible about the possibility of employees losing jobs. She called the officers a bunch of crooks and Scrushy a "bozo." She continued her attacks against the company and a boss who, she said, had tried to have an affair with her. "Don't be angry with me for posting the truth—IT IS THE TRUTH," she posted.[38]

In spite of warnings from other posters and Krum's humiliating settlement in October of 1998, Landry never saw the suit against her coming. **HealthBizz** probably had suspicions the night of October 29, and he gave Landry a vague warning in his final post ("They will track us down."), before vanishing from the message board. HealthSouth filed a defamation lawsuit against Landry, accusing her of having written defamatory statements against the company, Scrushy, and another Health-South executive. In the July 1999 *Wall Street Journal* article about Scrushy's lawsuits, HealthSouth is said to have cited postings in which Landry said that Scrushy and other senior management were megalomaniacs who "get off on their power and position," and others in which she called Scrushy a "bozo" and a "crook."[39] The company also cited postings in which Landry said that they paid too much for surgical centers, poorly managed and invested the company's assets, and that all of these actions would contribute to the decline in value of HealthSouth stock. In another article, the *Birmingham News* quotes HealthSouth attorney Donn Duttton as saying: "Her postings stood out as being more offensive than any of the others." To which Landry's attorney, Jill Craft of Baton Rouge, replied, "The last time I checked, this was still America and we still have the right to free speech."[40] Ms. Craft also was swift in her counterattack; on behalf of her client, she asked that HealthSouth turn over financial and personal records that Landry believed could prove that she was right in her assertions about HealthSouth's financial mismanagement. Among the records they sought were Scrushy's income and expense records dating back to 1995, along with flight records for the company's growing number of aircraft.

When the *Wall Street Journal* article appeared on July 7, 1999, many on the message board turned their discussion to the implications of the lawsuit—both for their right to express opinions on the message board, and also for what it revealed about Scrushy's relentless quest to silence criticism. Everyone agreed that the subpoena was an attempt to silence conversation; the First Amendment became the topic of discussion. In a post titled "WSJ Article thoughts," **jedlarson** wrote: "I just read the WSJ article on this company and am outraged at the behavior of Mr. Scrushy and his company. Don't we have freedom of speech in this country? It's like these people use their secret police . . . This is America. People can speak their minds . . ."[41]

Scrushyisasaint said: ". . . poor Screwshe. Imagine getting called a 'bozo' on a site discussing your own company. Thank goodness his company has lots of money and can hire lots of lawyers." A poster who claimed not to be a shareholder, **wintel millionaire,** urged everyone to read the article and think of the importance of the First Amendment. He wondered why a major CEO would waste his time on such trivia: "Who, save Mr. Scrushy, believes what they read on message boards?"[42] His concern, he said was free flow of ideas. Many posters agreed with his stance and several pointed out that the very newspapers that carried the story depend on the First Amendment for their survival. Yes, said several posters, but lies and slander are another issue; private lives should be out of bounds.

In Landry's defense, **hrcblows** wrote a message titled "Kim's Crimes," in which he listed Mr. Scrushy's salary and perks and then told the board that, in his opinion, Landry's appraisal of Scrushy as a megalomaniac, bozo, and crook was not only fair, but generous. Another poster, **kjmack,** using his real name, wrote in a message titled "Kim Landry Defense Fund": "I just talked to Jill Craft, Kim Landry's lawyer . . . She's appreciative that people have expressed support for Kim and interest in creating a defense fund . . ." **kjmack** rallied support for "anyone who believes in free speech, especially those who use Internet message boards." He pointed out that case law regarding speech, privacy, and libel on message boards was only now being developed, and that Landry's case might become a First Amendment landmark. Discussion on the board ranged from praise for Scrushy's willingness to stand up for his privacy, to dire warnings that "censorship is next."[43]

The topic was of national interest, and HealthSouth was not alone in its concerns. *The Wall Street Journal* Interactive Edition, in its "Heard on the Street" column of July 27, 1999, stated: "With an explosion of online corporate chat by investors, more companies are hiring private eyes to track down people posting anonymous messages they don't like . . . It's unclear whether tactics private investigators use to coax identities from people online could constitute an invasion of privacy, say lawyers who specialize in Internet issues. The SEC, for example, doesn't conduct undercover Internet operations, says John Reed Stark, chief of the agency's Office of Internet Enforcement . . . Adds Joseph Grundfest, a professor of business and law at Stanford University's law school, 'It's not against the law to say bad things about a company's stock and management and strategy.'"[44] Robert Lemos, of ZDNet News, quoted Ari Schwarts, policy analyst at the Center for Democracy and Technology, as saying: "Technology has always pushed policy . . . In the privacy arena, especially, technology is going to be a major part of the solution."[45]

And so the debate continued, as did Scrushy's efforts to silence critics on the message board. In a later posting, a member wrote that after the *Wall Street Journal* article had appeared, he was "ferreted out" by HealthSouth investigators and still had the court orders where he had been one of a hundred John Does they were seeking to identify. The poster said that he was contacted by the attorney who was handling HealthSouth's case, who revealed that he knew "everything" about the poster. He went on to say that he was told the lawyer would be in touch in the future if Richard Scrushy wanted to pursue him for further action. He stopped posting on the board shortly thereafter and became a lurker.

But perhaps the most chilling demonstration of Scrushy's efforts to intimidate the message board participants into silence happened in response to a message posted by **Bopper63**— a fairy tale parody, based loosely on George Orwell's *Animal Farm*, titled "Tale of the Porcine Ones."[46] In it, **Bopper63** compared the fate of three Birmingham entrepreneurs, Richard Scrushy, Larry House of MedPartners, and R. Brad Martin, CEO of Sak's Department Stores. All three CEOs led high-profile, privileged lives in Birmingham, but their shareholders had fared less well. When **Bopper63** wrote the tale, HealthSouth stock had fallen from near $30 to about $5, MedPartners had died an expensive death, and Sak's stock had fallen from near $40 to about $10. A June 1999 *Fortune* article, "Vulgarians at the Gate," had featured Scrushy and his entanglements with House; the article referred to the men as "two CEO hustlers," and went on to say: "Their contorted relationships turned a promising enterprise [MedPartners] into one of 1998's biggest Wall Street fiascos."[47] Below is the post (unedited) that led Scrushy to a blatant demonstration of his desperation to stamp out all criticism of him and his empire:

---

bopper63:   Tale of the Three Porcine Ones #12198

"Once upon a time in Birmingham, Alabama, there lived three hungry guys aspiring to get fat like an animal inclined to porcine proclivities. We will call these three Brad, Larry and Richard. Two of these guys chose for profit healthcare, while the other the department store business. The two healthcare guys raised tons of money from investors and soon became known as Vulgarians. They grew fat at the trough of healthcare. They drew porcine salaries, built mansions, acquired airplanes and helicopters and acquired all the trappings of the leading characters in Animal Farm. The other prospered in the department store business but was not happy making lots of money in the medium city market. Inclined to be porcine, he needed to own something prestigious, SAKS 5th Avenue. He acquired SAKS, drew an even bigger salary and looked down at his

---

two B'ham contemporaries. This distressed the other two. Soon Larry bit off more than he could chew; Richard began calling the citizens of B'ham, 'the little people'. Brad started working in earnest to make the stock in his company worth far less than when he acquired SAKS. Richard, not to be outdone, soon started working overtime to make the stock in his company worth even less than the stock in Brad's company. Larry, as is often the fate of porcine ones, disappeared into obscurity, his stock worth even less than Brad's or Richard's but his name forever enshrined with Richard's in Fortune magazine. As the remaining two more aggressively fed at the troughs of their respective companies, they forgot to do what they were being paid to do. They just fed and fed as their stock became worth less and less. Soon they began to behave like the leading characters in Animal Farm. They fed and fed, they discovered stock options and bonuses and they fed some more. This is good they said. Unfortunately, the other residents of this version of Animal Farm were left with something called common stock. Moral of story, if you want to get 'fat' in the stock market invest in companies with a 'lean' management team. End of Story."[48]

By message board standards, this posting hadn't been particularly scandalous, but it elicited a furious response. Shortly after her husband posted this message, **Bopper63**'s wife, manager of a merged HealthSouth surgical center, was at her desk when she received a request by phone to meet an incoming private plane. When she arrived at the airport, two HealthSouth representatives, an officer and a lawyer, took her aside into a conference room. They showed her a folder filled with her husband's Yahoo! Internet message board postings, and told her that Richard Scrushy found them offensive. On the top of the pile was "The Tale of the Porcine Ones." As she later explained to her husband, the HealthSouth representatives threatened to fire her unless he would apologize and cease posting. **Bopper63** was angry and upset. **Bopper63** later told me that he wrote what he felt was the narrowest possible apology and sent it to Richard Scrushy, and briefly considered limiting his comments on the message board. But after time for seething thought, **Bopper63** returned to the message board, blade sharpened to make his point with greater precision and to take a leading role in the anti-Scrushy camp.[49] In years to come, following the FBI raid, **Bopper63** would play a major role in evaluating the investment value of the fallen company with others on the message board.

>>> HOW SWEET IT IS

Later events would serve to prove that many of the negative claims against HealthSouth and Richard Scrushy were not only relevant, but accurate and among the first public information offered about the problems that were accumulating with the organization. Though Scrushy's lawsuits against the message board may have temporarily stifled some of this information, in the end, the growing problems within his company made cover-up impossible.

HealthSouth's lawsuit against Landry didn't stifle her, nor did it end as she had planned. True to her promise, Landry did not seek immediate settlement and continued to post on the board under the names of **OuchSuit** and **kllmissions,** though she remained convinced that she had been denied employment several times because of her involvement. Her later settlement with HealthSouth did not require her to recant her posts, and she maintained: "It is all true."[50]

In 2003, after the FBI raid on HealthSouth headquarters, I posted this message to Landry on the Yahoo! message board: "Told ya so! No one likes a wise ass, but having Bopper's and my opinions (gained through no little personal discomfort) confirmed is refreshing justification. My sympathies to Ouchsuit/kllmissions/rehab1KL, and all of those who told the truth about these high-flying bastards over the many years we have followed this board. Even makes you feel a little bad for Dirk Diggler."

In response, Landry wrote: "I said it four years ago and they sued me! What is so hilarious about the entire ordeal is that they sued me for telling the truth!!!! Now who is going to have the last word! ME . . . Ohhhh, how sweet it is![51]

>>> THE EMPIRE STARTS TO CRUMBLE

Although those on the Yahoo! message board didn't realize it in 1998, Scrushy's attempts to intimidate Krum, Landry, and other posters had little to do with them as individuals, and a lot to do with Scrushy's own need to control the spread of negative information about his teetering empire. The age of Imperial CEOs was not yet finished, analysts still held sway, and most people failed to mine information from Internet message boards. Nevertheless, by the year 2000, Scrushy's ability to control the buzz about HealthSouth was diminishing, and the power of message boards and blogs was growing. As HealthSouth's stock price suffered and damning information about the company escalated online, the meltdown of Health-South began. The marketplace, as always, was about to claim the last word.

CHAPTER *five*

The Meltdown

The year 1999 had been the beginning of a difficult struggle for Richard Scrushy, as he fought to promote HealthSouth in the face of mounting criticism and falling share prices. His company's fortunes were continuing their serious dive. In spite of Scrushy's assurances that the company was "poised for recovery" from its dizzying plunge in value during the preceding year, many inside HealthSouth recognized that the company was suffering from a cash shortage. Internally, according to testimony in Scrushy's 2005 federal court trial, accounting manipulations were taking more employee time and progressively distorting financial reality.[1] What began in the late 1980s as small but fraudulent adjustments to records, had evolved by 1999 into the manipulation of thousands of accounts; it was called "pixie dust" and filling "the hole" by the conspirators.[2] And the financial manipulations were continuing to fuel at least some favorable coverage within the mainstream media.

After a partial recovery early in the year, *Smart Money* magazine had given the company a boost with a highly favorable report.[3]

Although Scrushy had silenced some of his most vocal critics, the Yahoo! finance message board continued to offer some of the most accurate information that could be had about HealthSouth and its operations. Opinion on the message board was that HealthSouth might well be oversold from a technical viewpoint, having fallen too rapidly, but that press coverage such as the *Smart Money* piece was simply "fluff" that seemed to ignore lawsuits against HealthSouth as well as current economic pressures on health care. A poster who said he was a CPA wrote that *Smart Money*'s reporting was so unclear as to be deceptive.

Then, in June of 1999, Scrushy announced that Health-South would divide into two separate companies. He billed the split as a path to new jobs and better growth, though the maneuver likely was an effort to stifle some of the growing concern among shareholders and boost the price of HealthSouth shares. He was quoted in the *Birmingham News* as saying: "You will have two $2 billion plus companies in Birmingham."[4]

On the message board, **sistersavant** had wondered about Scrushy's figures for growth and volume.[5] None of us could contribute any hard data to explain the size of management's write-downs, but HealthSouth became suspect for its quarterly one-time adjustments, the most common of which were write-downs of unadjusted accounts receivable.

Although the announcement brought an initial boost to the company's stock price, within a few months, the news was less encouraging. By August of 1999, the mainstream press was reporting a decline in HealthSouth's earnings, and many analysts were questioning whether the company's stock split was actually going to take place. Then, with the stock near new lows, the *Birmingham News* published the September 10 announcement that the spin-off plan was scrapped, only days after Scrushy had denied any change in plans. The cycle of optimism to gloom took less than three months. Analysts downgraded HealthSouth after the failed split, and shares plummeted by more than 30 percent. HealthSouth (HRC) became the New York Stock Exchange's most heavily traded stock of the day at 25 million shares, and analysts began to speak of worries about management:

---

flymeahelicopter: FLY FLY FLY   **5/18/99**

"HS is going nowhere if Scrushy doesn't quit frivolous spending. The latest expenditure . . . a 1 million dollar helicopter. Scrushy said the 20 mins it took to get from the headquarters to the airport was far too long.

Give me a break . . . when will such practices be stopped????"[6]

---

hospital_boy: HRC 10Q is interesting

". . . as far as the helicopter goes - this is a 5 billion dollar company on its way to being a 50 billion dollar company in 10 years. Think big, will ya?"[7]

The message board had been the first to spot decay. Postings painted a continuing picture of shareholder frustration and disbelief at lavish executive perks, musical-chair reorganizations, and a lap-dog board of directors that was ever ready to approve bonuses or forgive sweetheart loans. Scrushy's September announcement of a deal to link HealthSouth clinics to the Internet in a venture with Healtheon/WebMD, included the news that he and other officers would support HealthSouth's share price by buying shares on the open market. Few of us on the message board were bamboozled by a move so obviously slanted to promotion. This time, skepticism extended to the mainstream media as well. In an interview on CNBC, Bob Gabele, director of the insider-trading research division of First Call/Thompson Financial, noted that insiders had financed the purchase of shares through a loan from Health-South and that the collateral was the shares themselves. The message board agreed that the deal offered insiders an opportunity to profit without taking any risk. Said one poster: "These guys have nothing to lose and everything to gain. I have a lot to lose . . . and a lot to gain."[8]

Not to be put off by the growing rumble of investor discontent, Scrushy staged a lavish Christmas party at his Birmingham mansion. The local paper gave it glowing coverage: "Guests were met at the door by Richard Scrushy and year-old daughter Chloe. The party of the season was complete with flowers, gourmet food and live entertainment, including a command performance by host, Richard Scrushy, playing with his friends from "the band," Dallas County Line . . . It was a reunion for politicians, university Presidents, sport stars, neighbors and friends . . . Dancing to the music of Foxxy Fats and clapping to the music of Scrushy's boys . . . The fellow-founders of HealthSouth were there to play with guitar-man Scrushy and to hear Scrushy favorites, 'I've Got a Woman' and 'You're Too Good Lookin' to Still Be Lookin'.' Fresh salmon by candlelight and fine wine . . . a special treat for all of his friends."[9]

>>> GOOD TIME NOT HAD BY ALL

As 1999 drew to a close, however, not everyone associated with HealthSouth was having a good time. Investors on the message board were, for the most part, under water with HRC shares. The furious pace of trading had brought many day traders to the stock and to the message board, but the more thoughtful investors, those who intended to hold the stock until recovery, were not able to put aside their concerns with HealthSouth's reporting accuracy and timliness:

Quiterisky: Patience   # 9752   12/28/99

"Patience . . . Sure, if HRC meets the 2000 numbers, we are right back up to $15-$20. I'm just getting skeptical of the numbers based on the present price of HRC. After all, if we see the potencial, why don't others see it??"

Quiterisky went on to complain about the surprises brought on by asset write-downs: "Investors have confidence in the business, but nobody likes surprises. Scrushy and his pals have been full of surprises, negative surprises, and that pisses off investors . . ."[10] **SinclairKnow** looked for a tough year: "HRC is in for a tough year 2000 and will be facing quarter over quarter decreases in EPS . . . HRC should have its cost savings measures in place by 2001 (and no more large charges)."[11] And **jkesoc,** answering a thread of discussion on confidence, said what many who were tired of promises and waited for the chance to get out were thinking: "I have the stock, think it will go up, but would never buy a share more. And I will sell it as soon as it goes up and put the money somewhere else, where I am competing not against the managers of the company but the competitors of the company . . ."[12]

The new year brought hopeful words from company headquarters, as reported in the *Birmingham News:*

AFTER 15 ROCKY MONTHS, SCRUSHY UPBEAT ON 2000

HealthSouth Corp. spent the past year suffering one occupational hazard after another on Wall Street. In fact, 1999 was so bad that officials at HealthSouth—

which bills itself "the health care company of the 21st century"—will be glad to put the 20th century behind them.[13]

By January 2000, it had been nearly 18 months since the all-time high for HealthSouth stock. It had been a difficult period due to government cutbacks and pressure from HMOs; most health care service companies had been hurt. Health-South's straight-down plunge was made worse by reports of insider trading (directors' sales as well as Scrushy's), the large write-off for the sale of HealthSouth's Home Health Care division, and chronic troubles with accounts receivable.

Scrushy looked forward to receiving more Medicare money for inpatient physical therapy and to profiting from computerized medical records. Internet deals will "save up to $100 million," he suggested. He played the "global Health-South" card whenever he found an opening: "We are looking at deals in South America . . ."[14] On the message board, a few posters agreed with Scrushy, but more agreed with **Bopper63:**

Bopper63:   You don't get it #10123

"Today COL, UHS, THC and HMA all finished higher. Why? Because they have management teams that know what they are doing. I'll keep repeating it: we need a change in sr. management. The argument that all of the bad news and the resulting plummet in the company's stock is the fault of the government, HMO's, politicians, etc is so much smoke . . ."[15]

At the next quarterly report, Scrushy again announced satisfactory earnings. That part of his strategy remained unchanged, and the *Birmingham News* duly announced in its "Money Briefs" column that "HealthSouth will report fourth-quarter and annual 1999 earnings . . . in line with analysts' expectations . . ."[16] But the stock price did not respond. Actually revenues had been down by $40 million from the previous year. Even after Scrushy had appeared for an interview on CNBC and discussed his satisfaction with operating income, share price dropped 9 percent to $5.14. Major brokerage houses were more kind. A message on the board quoted Joseph Chiarelli of J.P. Morgan Securities as saying that with improved prospective payments, "HealthSouth, by my calculations, would probably receive about a 12% increase in its reimbursement . . . As a result, there appears to be upside potential to current earnings estimates . . ."[17] In the next few weeks, HRC shares bottomed and started a new run upward. I had been skeptical in March and I hadn't changed my mind: "HRC is not a good company; its top officers borrow money from the company at low rates to buy stock, and the company has more airplanes for executive travel than the Tunisian air force. But it is worth more than $5 per share."[18]

>>> THE PRESSURE MOUNTS

Scrushy's compensation remained a polarizing topic on the message board. In a message thread entitled "Scrushy Received a $10 million Bonus for What?" posters discussed another troublesome incident, in which management had provided a private equity fund for Scrushy and other insiders. After investments didn't pan out, the fund was transferred back to the company, leaving shareholders to absorb the loss. Once again, many on the message board shouted that the board of directors' compensation committee should be replaced. This was a growing sentiment and was reflected by other, larger investors who had called for more independent directors. Scrushy reacted to the growing pressure by announcing in another *Birmingham News* article that he would take a pay cut. ". . . that should keep him from making any 'highest paid' lists this year," the article stated.[19]

A salary reduction left Scrushy's 1999 pay at $1.6 million, down from $2.7 million in 1998 and less than half of the $3.4 million he earned in 1997 when his total pay neared $106 million. Scrushy commented: "When you get a couple of hundred million dollars cut, you have to make adjustments and that includes my pay. I've always been taught you're supposed to lead by example." The newspaper went on to quote Scrushy as saying: "When you look at the stress and the number of hours that goes into managing a company this size, I doubt many people would trade places."[20] His pay for 2000 would resume its normal scale of $3.6 million.

HealthSouth's problems were becoming familiar and were beginning to look very much like those common to other health care companies. The Scrushy magic—growth plus earnings—had disappeared. As testimony at Scrushy's trial would show, the company was increasingly short of cash. Money was being borrowed to pay taxes on nonexistent profits.

HealthSouth guided analysts to expect lower earnings and then, as expected, the company hit the analysts' new lowered targets. The second quarter of 2000 was reported in July and earnings were 17 cents per share, down from 27 cents for the same quarter the past year. There was no earnings surprise—a possibility that had teased investors:

Bopper63: Disappointment   #15910

"Obviously, word had leaked out that there would not be an earnings surprise. As usual shareholders were the last to know. The sale of over 1 million shares by a director at $8 should have alerted all of us, no matter what spin you put on it."[21]

Two of the message board's most regular and best informed posters, **Zman492** and **Bopper63,** discussed the prospect of another "September Surprise." **Zman492** was an investor who did his homework and had, in the past, trusted management; **Bopper63,** of course, had been burned before and was hopeful he would find an opportunity to sell the large position in HRC stock he inherited by merger. Both were wary of third-quarter reports:

Zman492:   August/September   #16570

"In the past three years there have been four months where HRC lost more than 20% in the month: August 1998 : down 24.8% — September 1998: down 47.5% — August 1999: down 33.8% — September 1999: down 25.8%. That concern, while still present, has been reduced by the fact that we made it through August 2000 with a 4.5% increase in the stock price. Even if we make it through September without bad news, I will wait until the third quarter results are announced (assuming there is no bad news reported along with the earnings) before I stop worrying about a nasty surprise . . ."[22]

Bopper63:   Re: August/September/Julius Caesar #16573

". . . For those who didn't know how a company could lose 85% of its market cap, your figures clearly show how it happened. To me, Sep 9th is HRC's 'ides of March'. If we make it safely pass this date then perhaps the worst is over. Prior to the last announcements, the street had become aware of the impending bad news and had been selling . . . Last summer, six weeks before the Sep 9th announcement, 3 million shares were unloaded in one sale. I called Piper Jaffray to see if anybody could find out the reason. Answer, nothing, and all analysts have the stock as a buy. Six weeks later, kiss my ass good bye."[23]

The thoughts expressed from members of the message board who gave indications that they were employees or otherwise connected with HealthSouth are particularly revealing. **Sistersavant,** like **CrazyCPA,** posted as a Birmingham local and had respectable credentials of longevity and experience. Her posts and others raised suspicions and stimulated reinspection of HealthSouth's reports. A long-time poster, **sistersavant** saw something wrong. When I read this message, I suspected that she smelled a rat in HealthSouth's reporting:

> **sistersavant: Z, or someone who actually reads Q10 #16570**
>
> "Doesn't a 12% swing in the bad debt provision strike you as a bit radical? . . .
>
> Also what is with the almost 5% increase in corporate expenses—I thought they were trimming their corporate staff?"

Stock prices trended upward the entire fourth quarter of 2000. Those, including officers, who had bought at the low were ecstatic. Day traders, though, had to be careful of volatility. As the year drew to a close, regulars on the board knew that insiders would be tempted to cash in:

> **jbranger: Re: hrc be aware #17576**
>
> "Long time holders are aware of the insiders who bought heavily last year around the $5 level. do not be alarmed when some of them start taking 'some' profits for tax purposes . . . They could sell half their position, pay their tax and repay HRC and be left with 50% of their original purchase with a ZERO net cost."[24]

> **mdu51:   Re: Those who trashed Scrushy, Up 216%!   #17907**
>
> " . . . the ones who trashed the most bailed out first. Happy
> New Year to Mr. Scrushy and staff."[25]

>>> THE CHANGING HEALTH CARE SYSTEM

Outwardly, HealthSouth was ready, in 2001, to recover
from severe losses in payment brought about by Medicare and
Medicaid cuts, financial blows that had been made worse by
ever-tightening reimbursement by managed care companies—
increasingly no one remained to whom to shift costs. Health-
South's profit fade was mirrored by every medical practice
and hospital in the United States. Hospitals were closing, as
what was termed by insurers as "excess capacity" was wrung
out of the health care system.

Inside HealthSouth, however, more insidious stresses were
growing. The shortfall of millions of dollars per week below analysts' estimates was made worse by the fact that HealthSouth
had to pay taxes on income that it did not have. In federal court
testimony in 2005, Ken Livesay, HealthSouth CFO, testified
that HealthSouth claimed $407.5 million in income in one pe-
riod that led to a $145.5 million tax payment, but on only a real
income of $160.4 million.[26] Cash became so tight that borrow-
ing was necessary to pay bills. All facts that, according to his defense team, Scrushy was unaware of at the time.

Headlines from 2001 show widening cracks in Health-
South's company façade, as troubles mounted in the form of
lawsuits, government investigations, and shareholder rebel-
lion. But, the year began on a high note. In a January 28 article
in the *Birmingham News*, Scrushy was quoted as saying that he
was confident of a turnaround: "We don't see any negatives on
the horizon this year. We feel like we've turned a corner."[27]

FIGURE 5.1

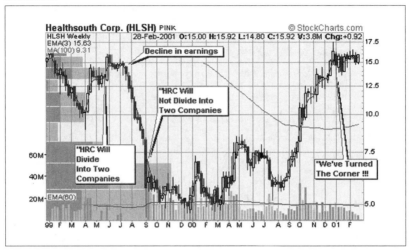

HealthSouth started the year at about $17, and its price began dropping in the first week.

On the message board, some posters remained guardedly upbeat.

Zman492 spoke of increased payments, reductions in debt, and earnings growth. He intended, he said, to hold his stock, but, he noted, unpleasant surprises can happen.[28] The investment bank UBS Warburg had lifted its target from $15 to $24 per share, and its analyst, Howard Capek, said that Health-South was the company's top pick for 2001.[29] (Analyst Capek later was forced out of UBS because he was found to have sent an e-mail to an institutional investor in September 1999 saying: "HRC, what a mess. I would not own a share . . ." despite being one of the last analysts to downgrade his recommendation.[30])

Despite Scrushy's published comments to the contrary, HealthSouth had not turned the corner—it had merely begun bouncing downhill. During the first quarter of 2001, share prices quickly dropped. At the HealthSouth March Conference Call, Scrushy promised that the company would meet analysts' estimates, but shares dropped from $15 to $12½, then bounced and dropped again. None of the posters on the message board could find a clear reason for the drop, and the mainstream press wasn't speculating on HealthSouth's declining value.

Scrushy then turned to another tried-and-true strategy for driving up stock share prices—expansion. He announced that not only had fourth quarter profits increased, but HealthSouth would build nine new rehabilitation hospitals. To some on the message board, his announcement seemed to be a testimony to HealthSouth's renewed commitment to sustained expansion:

---

svangil: Birmingham News #18525 3/7/2001

"Article in Money section says Scrushy expects to rapidly expand the number of rehabilitation hospitals it operates. Nine are under construction now (the most the company has built at one time in its 17 yr history) . . . 'Things are looking great right now' Scrushy said."

Scrushy had more big news. He would combine science with the Internet, inpatient with outpatient, and make a HealthSouth hospital the digital hospital of tomorrow. On March 26, Scrushy announced that HealthSouth would create "the first fully automated digital hospital."[31] With its partner, Oracle Corporation, HealthSouth planned to build the 219-bed, 500,000-square-foot, "smart" hospital. Doctors would work through the Internet and sign medical orders with a thumbprint; patients would have computer access at the bedside. Alabama Governor Don Seigelman, to whom Scrushy had been a generous campaign donor, came through by backing special legislation exempting HealthSouth from regulations requiring a certificate of need; these certificates are required by Alabama state law in an attempt to avoid overbuilding and duplication of health care facilities. The competing hospital facilities in and around Birmingham quickly worked to oppose Scrushy's digital hospital, but his political connections and public relations machine were too much for them, and he won the battle.

On the message board there were severe doubts about the viability of Scrushy's digital hospital plan. Company loyalists and local Birmingham residents wrote to the message board to express their support for the $250 million project, but many of us felt that it was too expensive and it was not a particularly new concept. I was aware that many of the promises of software are not frequently realized by early adopters, and expressed these concerns in a message to the board, to which **Bopper63** added his doubts:

Charon_xxx: bopper, Zman492, ranger.HRC/Oracle Hospital: Been There! #18684

"The digital press release doesn't answer many questions for me . . . So far the paperless record revolution is underway, but has yet to deliver profits . . . Electronics is still not secure—witness the hacking of Microsoft Headquarters—and wireless access only increases problems. At the end of the day, surprisingly little labor is saved—templates and forms seem to grow in complexity making navigation time consuming. Bandwidth will be a big help. But, inertia is a powerful force in health care and change will always come more slowly than predicted."

Bopper63: Hospitals are not HRCs Core Business #18682

"I find the announcement about the digital hospital peculiar. HRC advertises that it is a rehabilitation and surgery center company. Recently it announced the sale of an inpatient hospital in Virginia, proceeds which are being used to reduce debt and to focus the company on its core business. Why expend all the effort and capital in a business which

> is peripheral to your mission when a digital rehab hospital or surgery center would make more sense?"[32]

After Scrushy's original announcement, estimates on the cost of the digital hospital increased in price by nearly $100 million, to about $1.6 million per bed. Over time, the project would drag HealthSouth into a court battle against local hospitals, embarrass the board of directors, and become a digital white elephant. But Scrushy was not deterred, and plunged ahead with his plans. He released HealthSouth's annual report in April, with the announcement: "Things are looking great." The board of directors showed their appreciation by increasing his salary to $3.65 million, plus options on 80,000 shares of HRC. Salomon covered the stock and issued a buy, with a price target of $21. Lehman Brothers agreed with a "strong buy" recommendation.

Then, in May, HealthSouth announced that it was leaving the occupational health business; the company soon sold its OT operations to HealthWorks. HealthSouth's announcement cited the usual reasons for the sale: The company wanted to focus on its core business. In retrospect, however, it seems likely that cash was short and the CFOs needed an infusion of dollars for Scrushy's expansion plans. The marketplace did not view the sale as good news, and shares fell back toward $11.

As the second quarter of 2001 got under way, HealthSouth stock continued to flounder. Shares had not been responding to good news, and Scrushy had failed to convince investors that problems with costs were under control. In May, the company had paid $8 million in the settlement of a 1997 whistleblower lawsuit for Medicare overbilling. The government's case arose from a suit filed under the False Claims Act by Greg Madrid, a former HealthSouth billing clerk (Madrid would get $1.48 million as his part of the settlement). The government

FIGURE 5.2

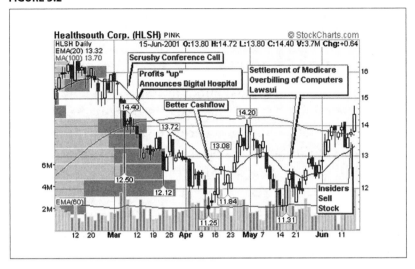

charges stemmed from HealthSouth's purchases of computer equipment from a company owned by Scrushy's parents at prices two and three times the going rate—overcharges first pointed out by some on the Yahoo! message board as early as 1998. These overcharges, in turn, inflated HealthSouth's expense ratios, which the government uses when calculating the overall Medicare reimbursement rate. As a result, HealthSouth had overbilled Medicare, and the government had sued the company for filing false claims.

In the announcement of the settlement, Tadd McVay, HealthSouth treasurer, said that HealthSouth admitted no wrongdoing and that government allegations "involved highly technical accounting issues" rather than patient care services. "This is the government's accountant disagreeing with our accountants," he said. "We would have spent more money litigating these issues than settling for the $8 million," spokesperson McVay was quoted as saying.[33] Many on the message board saw the situation as an unintended consequence of an unethical practice, but others considered the overbilling as outright fraud:

---

rehabbiz: Re: Birminham News Article #18964

"THE NO SPIN ZONE WANTS TO KNOW: How did a billing clerk uncover these 'highly technical accounting issues'? What was this guy making $5.50-10/hour."

---

bopper63: Minor Technical Disagreement Costs Millions? #18968

Why did HRC and ultimately we shareholders have to pay a fine that involved a company owned by the parents of Richard Scrushy? This was no 'arms length' transaction. The fine should be paid by those who benefited from it not the long suffering shareholders of this company. Minor technical accounting details do not result in multi-million dollar fines."[34]

>>> INSIDER SALES CAUSE FOR ALARM

With the threat of more serious charges of Medicare fraud gone, and with brokerages recommending "strong buy," HealthSouth announced personnel cuts. Investors perceived this announcement as ushering in positive changes; as the company appeared to be attempting to get costs under control, share prices climbed. Several employees posted to say that layoffs were mostly at large regional offices, but under the alias **Ken**, one poster wrote about the 60 layoffs in Tennessee. "Now wait for calls to the Inspector General," he predicted. "We will have more Whistle Blower Lawsuits."[35] **Ken** may have been correct. Without knowing the details of the official investigations, we'll never know with certainty who finally caught the ears of the FBI, the SEC, and the Inspector General. But several from the message board wrote complaints to regulatory agencies. On the message board, **Bopper63** posted again in disgust, and I replied that I was no longer a long-term investor in HealthSouth:

---

bopper63:   Take a Look #19049

"As many of you know, I am not a real big fan of this company. I have often pointed out the disparity between the stock price of this company vis a vis its competitors. I have often pointed out how the market loves the business but dislikes this company . . . you simply have to ask, what the hell gives with HRC. Many of you know the answer."[36]

---

charon_xxx: Re: Take a Look #19053

"I agree. Since I sold out my position, HRC has not broken out of its trading range. Good luck to those of you with staying power."[37]

As fate would have it, I sold too soon, at least by short-term measures. The stock hit $18, in a gain spurred by "greater than estimates" earnings announced in July, higher Medicare payments for rehabilitation, and an announcement that long-term debt would be reduced. This price bump was too great a temptation to the insiders. On August 8, a poster named **Walkstreet_2000** asked: "What happened at 1 PM on Wednesday? The stock took a big tumble on large volume."[38]

A poster new to the board asked, in regard to news that HealthSouth CFO Weston Smith was selling off shares: "Why Weston, why are you selling? Do you know something we don't?"[39] And the next day he asked again: "Why is the CFO selling?"[40] Indeed, that was a mystery. But the hints pointed to oddities that remained a mystery until the federal indictments. On August 1, for example, Scrushy had resigned as

FIGURE 5.3

president of HealthSouth, and named Bill Owens as the new president and chief operating officer. Then Rob Thompson, the president of the hospital division, was fired. Poster Ken Duval wrote about Thompson's leaving, wondering at the way Thompson, almost a founding father, had simply vanished.[41] Something was going on in the executive suites.

On September 7, **Zman492** and **cmnae** began a long message thread that explored the possibilities raised by the insider sales taking place at HealthSouth. **Zman492** started the thread by remarking: "I would not say that you should ignore insider sales, but you should keep them in perspective. As of the last annual report, officers and executives owned over 30 million shares of HRC. The sum of all shares covered by 'potential future sales registrations' is less than one million shares, only 3 percent of the shares held by officers and executives . . . Also remember that they have to sell some shares sometimes if they want to enjoy profits from those shares, just as you and I do."[42] His explanation was met with scorn by poster **cmnae,** who said it was only a signpost, a warning:

> **cmnae: Re: Today's Announcement #19319**
>
> ". . . Do you really believe that all these insiders suddenly needed big cash for a new mansion all at once? Would you believe some of them were taking money off the table before the stock started trading down? Naw! Not the leaders of our company! . . . They would be adding to their positions if only they had the money available. Yea, right! Think, Z. CM."[43]

Cmnae read the tea leaves correctly. His final post in the matter spoke to another suspected problem hidden by Health-South management. The combination of debt and insider selling was enough to depress the stock:

> **cmnae: Today's Announcement #19328**
>
> ". . . It's very interesting how money from bonds, many times, doesn't add to equity—isn't it? Long term debt to equity below the industry average with the new 500M loan? I doubt it . . . CM."

>>> DOWNWARD TREND CONTINUES

As the final quarter of 2001 progressed, HRC was volatile, but the stock's overall direction was downward. When **cmnae** returned to claim his rightful credit, **Bopper63** replied:

> **bopper63:   cmnae 10/13/01**
>
> "Where are you getting your info? The insiders in this company have consistently bailed out ahead of bad news.

However, as a reward for driving the stock from $30 to $5, the Board loaned $35 million to CEO and others to buy stock at the reduced price. Some of these people are gone and no longer are under rule 144. In any event, Scrushy is on the record since the attack as saying that the company will meet street expectations."[44]

By October 26, the *Birmingham News* carried an article trumpeting the tidings that HealthSouth's third-quarter profits were up 11 percent. According to the article, HealthSouth attributed the increase to higher prices, cost cutting, and more patient visits. Net income increased to 20 cents per share, up from 18 cents a year earlier. But on the release of this seemingly positive news, HRC dropped 14 percent to close at $12.50. As **Bopper63** said: "Déjà vu! What can one say?" Carl, **cmnae**, returned for a last comment; it may have been meant for short-term traders, but as events unfolded, it provided a guide for all who owned HealthSouth shares:

cmnae: Re: No cashflow . . . #19471 10/28/2001

"When the insiders sell, I sell . . . To anyone concerned with their HRC investment, I would like to direct you to HRC's price and volume charts. For those of you who know how to read them, you may be viewing them with some alarm. Looks like a serious breakdown to me, implying that something is afoot . . ."

>>> THE ROLLER COASTER RIDE CONTINUES

HealthSouth began construction of the digital hospital in late November with great fanfare, but there was little other good news to support a strong rally. December ended with HRC shares lower than the year's starting price. From the viewpoint of its critics, HRC had not answered questions about its collections of accounts receivable, leaving days of outstanding service at a level worse than its peers, nor were the old timers' views of management competence and honesty helped by the company's settlement with the Medicare Administration for overbilling. Because many who posted on the board were employees with shares in their company 401(k)s, and others were investors who had received large numbers of shares through a merger with HealthSouth, their options for exit were limited. They felt locked in until a more comfortable sales point could be found. Short-term traders were in the driver's seat and they loved HRC's volatility.

Forbes magazine, in a January 2002 article titled "Back to Life," summed up the situation at HealthSouth in the article's tagline: "HealthSouth's meteoric rise was matched only by its rapid descent. Now in recovery mode, Richard Scrushy faces his biggest challenge yet."[45] Monte Burke noted in the article that Scrushy had "regained his old swagger." In a favorable report, the article said that he was ready to digest and streamline his many acquisitions; he was credited for breaking new scientific ground with plans for his ten-story digital hospital. "'I'll be able to see it from right here,' said Scrushy at the window of his penthouse office. 'It's going to be great,'" said the *Forbes* article.

Under the new Medicare program, the profit game was won by reducing costs and by shortening patient stays and cutting services, because the same dollar amount was paid for each diagnostic code. HealthSouth reported that it cut its per-patient cost from $11,200 in 1997, to $9,600 in 2002, leaving a gross profit of $1,600. Scrushy reported that they would be able to cut costs even further to $8,000. Analysts computed that his current cost structure would allow for profits of 92 cents per share and a stock price in the $20s. HealthSouth was, once again, on the mend; Scrushy made headlines in his support for analysts' optimism. But skeptics on the message board didn't share in the rosy outlook:

> **bopper63:   Short Position   #19660**
>
> "Today's *WSJ* shows the short position in HRC going from 5,244,596 on 11/15 to 6,521,251 on 12/15 for percentage increase of 24.34. This is quite an increase which shows that a lot of people think the stock is overvalued at current levels. Any comments on this?"

>>> THERE'S NO BUSINESS LIKE SHOW BUSINESS

As was frequently the case at HealthSouth, however, a shakeup of sorts was already in the works. Many of us shook our heads as we read this headline from the *Birmingham News*:

THE HEALTHSOUTH YEARS

ACTOR LEAVES HOLLYWOOD
TO HEAD SCRUSHY'S MEDIA PROJECTS

"Former child-actor Jason Hervey, now Senior Vice President, Marketing, made the leap from Hollywood glitz to lead HealthSouth show-business projects such as the "Go-For-It Road Show" and the new MTV-like television show for children . . . 'Birmingham is terrific,' said Hervey who was best known as Wayne, actor Fred Savage's brother, in the '80's television show 'The Wonder Years.' . . . Why did Hervey leave Hollywood to become Senior Vice-President for Marketing? 'Two words: Richard Scrushy,' said the happy Hervey."[46]

It would be difficult to overstate the value that Scrushy placed on show business and spectacular public relations efforts. He was a salesman and a showman. In 2000, Scrushy had bought into a sports TV network, citing an opportunity to build the company brand name. He furthered his "brand-building" activities by launching a live road show, "Go For It!" and later "Go For It! TV: The Real Challenge," described in a press release as "a reality-based show created for kids by HealthSouth and Coca-Cola." The live road show had originally been presented as an opportunity for celebrity jocks to appear before groups of school kids to deliver important messages about staying fit and healthy. The show turned out, however, to be a vehicle for 3rd Faze—a Vegas-style girl group Scrushy commissioned from the same producer who helped craft the Backstreet Boys.

The Go For It! road show drew criticism from some parents for the singing group's scanty costumes and suggestive dance numbers. And many on the message board had questioned the value of investing company money in such a questionable pursuit of "branding." But nothing had angered employees who posted to the board more than Scrushy's hiring of Jason Hervey as vice president in charge of marketing, at a reported salary of $300,000.

Jason Hervey was criticized for many things: youth, inexperience, inability to spell, and his wife, Angel Hart. John Helyar's *Fortune* article, "The Insatiable King Richard," described reactions to Scrushy's hiring of Jason Hervey: "People at HealthSouth were shocked. Scrushy had taken a 29-year-old movie brat with no healthcare experience and put him in charge of marketing and communications. Hervey's main job was to be the latest Scrushy sidekick. There was even more shock when some employees discovered that Hervey's wife was a former porn star known as Angel Hart . . . The two [Scrushy and Hervey] became inseparable as Hervey reinforced Scrushy's show business obsession."[47]

>>> **HEALTHSOUTH TAKES ANOTHER HIT**

In late January, HealthSouth was hit with another govern-ment lawsuit when the U.S. Department of Justice (DOJ) joined a lawsuit brought by an employee who charged that Health-South had violated Medicare regulations governing the use of physical therapists, billing for services of an unlicensed techni-cian at professional rates. HealthSouth replied that the suit was without merit and took an aggressive rather than a compliant stance. (The company later paid the United States $325 million to settle this and a subsequent Medicare fraud allegation.[48])

Many who posted about this lawsuit complained that the DOJ action was a mere nuisance—little more than extortion. Several on the board noted that these payments only involved 1 to 2 percent of revenue. One poster, **buyabargain,** said: "HRC is the cleanest in the industry. They picked on the wrong company this time."[49] I replied from experience and to the contrary. I reminded **byabargain** not to underestimate the power of the DOJ or the Medicare Administration. When Medicare officials examine a provider—whether a coporation or an individual physician—and no matter what part of the business is being examined, even a minor or unintentional transgression can be fined at $10,000 or more for each in-stance, then tripled and multiplied once again by the esti-mated times it "may" have happened throughout the entire system. Having records stirred through distracts employees and is bad for business; taking a fighting stance rather than a cooperative stance ordinarily makes things worse.

The aggressive posture against the lawsuit seemed to work for some time. Lehman Brothers had recommended a buy with a $22 target and, despite the share price's recent declines, several, including **skyguy12345,** called a bottom in early March, saying: ". . . we're grinding out a bottom, and I stand by my earlier near-term target of high $13's for now."[50] It was a beautiful prediction, but troubles, seen and unseen, were mounting. HealthSouth's shares would never be this high again.

Then, the other shoe dropped: The Department of Justice announced that it would join in yet another lawsuit against HealthSouth—this one being pressed by the states of Texas, New York, Florida, and Alabama—that alleged HealthSouth billed the government for one-on-one therapy sessions actually done in groups.[51] The suit also alleged that HealthSouth had used a maintenance man to perform physical therapy on a patient. As the whistle-blower lawsuit gained strength, so did a movement spearheaded by local hospitals in competition with Health-South to stop the building of Scrushy's digital hospital. Republican gubernatorial candidate Tim James had criticized passage of a bill allowing HealthSouth to bypass the state certificate-of-need law. Scrushy demanded that James retract a letter accusing the company of using money and influence to get legislative help for its digital hospital; Scrushy's demand made headlines in the *Birmingham News*.[52] This response was vintage Scrushy. Where silence or a private response may have spared the company more adverse publicity, he chose the aggressive course.

It remained to be seen if his old strategies would continue to serve him well. Show business promotions, expansions funded by mounting debt, and a constant attacking offense worked wonderfully in a rising market, when health care was robust, and when HealthSouth enjoyed near-universal goodwill. But those factors had all changed by mid-2002, and message board critics, once cowed by Scrushy's lawsuits, gained strength. Messages squarely targeted management problems: "Birmingham Temple $75 million over budget," one message read. "It gets worse . . . a number of the so-called original partners . . . are rotating out!"[53] It was true. Scrushy announced that Siemans would replace Oracle for much of the electronics and the budget continued to climb; share price didn't follow. It was stuck at about $12. Messages focusing on old, unanswered questions appeared regularly as **nikgabpups** asked, "Does anyone have an explanation of why HRC reports earnings so late? . . . they do it every year . . ."[54]

Scrushy's pay was a particularly sore point because he was paid more than $10 million while HRC underperformed the industry. Net income was down as was cash from operations; many wondered why Scrushy deserved a bonus at all—particularly in view of his sale of Occupational Medicine to HealthWorks and HealthSouth's Richmond center to HCA at a loss to the company of over $100 million. I wrote to the message board:

---

charon_xxx: Bopper and Enron Lovers Everywhere #20460

"Don't you just love derivative financing deals, off book leases, obscure financial guarantees, interlocking directorates, big statues of wagons, huge corporate offices, laser light shows and country music? Is this a fun company, or what? . . . Vision like this is worth much more than $10 million a year. Some day we'll all be grateful . . ."

Forbes, it seemed, agreed, and in its May 13, 2002, list of the country's worst CEOs, it gave Scrushy an "F" grade for his efficiency and named him as number 4 in its list of the country's worst CEOs, noting that while he had taken a reduced salary for the preceding two years, he had also taken a $6.5 million bonus, even as the company's earnings per share dropped 28 percent.[55] The company responded by issuing a formal press release refuting *Forbes*'s claim—bringing more attention to the article. In the article, HealthSouth stated: "HealthSouth regrets that Forbes has found it necessary to use arbitrary calculation periods and incomplete information in order to give a misleading air of sensationalism to its reporting on executive compensation matters."[56] On the message board, posters responded to the company's weak defense:

> **Northern_European_American: That was a silly press re-
> lease #20672**
>
> "The Forbes methodology penalizes those chief executive
> officers who make decisions, such as the divestiture of
> non-strategic assets, which result in charges to income in
> the short term, but are in the long-term best interests of
> stockholders."
>
> How did the assets become nonstrategic in the first place?
> Management made a bad decision somewhere along the
> line and should be held accountable. That is the most rep-
> rehensible spin I have heard someome put on a screw-up
> in a long time

> **Zman492:   Re: CEO for Life #20570**
>
> "I don't think you will find anyone on this board who be-
> lieves that Scrushy is not overcompensted, both in salary
> and perks. However, I do not see much to indicate this is
> causing excessive harm to the financial well-being of the
> company. I strongly disagree with the accusation that the
> books were cooked. HRC financial reporting is quite
> straight-forward. There may be some minor juggling of
> goodwill, but probably less than most other companies
> with similar amounts of goodwill. The large decline in the
> stock price from the $30 level was due to the Balanced
> Budget Act passed by Congress more than anything else
> . . . Good Luck, Z."[57]

>>> WHERE DID THE MONEY GO?

It cannot be overstated that HealthSouth focused on share
price. Highly valued shares gave Scrushy a necessary advantage in mergers, and they made stock options for executives a

freeway to wealth. If that focus had been excessive in the past, it was to prove a major error for Scrushy in the month of May. According to the federal indictment, and to later testimony in the federal trial, HealthSouth was short of cash and had been scrambling to unwind the fraud.[58] Early in May, HealthSouth stated that its first-quarter profits were up by 44 percent; operating costs were lower and rehabilitation services were paid more, the company claimed. Net income was stated at $107.7 million, 27 cents per share.

Immediately, a new alias, **red_eye_treefrog_liberation front** from Birmingham, answered with a pointed question: "'Tangible Book Value per share:' In 1992 it was $2.52, and in 2001 it was $2.74—only 22 cents gain in book value in nine years. If earnings are real, where did the money go?"[59] he asked. It was true that no dividends had ever been paid, and the question was a good one, and one that analysts following HealthSouth might well have looked into. The marketplace, now, seemed to have reached a similar conclusion. HealthSouth's good news was ignored, and HealthSouth shares began falling, once again.

Scrushy's appearances at conference calls and on CNBC had never matched his reputation as a promoter and salesman. It may have been that his magnetism worked best at live musical performances, but his radio and television interviews were ordinary by comparison. In his May 2002 appearance on CNBC, Scrushy gave a confident message. He was disappointed at the market price for HRC shares, and when asked, he stated straightforwardly that the stock should trade "north of $20." On the message board, although some thought he'd handled CNBC well, everyone agreed that it was unusual for a CEO to state a share price; most tended to skirt that issue, if for no other reason than to avoid criticism and liability. Some took Scrushy's unhesitating assessment of HealthSouth's stock value as a very good sign. It would be too risky, they thought, for him to go out on a limb so boldly. And so, it was a great shock when it was announced that Scrushy had sold over five and one-quarter million of his own shares of the stock he'd recently valued at "north of $20" for less than $14 per share. The news was announced in his hometown newspaper:

Birmingham News, May 15, 2002

SCRUSHY PROFIT $56.3 MILLION

HEALTHSOUTH CEO EXERCISES
LONG-HELD OPTIONS ON 5.28 MILLION SHARES

The story said that his option price was $3.78 per share, giving him a profit of about $56.3 million before taxes. Scrushy's sale brought a storm of protest, shareholder lawsuits, and pleas for an SEC investigation:

---

bopper63:   The Scrushy Factor #20777

"When you appear on CNBC and look the camera in the eye and say the stock should be valued 'north of $20' and two weeks later unload 5 million shares at $14, you are sending a message about the stocks true value. Not even Richard Scrushy would leave $25 million on the table. You also provide yourself an opportunity to unload because everyone's eye is off the ball . . ."[60]

Zman492:   Re: The Scrushy Factor #20824

"Let me be the first to pooh pooh your comparison of Adelphia and HRC . . . The deregulation of the communications industry, coupled with unrealistic growth expectations for telecom, led to excesses and 'creative accounting' gimmicks which have devastated the whole industry.

> The health industry is and probably always will be highly
> regulated. HRC has never used the kinds of gimmicks com-
> mon in the telcom industry. About the most HRC does is a
> little fiddling with things like reserves for uncollectible re-
> ceivables, something done in almost every company the
> size of HRC . . ."[61]

> **northern_european_american: Re:The Scrushy Factor
> #20827**
>
> "About the most HRC does is a little fiddling with things
> like reserves for uncollectable receivables, something
> done in almost every company the size of HRC"(?)
>
> How soon we forget, do you recall the $8 million fine the
> company paid recently for buying from Mom and Dad.
> 'Our accountants disagreeing with their accountants . . .'"[62]

In keeping with Scrushy's aggressive strategy, the company answered critics with a formal statement, one designed to answer questions and quiet the market. The statement concluded by saying: "There are no additional options held by HealthSouth executive officers remaining to be exercised from the pool of options expiring in May and June, and Mr. Scrushy has no intention of selling additional shares in the near future."[63]

Many investors weren't mollified by the company's reassurances, however. "Subpoena Anyone? I can't spell it, but I can smell it! . . ."[64] was a discussion thread that looked at the dark side of the investors' predicament. Rumors were posted that providers had been asked by the Medicare Administration for data to support charges of HealthSouth billing fraud. One post emphasized that collections had again lagged and DSO (days of service outstanding) numbers were up once again from the last quarter despite HealthSouth promises that they would drop into the 70s that year. HealthSouth, in late May, sold $500 million of ten-year notes, underwritten by UBS Warburg along with Bank of America and Deutsche Bank. The debt was rated BBB by Standard & Poor's; the lowest investment grade, this labeled the stock barely above junk. Total bond debt extended to nearly $3 billion.

In the days and months that followed Scrushy's stock sale, a flurry of lawsuits were brought against HealthSouth. On May 15, Brookwood Medical Center and Baptist Health System sued the state citing special legislation for HealthSouth's digital hospital that allowed it to bypass regulatory review. The two hospitals' spokesmen said that HealthSouth had misled legislators. The Department of Justice, on May 29, joined yet another whistle-blower complaint, filed May 23, 2002, in San Antonio, Texas (HealthSouth settled this complaint in December 2004).[65] In late June, the Alabama Hospital Association joined the lawsuit against HealthSouth's digital hospital.[66] In the face of these mounting legal issues, HRC shares dropped from $14 to just over $12. Declining profits were spent to support HealthSouth's law firms.

Richard Scrushy's carefully protected world was beginning to unravel. Despite his efforts to silence the Internet and keep a lid on information, rumors began to circulate widely. As HealthSouth headed for a stock price drop of 21 percent, the largest weekly drop since September of 2001, Scrushy lashed out in the press:

The Birmingham News, July 12, 2002

HEALTHSOUTH HIT, REBOUNDS

SCRUSHY BLAMES UNFOUNDED RUMORS ABOUT ACCOUNTING

HealthSouth CEO Richard Scrushy blamed unfounded

rumors about the company's accounting practices for sending his company's stock in a downward spiral Thursday before rebounding . . . It closed at $10, down 6.5 percent for the day, as the company repurchased shares.[67]

Other events were happening in Richard Scrushy's private life that also were to have a major effect on federal efforts to uncover the fraud. They involved William Massey, Scrushy's private CPA and the man who tended to the many corporations he maintained to contain his growing fortune. Massey served as Scrushy's private CFO for Marin, Inc., which acted as an umbrella organization for a number of companies—those associated with Scrushy's country band Dallas County Line, the showgirl-troupe 3rd Faze, his real estate investments, and other side operations. Five of these companies were run from his office at HealthSouth.[68] As Scrushy's personal accountant, Massey had advised him against making the large stock sales that had triggered such a furor in May, fearing that the sale would draw unwanted attention to HealthSouth's finances and to his boss.[69]

According to journalist John Helyar, during the week of July 22, Scrushy learned that Massey had stolen some $500,000 from Scrushy's accounts. Scrushy also claims to have learned at the same time that the 37-year-old Massey—the married father of two children—was involved in an affair with Hope Launius, an employee of Leslie Scrushy's clothing company, Uppseedaisees. In his *Fortune* magazine article, Helyar stated that sources "familiar with the matter" claimed that some of the stolen money had been spent on Launius, paying for gifts and outings. Reportedly, Scrushy was furious at the revelation of the theft, but he didn't immediately report it to authorities. He suspected that Launius was involved in the theft, which she later denied.[70]

Then, on the morning of July 30, 2002, Birmingham police received a call from a security guard who worked for Scrushy at HealthSouth. The guard had found the body of William Massey, lying dead on a country road behind the suburban development where Massey lived; the former CFO and advisor to Richard Scrushy had been killed by a shotgun blast to the head. The county coroner ruled his death a suicide. The day after the body was found, Scrushy confronted Launius and reported Massey's alleged theft to the police. He is said to have contacted Launius's husband about her transgressions with Massey (Scrushy has denied those accounts); she was later divorced.

As news of the suicide surfaced, the public also learned of Massey's affair with Hope Launius, and her ties to the Scrushy family. None were aware, however, of the investigation that was now being conducted discretely by both local authorities and the FBI. The investigation would take nearly a year. As it unfolded, the meltdown of HealthSouth and its CEO's world had already begun.

CHAPTER six

The Raid

Richard Scrushy's omnipresent armed bodyguards, security cameras, and hidden microphones were well-worn topics on the Yahoo! HRC message board and around company head-quarters. When William Massey's body had been found lying dead on a deserted country road, a shotgun blast to his head, some on the message board couldn't resist speculating about the events surrounding his death. In the months that followed, I saw occasional posts on the message board asking for more investigation into the death of Massey, but Scrushy's dogged legal pursuit of message board posters in 1998 had taught the board to be cautious. Most messages that mentioned the murder simply asked "What about Massey??" and went no further.

In an article for the *Birmingham News*, Russell Hubbard reported that FBI agent Carmen Adams agreed with Pelham Police Detective Eddie Carter that the ruling of suicide in Massey's death would go unchallenged. "We don't expect anything to change; there are other facts surrounding this case that pertain to other investigations." The article went on to say that the FBI investigation involved all of Scrushy's businesses. It also quoted Vestavia police Sergeant Erwin Self as saying that Scrushy never followed up his Vestavia Hills police report that accused Massey of stealing money. "These were only allegations of possible theft. We never received anything from Scrushy but the initial report."[1]

Scrushy reportedly was furious with Hope Launius and suspected that she was complicit in Massey's theft. According to John Helyar's *Fortune* article, "The Insatiable King Richard," Launius had been the recipient of gifts from Massey. According to sources Helyar interviewed for his article, Scrushy asked Launius specifically what she knew about his financial affairs. Launius told investigators that, after she had lost her job at Upseedaisies (where she was a personal buyer for Scrushy's wife), Scrushy had reported her affair and involvement with Massey to her husband. The resulting mess ended in her divorce. According to Helyar, after she learned of a federal investigation into Scrushy's stock sales, Launius called the SEC and the FBI.[2]

Yet, after brief public furor, the investigation seemed to simply end. News articles about Massey's suicide faded from the local press, and the coroner's verdict quieted much discussion. However, taken with other adverse events at Health-South—Medicare overbilling, charges of billing fraud in physical therapy, shareholder complaints of insider selling—the death of Scrushy's personal accountant Massey brought even more investigative attention to Richard Scrushy's finances.

After reporting Massey's theft on July 31, Scrushy unloaded another $25 million of his HealthSouth stock holdings. July had been a disastrous month for share prices with intraday lows dipping to $7, a 50 percent loss since May. The stock had mysteriously dropped mid-month following Scrushy's transfer of his HealthSouth stock back to the company, in satisfaction

FIGURE 6.1

for a company loan. This second sale caused little stir in the financial community, but outraged many investors on the message board who felt that it was a violation of the company's announcement just months earlier that Scrushy planned no more sales "in the near future."

HealthSouth shares rose 27 percent the week following a *Barron's* report that suggested the stock might reach the midteens once people regained confidence in operations and finances. HealthSouth followed up on this news with a reported second-quarter profit (as opposed to the previous year's loss), attributed to better payments from the new Medicare payment system. Net income was said to be $57.5 million, which included a $53 million loss from the sale of five nursing homes plus another $3.4 million to retire debt. I posted my doubts regarding HealthSouth's ability to continue their strategy:

> **charon_xxx: Health care stocks: the sweet spot #20684**
>
> ". . . watching the board for several years, one would as-
> sume there is a relative consensus that out-patient is a
> sweet spot in health care investing. Maybe so. I'm not so
> sure that HRC is in the best position, and I'm not certain
> that the hospitals are in the worst . . . In my view, HRC is no
> shoo-in to be worth a premium to the market any time
> soon. They need to operate the business, control the AR,
> and at least meet the industry averages . . . for return and
> margins. So far, that has been beyond their reach . . . ??"

>>> A FAILED MOVE TO SPLIT HEALTHSOUTH

Share price continued upward and ignored more bad news; a new lawsuit from Baptist Health System, Inc., claimed that HealthSouth's $30 million tax exemption for "new technology" in the digital hospital was not warranted.[3] Then, on August 27, Scrushy appeared on a CNBC live news feed, where he was interviewed about the company and its progress. Scrushy was evasive when asked about his sale of stock in May and July. Scrushy first claimed he had no memory of the sales, and then claimed he had only exercised options. As the questions heated up, the news feed suddenly went dead. According to message board poster **dumas_46,** titled "Power was cut from Birmingham end," one of Scrushy's aides abruptly cut the news feed to end the interview "when his aide realized that he couldn't (shouldn't) answer the questions about insider sales."[4]

Combined with Scrushy's reluctant answers and final blackout in the CNBC interview, what happened next made HRC a penny stock and sent its market capitalization down from its high of $12 billion to a mere $2 billion, eventually to trade at rates below its 1986 issuing price.

In late August, Scrushy released a public statement in two parts that, at the time, seemed completely unrelated. In the first, Scrushy announced his plan to divide HealthSouth into two companies by splitting off the surgical center division. Stepping out of the role of CEO, Scrushy would be chairman of both companies; HealthSouth's chief operating officer, Bill Owens, would take over the position of CEO, as well as the day-to-day operation of HealthSouth. The federal indictment later alleged that Scrushy's plan was a ploy to extricate the company from unmanageable fraud on its books.[5] The indictment also alleged that UBS Warburg advisor to HealthSouth, Benjamin Lorello—the man for many years largely responsible for helping UBS Warburg underwrite HealthSouth's bonds—devised the plan. (To date, no charges have been brought in connection with these allegations.) Called "Project Cardinal," the plan would have split off a private outpatient surgery company that could then trade on public markets and hide HealthSouth's accounting fraud.[6] The announced plan never took shape, however; according to the indictment, a shortage of cash and disapproval from bondholders squashed its implementation.

Second, Scrushy announced a $175 million shortfall in revenue due to what he described as a surprise decrease in Medicare payments brought on by regulatory changes. Scrushy, in an interview with the *Wall Street Journal*, explained how he had been surprised by the memo and its meaning: "In June, one of HealthSouth's reimbursement lawyers happened across a May 17 transmittal on the Web site of the Centers for Medicare and Medicaid Services," he stated.[7] The Medicare Administration memo contained in the transmittal Scrushy referenced had clarified a simple rule: Grouped patients couldn't be charged at an individual rate. According to Scrushy, when the attorney brought the information to the company's attention, HealthSouth didn't think the rule applied to them because the memo clarifying the rule wasn't sent to the Medicare contractor that processed most of HealthSouth's claims.

The Medicare Administration immediately disputed both his estimate of the shortfall and his public denial that he was aware of the Medicare regulations.[8] Most of us on the message board shared the Medicare Administration's skepticism. Few could swallow the idea that HealthSouth's lawyer was unaware of this regulation—a ruling central to both the attorney's legal specialty and his major client's business—until he stumbled across the rule clarification while surfing the Internet.

I saw posts on the message board saying that lawsuits already had been filed against HealthSouth. There were indications that HealthSouth employees knew of the changes in Medicaid billing because of code changes made in documentation software in the clinics where they worked. On the message board, one poster claimed that one of the lawsuits charged that the code change had been planned by management for months.[9] Others on the board agreed. I posted a message that cited my conversation with a long-time HealthSouth therapist who managed several clinics:

---

charon_xxx: Therapist at HRC knew Medicare rule #24231

"I talked to a therapist at HRC and that person said that they have been talking among themselves about the group/solo problem of reimbursement for many months. It seems unlikely that management would be in the dark as was suggested by Mr. Scrushy. The conference call will indeed be interesting."[10]

After news of the $175 million shortfall was released, HRC trading volume surged with more than 42 million shares changing hands, and the stock plummeted to $5.05 by Wednesday. William Borden, writing for Reuters, reported the drop of share price of 57 percent in two days, blaming it on investor disappointment that "only a few weeks ago HealthSouth reaffirmed guidance,"[11] That insight focused on a very real problem for Richard Scrushy: If he knew about the projected decrease in revenue announced by the May 17 transmittal, his sales of stock were improper under SEC rules governing insider trading.

True to form, Scrushy was steadfast. He maintained that he had no knowledge of the CMS (Center for Medicare Services) changes in procedure for outpatient rehabilitation care before the stock sale; according to his statements, the CMS transmitted the change to health care providers well after the stock sale. He went on to commiserate with other physical therapists, the little guys. Scrushy said that the CMS rule change would create serious difficulty for physical therapists, adding "I don't know how the guy out there in private practice is going to make it." He went on to say that bad news was over for now, and "I think you will start to see some positive things coming out soon."[12] Nevertheless, after the double blow of Scrushy's announcements and subsequent explanations, analysts quickly downgraded the company, and HealthSouth discontinued giving earnings guidance for the balance of 2002 and for 2003.

More legal trouble arrived at the end of August. An article in the the *Birmingham News* suggested that the hundreds of thousands of dollars HealthSouth and Scrushy donated to political action committees—including a $250,000 donation to a PAC-associated Alabama Governor Don Siegelman—had provided political influence for HealthSouth's Digital Hospital.[13] Siegelman denied wrongdoing.[14] (An indictment against Governor Siegelman was dropped by prosecutors in October of 2004.[15]) More importantly, an as yet unresolved suit brought by the Birmingham law firm of Hare, Wynn, Newell and Newton alleged misuse of corporate assets and trading irregularities with regard to Scrushy's $25 million sale of stock back to the company in July, alleging the transaction to be "a waste of corporate assets."[16]

>>> **THE APPROACHING STORM**

For those of us who thought things could get no worse, September was painful. Short sellers were drinking deeply at the trough. One long-term investor from Omaha commented: "Where have the profits from a decade gone?" Kim Landry, awaiting her day in court with HealthSouth, even dropped by the board posting as **Ouchsuit:** "Where were you in 1998 when I needed moral support? When I called Screwshy a Bozo, he sued me . . . Everyone else caved in. After the stocks crashed in 1998, I knew it was only a matter of time before this would happen again. Lots of luck to all of you."[17] Another alias, **Wallysparks_98,** probably bashing for the short sellers, made a prescient prediction that the stock exchange would halt HRC from its Index. Some posters began discussing what would happen if the share prices dropped to near zero; and some accurately predicted the stock would be removed from the S&P Index.[18] But few believed that a company of Health-South's strength and reputation would fall so low.

Suddenly, lawsuits were nearly too many to count. On September 15, the *Birmingham News* reported that HealthSouth surgery centers faced 14 new shareholder actions, all claiming that management withheld information regarding Medicare rules changes.[19] As lawsuits continued to mount in number, Scrushy continued his offensive in the press. On September 19, he announced that someone within the Medicare program's administration had admitted to him during a phone call that its rules were flawed. Scrushy also stated that an administrator, Tom Scully, had told him in August that changes to rules regarding Medicare reimbursement needed to be redone.[20] But these justifications were weak and much too late to bolster Scrushy's credibility. The SEC announced a probe, in part to determine when Scrushy knew HealthSouth's revenues would fall. To restore confidence in the company, Scrushy announced that two members of his board of direc-

FIGURE 6.2

tors would perform an internal probe. Upon the announcement of these two investigations, shares promptly dropped to $3—an 80% loss for the year. On September 28, Moody's rating service cut HRC's bond rating to Ba3, which is, essentially, a junk bond rating.

Undaunted by bad publicity, Scrushy's loyal board of directors publicly denied plans to dismiss him following the SEC probe. Board member Phillip Watkins denied any discussion of the matter and stated: "We have full confidence in Richard."[21] But, it appeared that the board of directors was indeed worried. After ignoring years of criticism and pressure to hire an independent board member, the board relented and elected Mr. Robert May, former CEO of the Internet company, PVN, Inc. The company then announced that he would head the committee investigating insider stock sales.

Burt Denton, president of Providence Capital, a mutual fund invested in HealthSouth, helped spearhead the movement to improve the company's board of directors by negotiating the placement of independent directors. Denton said that his fund had not determined whether a proxy fight would be needed to change the board. He led a group of institutional investors who, during a conference call, complained of a list of bad corporate governance practices that needed change.[22] Scrushy jumped aboard the bandwagon for independent directorships as investors threatened proxy battles at the annual meeting. "It may be we have to make changes among our board members in the future. We will hear from our committee and consider some new people if that is what is needed,"[23] he announced to the press. The message board was pleased; some called for a whole new board. **Murf** (**iammurfthesurf**) quoted a news clip from Reuters:

---

iammurfthesurf: They should sell tickets to that one.
#36577 10/16/02

"Reuters reports that HealthSouth's entire board is up for re-election at the next shareholder meeting. With all that is going down, one analyst (who preferred not to be named) said 'they should sell tickets to that one.'"[24]

>>> LAW FIRM FINDS NO WRONGDOING

At the very worst moment, HealthSouth, gathered in more bad publicity courtesy of its board of directors. Cozy dealings that might have passed without comment in previous years were now on view to a more critical public, and it was at this moment that the board approved what appeared to be a sweetheart contract for glass installation at the digital hospital. On October 6, local headlines announced that HealthSouth director, Larry Striplin, had won, by bid, a $5 million construction contract with HealthSouth.[25] Striplin's long history of buddyhood with Scrushy was public knowledge, because both served on the board of Birmingham's Banc Corporation and on the Birmingham-Southern College athletic committee—where the baseball field was named the Scrushy-Striplin field. Striplin also was a member of the two-man board of directors' committee investigating Scrushy's stock trading, a fact which further outraged many of us who were following events at the company. Shortly after the announcement of his winning bid for the glass installation contract, Striplin resigned from the investigating committee, citing "bad publicity" surrounding the contract.[26]

On October 14, **The_Emerging_Analyst** posted: "The spinoff is not assured. They must make a deal with bondholders . . . and they need SEC approval . . . both are doable, they are not assured."[27] A few days later, HealthSouth made the announcement that the plan to split the company had been abandoned; the announcement cited poor market conditions and concerns from investors. On October 31, the *Birmingham News* reported that Scrushy had announced in an interview that he had been cleared of charges of wrongdoing in his stock sales by an independent law firm.[28] Under the headline "Lawyers' Probe Clears Scrushy: Firm Hired by Company Finds No Wrongdoing in His Stock Sales," the article quoted Scrushy as saying that the Houston-based law firm, Fulbright & Jaworski had, after a six-week investigation that involved examining 546,000 pages of documents, searching computer hard drives, and interviewing 19 key employees, concluded that Scrushy new nothing of the unfavorable Medicare ruling prior to selling $100 million of his company stock.

"As far as I'm concerned, it's done," said Richard Scrushy. "This investigation was as thorough as what the SEC is doing. Now we're working on getting our stock back up and keeping our customers happy."

A spokesman for Fulbright & Jaworski was less positive; the law firm announced that it had not written Scrushy's press release, and that the results of the investigation could not absolutely confirm the claims of HealthSouth management. Morningstar analyst Tom Goetzinger commented: "I'm not sure this will increase investor confidence a lot. That probably won't happen until, or if, the SEC clears the company. That is the real investigation."[29]

Scrushy's critics on the message board made caustic remarks. Said one message: "Bow Wow. If I had a lawyer, I would feed him every day . . ."[30] Said another: "Let me assure you, your President is not a crook. You can't make this stuff up!!"[31]

The year ended poorly. Scrushy said results would be down, and on schedule, HealthSouth reported lower profits due to Medicare cuts, fewer patients, and higher labor costs. HealthSouth announced a 2 percent cut in labor force, for a loss of 1,000 jobs. Profits for 2003, they said, would fall short of projections by 4 cents per share.

>>> MUSICAL CHAIRS: SCRUSHY RETURNS AS CEO

After the steady building of bad news through the end of 2002, January 2003 began on a mellow note. In the first week, the *Birmingham News* noted, as somewhat of a surprise, that a bounce was seen for HealthSouth stock prices. Scrushy also dominated the January news with a story that he bumped Bill Owens out of the position as CEO, to reclaim his old job as head of HealthSouth, now that a plan to spin off the company's surgical centers had been reluctantly withdrawn.

But the relative quiet surrounding HealthSouth at the beginning of 2003 didn't last long. By February, financial difficulties forced Scrushy to cancel the much-criticized "Go For It!" road show—a move that delighted many of us on the message board. The FBI revealed that it was probing SEC violations, and that it had interviewed employees and issued subpoenas. The SEC raised the level of its probe to formal status, which indicated that it would issue subpoenas also. To cap off a bad month, Scrushy announced that HealthSouth had suffered an astonishing $406 million loss—news that triggered a drop in bond ratings.[32] HealthSouth debt now had junk bond status—the company was $3.3 billion in debt, and had fallen below investment grade.

Investors complained about Scrushy's return as CEO, and filed more shareholder lawsuits contending that HealthSouth executives had been adequately warned by their own therapists and supervisors in April of 2001 that company Medicare billing practices were illegal. Then, in March, the board announced that two firms had been hired to seek out new, independent directors. Betsy Atkins was a new board member chosen by that search process, and reportedly was enthusiastic about taking on the huge challenge.

In an account she wrote for *Corporate Board Member* magazine, Atkins stated that she first met Richard Scrushy on February 6, when she traveled to HealthSouth headquarters for a meeting that also included Bill Owens.[33] In her article, Atkins noted that Scrushy was very articulate and compelling in his description of the company. "He was charismatic," she wrote, "almost like a revival preacher." At the time of their meeting, Atkins was aware that Scrushy was the target of a six-month SEC investigation into charges of insider trading. Atkins said that she immediately began to question whether either Scrushy or Owens should retain their positions with the company, regardless of the outcome of the investigation. She was uncertain, she wrote, about their "scalability," and whether they would be capable of continuing to develop and grow the company.

After being voted onto the HealthSouth board, Atkins quickly began reviewing the company's bevy of legal council, trying to determine why so many attorneys were on the payroll. Atkins writes that as she conducted her research, she came to believe that some other members of the HealthSouth board of directors, most of whom had been chosen by Scrushy, were "perhaps overly influenced" by him. Atkins also notes she believed Scrushy even tried to gain influence over her, calling her at home to offer his version of the back story on HealthSouth and its current problems. Atkins rebuffed these attempts, however, saying that she wanted to interview Scrushy only in the presence of the investigative committee's independent attorney.[34]

>>> FBI MOVES IN

Atkins tenure on the HealthSouth board lasted only 16 days—but those days encompassed a tumultuous period at HealthSouth's Birmingham headquarters. Sometime around 10:00 on the evening of March 18, a poster with the alias **poorcountrypreacher** dropped this message on the Yahoo! board:

"Local B'ham station is reporting that the FBI is searching HealthSouth headquarters tonight. Don't know what it means, but thought you guys would be interested." [35]

Suddenly, without warning, an FBI raid had closed the company's doors. Within minutes, posters began flooding the message board with the news; many were residents of Birmingham who were watching the news unfold on their local television stations:

---

love_uppsie_dazeies: FBI just down the street #50121 3/18/03

"HealthSouth . . . surrounded by FBI agents . . ."[36]

BestTimesNow: Re: FBI just down the street #50115

". . . It was on live TV." [37]

Murf_the_surf: How Perfect. #50228

"Scruffy and Saddam Out Same Day! 'The irony of it is so sweet!'" [38]

---

jmanwepit: What the hell? You got to be kiddin me #50879

"i only found out about this disaster! holy hell! i have most all of my retirement savings in this stock! i'm ruined! why does this sh*t always happen to me? good night! i have virtually nothing left! if you can't trust what you read in companies financials, then how the hell are you supposed to make an educated investment decision?

there goes 31 years of working hard!! goddamn it all to hell. i'm in total shock!"[39]

---

fraudsrevealed: Scrushy to share cell with Jff_Sux #50227

"JFF_SUX was right on when he ripped on Scrushy."[40]

The next morning, headlines reported what the group already knew:

MARCH 19, 2003

HEALTHSOUTH RAIDED BY THE FBI

Yesterday FBI agents raided the Birmingham, Alabama, headquarters of HealthSouth. The FBI took away current and historical financial records as well as serving the company with a grand jury subpoena from the U.S. attorney's office and several employees with individual subpoenas.[41]

And that morning brought another surprise to those of us still following the message board. The SEC suspended trading on HealthSouth shares on March 19, citing an investigation into accounting fraud. Although the SEC initially halted trade only until March 20, in fact, trading would not resume until March 25, and then only for half of the day.

>>> MESSAGE BOARD BECOMES RELIABLE SOURCE

I was amazed at how quickly the message board found every shred of news and gossip from within the company. Many Birmingham employees must have read the message board, and it seemed clear that many posted to the message board straight from headquarters. From time to time, **les majeste2003** or **ejauburn** would report from the company's airport hanger to chronicle the comings and goings of corporate jets. Messages already contained speculation about who would be indicted and who would confess. Many who had been in hiding from Scrushy surfaced and began posting new messages. The message board would come to be the best and most reliable source of information about HealthSouth, as investors posted messages regarding the growing financial disaster.

Ivry_tower: Sell HRC stock on EBAY #51353

"Certificates will be collectors items - there's a definite market for these . . ."[42]

Whatsup3000202   Massive fraud #50343 3/19/03

"the board of directors are suckers too . . . they claim scrushy is the best choice for the job . . . they don't look so independent . . ."[43]

>>> **THE HOUSE OF CARDS CAVES IN**

The unfolding events were, as Betsy Atkins recorded in her notes for March 19, "cascading at a rapid pace."[44] Unaware of the previous evening's events, Atkins began receiving calls from other board members about the raid on the morning of March 19. In her diary, as she relates in her *Corporate Board Member* account of events, Atkins spent the morning engaged in a series of nonstop phone calls as she attempted to gather information and formulate a response in her role as chair of the Special Litigation Committee of the board. She recalls that, after consultation with several board members, she participated in a Special Investigation Committee call with attorney Bruce Vanyo, and that about noon, she spoke with HealthSouth's largest shareholder and the chairman of its board of directors, Joel Gordon. By 5:00 PM that afternoon, Scrushy and all available board members (except Bob May, who was on a cruise) spoke by phone, a meeting that she describes as being made chaotic, both by noise on the phone lines and by the presence of multiple attorneys representing nervous clients; identities and relationships became impossible to untangle on phone lines. All agreed that HealthSouth would be fully cooperative with the Department of Justice.[45]

By that evening, the board held another meeting, this time without the participation of Scrushy and Bill Owens. Among the agenda items Atkins prepared for that meeting was the question of how the board should handle the removal of Scrushy and Owens. To avoid triggering Scrushy's $15 million severance contract, the board determined to place both officers on administrative leave. Scrushy and Owens had to leave the building immediately and would not be allowed to reenter. The board also voted to deny Owens and Scrushy access to HealthSouth's airplanes, to avoid the risk of their flight from the country.

Of primary concern was who would run the shop. The board's decision was to split the job between Chairman Joel

Gordon, who had intimate knowledge of health care, and Bob May, who agreed to accept the title of acting CEO. Acting CEO May had come to the HealthSouth board as an independent director only five months before the crisis. Gordon, 75, had come out of retirement to become chairman of the board of directors. He had been a board member since 1996, when he sold his Nashville-based surgical centers to HealthSouth, but was a relative outsider with regard to the board's interactions with Scrushy.[46]

Ms. Atkins, as sole member of the Litigation Committee, had concerns about Scrushy's insider trading charges and the number of Birmingham attorneys hired by HealthSouth. She elected to hire independent counsel for the committee, choosing Bruce Vanyo—in part because a Delaware Court had publicly criticized the previous board committee for lack of independence. Atkins also pressed the board to hire a forensic accounting firm to provide a true picture of HealthSouth's finances. She also advised the board that they must immediately begin considering the ramifications of taking the company into Chapter 11. Equally essential, Atkins began the process of finding a crisis management firm to lead the company through the coming storm.

On March 22, Atkins received word that Chubb, the providers of HealthSouth's directors and officers liability insurance, had returned the company's check and cancelled its coverage. Unwilling to put her personal assets at risk by continuing in her role on the HealthSouth board of directors, Atkins called George Strong, head of the audit committee, and resigned immediately. In the three working days following the raid, the board began interviewing forensic accounting firms (they would ultimately choose PricewaterhouseCoopers). Atkins also had succeeded in getting the board to agree to hire a crisis manager and to let go of a group of the attorneys retained by HealthSouth—". . . a group that included many of the Birmingham outfits," Atkins wrote.[47] A main creditor, J.P.

Morgan Chase, was on call with the board and urged them to hire New York crisis management firm Alvarez & Marsal. By that weekend, partner Brian Marsal was in Birmingham, with a team of 26 accountants.

>>> THE AFTERMATH OF THE RAID

Trading had been expected to resume on March 20, but after the public announcement that charges of accounting fraud had been brought against the company by the SEC, the New York Stock Exchange abruptly halted trading. Trading initially was halted for four days, then suspended permanently by the NYSE. With trading halted, the board had a respite, but HealthSouth finances were in desperate shape. Shares that had last traded at $3.91 were expected to take a huge fall, and HRC bonds already had a junk rating. During the trading halt, most assumed that HRC would be traded on the NYSE after time had passed to let events stabilize. Then, abruptly, HRC was removed from the exchange, delisted, and therefore immediately dropped from the Standard & Poor's 500 Index. HealthSouth would trade no more under the symbol HRC. After being removed from its prestigious position as one of the 50 most important health care stocks, it would eventually resume trading as HLSH.PK, the PK suffix marking it as a stock supported by no exchange. The stock would then dwell on the bulletin boards with lowly penny stocks while the company awaited the very real possibility of bankruptcy.

During this time rumors flew and information continued to trickle on to the HRC message board. HealthSouth's bank accounts were frozen, as the SEC charges alleged that the report of an earnings shortfall at HealthSouth was tactical and fictitious, and no more than a device used by the conspiracy to help unwind the fraud. Investors were poring over details released by the SEC and in the media, and many on the board were debating the facts and their implications:

The_Emerging_Analyst: Re: Cash-This is what happened #52900 3/23/03

"... The company its shareholders, debt holders and employees should not be destroyed ... HRC a week ago was a company with over 1500 facilities and over 50000 employees that was providing needed quality health care ... It was current on ... payments and still providing positive cash flow despite Scrushy's extravagant spending and probable fraud ... The same facilities are still there ... What is needed is that everyone do the right thing ... This turnaround can be accomplished ... The scum that get on this board and are calling for liquidation are either short the stock, trying to scare investors to sell at pennies so that they can buy or just miserable beings that enjoy human suffering."

---

zaruthrustra101: What were the warnings signs?/ where is_my_salmon! #53447

"The fact that you had sociopathic trash as a CEO ... (naming things after himself constantly, showing off his money, bragging on his radio show about his flown in salmon) was reason enuff."[48]

---

outman27   More bad news coming #51224

"<Mr. Smith, 42 years old, of Hoover, Ala., has agreed to cooperate with the federal government's ongoing investigation of corporate fraud at HealthSouth. He has agreed to forfeit any proceeds derived from illegal activity.>"

> I have heard (and no reason to question the source) that criminal indictments are to be handed down today from the Grand Jury in B'ham. Arrests are to be made. I won't trade tomorrow if this hasn't yet occurred, but will after this news is out. HRC is too strong to not recover. The shame of it is that a number of families are going to be destroyed by this through no fault of their own."[49]

As **outman27**'s message indicated, HealthSouth CFO, Wesley Smith, had been indicted and pleaded guilty to fraud; he then implicated other officers, including Richard Scrushy. With more indictments on the way, news began to filter through the press that multiple HealthSouth officers were cooperating with the investigation.[50] Smith, we would later learn, had approached prosecutors and offered to cooperate fully with the government's investigation; many other Health-South executives soon followed suit.[51]

In Scrushy's 2005 trial, jurors would listen to taped conversations between Bill Owens and Scrushy, made through a hidden "wire" Owens wore to the meetings, in which the two discussed how to deal with the looming disaster that followed the SEC filing. After Owens and Scrushy were placed on leave, Owens was formally charged by the Department of Justice.[52] In all, U.S. Attorney Alice Martin would gather 17 cooperation agreements from HealthSouth executives who reported to Scrushy, including all five of the company's CFOs.[53] Scrushy himself would be indicted on 85 counts of fraud.

>>> GLOOM FOR HEALTHSOUTH IN THE PRESS

Although the mainstream press had been slow to investigate Scrushy and his company before the scandal, now Health-South news filled the wires. Richard Scrushy would be the first executive tried under the Sarbanes-Oxley Act, and the press was eager to report on developments associated with the case as they unfolded. Prudential analyst David Shove wrote that he saw a strong potential for bankruptcy, and admitted that neither he nor his fellow analysts had "raised red flags" about HealthSouth.[54] *Barron's* March 24 "Trader Column" offered a mea culpa ("count us among those duped by the scam . . .") and observed that "it was not an attractive proposition" for shareholders to be at the mercy of bankers.[55]

Russell Hubbard's March 21 article for the *Birmingham News* chronicled all of the known elements of the fraud.[56] The article contained a quote by Kemp Dolliver, an analyst for S.G. Cowen Securities: "They're toast. I don't know how they are going to make it, and I don't see how they could get new credit in ten days." As to bankruptcy: "It's hard to imagine Health-South avoiding it." The article also noted that the frozen bank facility had been a $1.2 billion line of credit and the payment due on the convertible bonds was cited as $345 million. Curiously, no large Alabama bank participated in the syndication of the bank facility. Scrushy's financiers were located far away from Birmingham.[57] Several on the HRC message board wondered if local money professionals had known of—or suspected—problems with the company.

Simon Romero and Reed Abelson, in a *New York Times* article titled "HealthSouth Officials Seek to Cut Deals with the U.S," asked how the fraud could have gone undetected for so long.[58] The two noted that several officials were "scrambling to offer evidence and strike deals." Many posters also were at a loss to understand how HealthSouth's auditors had missed such massive fraud. Expectations were that Ernst & Young would be involved in civil litigation and that they would be forced to settle. The *Birmingham News* reported that both Ernst & Young and the investment bank UBS Warburg were to be investigated in connection with the HealthSouth scandal.[59] (Both companies testified to Congressman Tauzin's Commerce Subcommittee; no action has taken place to date.[60]) Dozens of posters suspected foul play and predicted criminal charges. Many posts noted that Ernst & Young were not only the company's auditors, but also that several of HealthSouth's top officers had once been employees of Ernst and Young.

In a March 24 article for the *Birmingham News*, Russell Hubbard returned to the HealthSouth case, as he reported that the Alabama Secretary of State had listings for ten private corporations (including Scrushy's private charitable foundation) that listed Scrushy as member or registered agent.[61] Four of the corporations listed HealthSouth Corporation as their address. Scrushy was connected with firms that managed money, operated aircraft, and dealt in a wide range of show business activity. The article quoted Doug Jones, a former U.S. attorney in Birmingham, saying: "With HealthSouth, it's hard to tell if there was a line between what was Richard Scrushy's and what was the corporation's. Government investigators would be duty-bound in a situation such as this to investigate all the affiliated entities."

According to Hubbard's report, companies listing Health-South as their address included Marin, Inc., Dallas County Line, LLC, and Marinda Productions, Inc. Marin, Inc., is listed as an investment management company managed by William Massey, who had died prior to the SEC investigation. Marin was the vehicle for investing much of Scrushy's $55 million in compensation (dating to 1996), money from his sale of Capstone Capital (the company that leased properties to Health-South, later sold to Healthcare Realty Trust), and the $100 million from his millions of shares sold. Dallas County Line, of the same name as the band in which Scrushy played guitar, was a musician management company and record producer. Marinda Productions produced sound and video productions. It was obvious that HealthSouth's expenditures for show business, girl shows, and music were filtered through Scrushy's private companies. The same seemed true for his real estate interests with Capstone. The newspaper article noted that companies are required to disclose in annual documents filed with the SEC any companies that are joint ventures or general partners of the filing corporation. None of the four companies were listed in HealthSouth's 2001 filing.[62]

>>> HEALTHSOUTH RESTATES ITS NUMBERS

HealthSouth released restated figures for its income growth. Growth for 1999 had been reported at 143 percent and adjusted for fraud down to 3 percent; it would come out in trial testimony from the CFOs that HealthSouth was cooking their books at a rate of $10 million per week during some stretches in 1999. The following year had been reported as an 89 percent increase and corrected to 8 percent.[63] Ernst & Young declared that only information from the guilty plea of former CFO, Weston Smith, had unearthed the fraud. In a later appearance before a Congressional Committee investigating the fraud, Ernst & Young said: "When individuals are determined to commit a crime, a financial audit cannot be expected to detect that crime."[64] No mention was made regarding the hundreds of millions missing from a cash account.

On March 25 came news that the NYSE had "determined that the Company's common stock is no longer suitable for continued listing on the NYSE."[65] On the message board, we continued to speculate on the fate of HealthSouth:

> **leadtheherd: Re: NYSE Press Release . . . What !!?? #53428**
>
> "NYSE: abandons the individual shareholders of America . . . [66]

Jrm30655   Re: Raid   #52423

"If you will look back over my posts, I have stated that I thought that there were some people in middle management that knew of the CMS changes first and probably traded ahead of the news. I've also stated that Scruchy would probably skate free on the insider trading charge. I still think so.

Take a look at PLMD and see what happened. Could be a great buying opportunity if HRC really takes a dump at the open. The good thing about this is I think this is the first day of the last days of Scruchy. He may never be found legally liable, but like Saddam, his days are now numbered."[67]

Bramblebush: JRM any opinion?   #53322 3/25/2003

"http://www.alvarezandmarsal.com/founding.asp?d=3 Here's a link to the crisis managers just hired: Alvarez and Marsal. I've been trying to find an example of a turnaround by these guys that avoided BK. They appear to be running HRC now. Anyone familiar with the companies they've helped?"

>>> CRISIS MANAGERS ARRIVE IN BIRMINGHAM

At HealthSouth, Bryan Marsal and his New York City professional services firm, Alvarez & Marsal, were attempting to manage the company through the critical period following the FBI raid and indictments. The company employs a methodical approach to crisis management that involves a five-step process: stabilize, diagnose, plan, facilitate, and lead. In a later phone interview, Marsal described for me the chaos he inherited when his crisis management firm first took over the operation of HealthSouth.[68] Citing one example, he explained that

HealthSouth's security guards—those ever present forces so often complained about by employees who posted to the message board—were to be evaluated by the new management. A
meeting was called with a head member of the security force
to seek details of security operations as well as explanations
for several complaints. The guard did not report to work the
following morning and left the employment of HealthSouth.
Over $200 thousand of guns and security equipment was not
accounted for. Restoring order in the face of social disruption,
a lack of solid information and financial hemorrhage was a
very large task.

For Marsal, a cash drill is the first and most vital step in
staunching the bleeding of a company in crisis.

A "cash drill" involves a nonstop effort to define the company's cash position: the amount in the bank, liquid assets,
and importantly, how long the cash can last. A general view of
the fraud was outlined within three days, but each week new
details of malfeasance surfaced. Marsal's team found that $374
million was missing from the $500 million reported on the
books. They discovered fake bank accounts at nonexistent
companies with coined names such as "PNC Consolidated."
An early concern was that banks would lay claim to any available cash; these included giants such as Deutsche Bank, UBS,
J.P. Morgan, and Wachovia.[69]

Marsal had engaged former HealthSouth treasurer, Tadd
McVay, to assist with the cash drill; McVay, at first, said that
he was not involved in the fraud, but soon pleaded guilty to
District Attorney Martin, cleaned out his desk, and left.
Marsal froze all nonpatient-related expenses, stopped paying
interest on debt, and began to sell assets. He raised $20 mil-
lion from the sale of Scrushy's fleet of jet airplanes and the famous helicopter, Bonus One (so named by employees because
they received no bonuses in the profit-poor year that Scrushy
had bought it to ease trips to the nearby airport and his Lake
Martin retreat).[70] Also discontinued were the company's

many show business expenses, including the $300,000 salary and services of senior VP of marketing, Jason Hervey, and the 3rd Faze show girls. The crisis team also began cutting staff, including one employee who posted to the message board as **Inman** (he was later rehired to a better job as a project manager).

As Marsal's team worked on securing the company's cash, CEO Bob May turned his efforts toward regaining employee confidence and morale. HealthSouth corporate culture was very much as it had been described on the Yahoo! message board. May had his assistant conduct a survey among the HealthSouth workers to determine the ten things that "really piss off employees."[71] First on the list was Scrushy's private entrance into the HealthSouth Campus, used only by top officials. All employees other than this elite few were expected to use the main gate, exiting off of the main freeway, Route 280, a trek that caused rush-hour gridlock and long delays. When May opened the private entrance for employee use, he reported that "you would have thought I'd given them a million dollars. It was clear the employees had been really angry for a long time."[72] Another casualty was the huge statue, "Pulling the Wagon," forged from steel to match Scrushy's stick-figure drawing, and prominently displayed outside the entrance to headquarters. Like the statue of Saddam Hussein we had all watched topple in Baghdad just weeks earlier, Scrushy's own monument was unceremoniously pulled down and dragged away.

>>> MESSAGE BOARD COOPERATION LEADS REBOUND

For those on the message board with investments and pensions laid waste by the HealthSouth scandal, delight at the toppling of a fraudulent regime at the company was tempered with real concern about how to best react to the financial disaster.

Although the new board was making good decisions, Yahoo's HRC message board seemed to be the only group paying attention. Just as **JRM30655** had predicted, a rebound did occur when trading started for half a day on the afternoon of March 25. The rebound wasn't led by Wall Street brokers and analysts or HealthSouth's old management. Instead, the advice and actions of many among the message board would lead the rebound, saving the pensions of some and making fortunes for others.

CHAPTER *seven*

The Rebound

The FBI raid was an earthquake, and all of us—employees, investors, partners—watched for several days as the after tremors subsided. As Bryan Marsal and his crisis management team performed their cash drill and worked to staunch the company's cash damages, we waited, knowing that the stock soon would be hit by a huge wave of selling. But halted trading left us in an information vacuum. The pre-raid numbers from filed SEC reports, annual reports, and analysts had been made irrelevant by allegations of widespread accounting fraud at the company. To understand fully HealthSouth's financial situation, we needed information from clinics, from headquarters, and from those who knew what the conspirators had faked. I suspected that hedge fund analysts and junk bond traders were evaluating the opportunity, and preparing to jump into a trading frenzy, but after HealthSouth's delisting, no investment analyst would report on the company's stock. The first open discussion of the situation at HealthSouth began on the Yahoo! finance HRC message board; at first, reliable information was drowned out by other message board noise, but as hours and days passed, the news on the board became increasingly useful and coherent.

As those stuck with investments in the company assessed their positions, they needed answers to two questions: Could the company survive without bankruptcy that would render its shares worthless? And, if HealthSouth survived, what was it worth? In attempting to determine the company's value and potential for survival, we sifted through what little information we had. We knew that the market capitalization of HRC had recently been at a low $1.6 billion (a substantial loss from its high of $12 billion). HealthSouth's $3 billion debt load seemed high and some convertible bond coupons were due for payment in only a few days. In the indictment, federal prosecutor Alice Martin had suggested more than a billion in fraud. So, could the company pay the bondholders? Would any assets be left after fines and audits? More to the point for stock investors, would any assets remain for equity holders when bondholders carried off what was left after the federal government recovered payments and levied fines? These were tough questions, and investors knew it was unlikely that any one person held all the answers.

Prior to the raid, company employees, and others like **Bopper63** and I, could contribute helpful information to the message board, based on our clinical experience and knowledge of HealthSouth company managers. With the company in limbo and trading halted, however, the group needed the advice of board posters with accounting expertise, experience in evaluating distressed companies, stock trading skills, and a broad knowledge of financial markets. Luckily, the message board was populated with several in each category.

While some veterans from the first days of the message board were still active participants, a raft of new traders now joined the board, including **iammurfthesurf, jbje2000, IndianaSteve2002,** and **itsabloodyfight.** I knew **JRM30655** would continue to be a lynchpin of the message board, both because of his timely analysis of issues and because of his experience in managing businesses. Posters **Outman, Inman, going_to_niceville,** and **Bhambamalady** were HealthSouth employees who knew the company intimately. The message board group also contained a number of CPAs, engineers, analysts, and stock traders. Together, the members of the HRC message board offered impressive credentials. And many posters willingly pooled their expertise to help the group understand the evolving situation at HealthSouth.

Hope remains, several said, posting messages supporting their hopes. **Carler98** was one of them. He said: "This said this is not an Enron, they make real money…Even if book value is cut in half from scandal they will remain in business."[1] **Mrktresrchr** demonstrated first rate research abilities and **jbje2000** contributed favorable "observations":

Mrktresrchr: Liquidity and Book Value #50304 3/19/03

"Book value was $10 per share. As of 9/30/02, at least $2 was phony, $800 million. As of 12/31/02, the company took a charge of $175 million to close facilities, etc. So, the bad assets are anywhere from $600 million to a billion. That puts book value at $7.50 to $8.50 per share. The problem is liquidity . . . The loans have to be renegotiated. The primary question is the $.55 to $.57 going forward. If the company can truly earn that much going forward and assets are impaired only 10%, then the company is fairly valued currently until the turnaround . . . Shareholders are not dead but Scrushy is."

---

jbje2000: **More Observations #50922 3/19/03**

"The headlines are devastating. However, it looks like that the recent numbers and projections are a reflection of the current business conditions. Assuming the company can earn at least $0.30–$0.40 and generate cash as it cuts capital spending and sell assets, equity value hear could still be $3. A massive sell-off on Friday could be followed by recovery toward that value . . . It will all depend on company's actions between now and then… Crisis management will be key to salvage equity value . . ."

Mrktresrchr: Re: Liquidity and Book Value #50345 3/19/03

"The news release from the SEC says assets were overstated by $800 million as of 9/30/02 . . . And please remember, market cap is already less than half of new lower book value so why should it go lower if the company can be turned around and actually produce a profit. Sell the jets. Stop Scrushy's salary. Cancel the pension and benefits for all guilty parties. Sue Scrushy."

Jrm30655: Remember WorldCom #51015 3/19/03

"< when fraud is found, there's often vastly more yet to be uncovered . . . >"

Ordinarily, I would agree . . . However, all this seems to have come out from the ex-CFO. They had quotes out of the boardroom . . . My guess is that most of it is out. In every other situation that I can think of, the SEC found the iceberg and had to keep digging to see the real size."

Many disagreed with these optimists. Media opinion overwhelmingly predicted bankruptcy, and it seemed that creditors were in firm control: "Never were there any real earnings here," said **BanjoJ.** "This is bk [bankrupt] for sure."[2] Understandably, many on the board focused their outrage on Richard Scrushy. A message was titled: "HERE: FUNDS THAT SCRUCHY SCREWED"; it listed 20 leading funds that held 203 million shares—Fidelity Funds alone held almost 54 million shares. Another message, titled "Litany of Lies," summarized the downward news spiral:

May 2002 Scrushy on CNBC says shares are worth "north of $20."

May 2002 he sells $70 mill of stock at $13, "to diversify."

July 2002 Stock drops from $10 to $7. HealthSouth reaffirms 2002 guidance and initiates buyback. Great value.

July 2002 *Barron's* reports: Scrushy says he'll sign certified financials; books are clean; no plans to sell anymore stock (2 days later he transfers another $25 million; says stock is compelling value at $10.

August 2002: Certifies and swears to financials.[3]

I found that scrolling from comment to comment was confusing. Messages made wild accusations about brokers, company officers, the board of directors, and the stock exchanges. It was group therapy, though not personally helpful. Then, I found an intelligent thread titled, **"Serious Discussion Only."**[4] It began the evening following the FBI raid, and involved **JRM30655, jbje2000,** and **IndianaSteve2002** with others joining during the early evening. **Jbje2000** started the thread with two hopeful messages, which were followed by 23 responses from investors who avoided emotion and instead focused on establishing the company's true value. Importantly, the thread helped to draw together an interactive community ready to dig into the problem. Similar exercises were to continue for weeks. During the five days of halted trade that followed the raid, this group of strangers came up with a remarkably accurate analysis of HealthSouth's situation.

Among the reports of disaster, the group took account of the good news that also surfaced. "Read the DOJ and SEC reports," suggested poster **jbje2000**. "The suggestion is that manipulation stopped in the second half of 2002 and they were still making money."[5] That meant that 2002 financial reports might best serve as an honest starting point for analysis. And there was other good news: half of inflated earnings had been written off; Scrushy, a spendthrift, was gone; there was cash on hand; and there could be tax refunds. Still, we knew that lawsuits were a problem and that institutions would dump their holdings, dropping share prices below $2. A lawyer on the message board addressed worries about lawsuits, reminding us that they were derivative lawsuits, filed by shareholders on behalf of others who own shares. Though legal fees would be a problem, he reminded us that most shareholders wanted to clean up the company, not to kill it.

At this point, most on the message board saw bankruptcy as certain, but **JRM30655** encouraged us to look beyond that fear and coolly analyze the government's allegations:

JRM30655: Re: Serious Discussion Only #51009 3/19/03

"I've read the legal filings and here is my take:

1. HRC made a "true" $157M the first 2 quarters of 2002, the best showing over the last 3 years in reality.

2. The CMS hit was in actuality $25M or .05 a share

3. The total hidden fraud was about 1.4B. I presume that the CFO came up with that number, so I presume that it is close.

---

4. All the antics in the 3rd and 4th qtr were to help hide the cover up of the fraud. I suspect that $600-700M was covered over those 2 quarters. That leaves about $800M left, most of it in 'virtual' assets.

5. The .55 per share this year seems real but may have been more with the extra going to recover the fraud account. Since they made $175M in the first 2 qtrs of 2002 they should have made about 300M this year or about .75 a share. All the reduced billing etc was just to correct back to real billing.

6. The funds can't dump. They own 300M+ shares and there is not that kind of market in the retail trade to absorb it. They will have to hold. Average volume is only 1.5M shares.

7. Everyone wanted Scruchy and his team gone so HRC could be run right. That has been accomplished.

8. Friday will be a real storm, but everybody has had 2 days to sort all this out, so I don't think it will be all that bad.

9. Scruchy just blew away $400M that he admitted to and probably more during the last 2 quarters and the stock went up 20%.

10. Lawsuits are a real unknown but the targets will be ex-management. Not the best but better than CMS (the Medicare Administration) looking for the company assets or massive fines for a toxic dump.

If you rip all the garbage off and view this as a mismanaged company with new management coming in, making at present .55 a share with good cash flow, you get a $5.50-$7.50 stock with improving prospects."[6]

>>> MESSAGE BOARD: HEALTHSOUTH IS STILL VIABLE

I read similar analyses by others who had independent conclusions. On March 20, 2003, a message by **louiswu_2000,** titled "Doing The Math," came up with a book value of $4.89 per share. He worked backwards from assumed earnings adjusted for fraud; his result was 18 cents per share after taxes. He used the amount of fraud proposed by the SEC report ($1.4 billion) and doubled it before deducting it from the reported 2001 year-end book value. Though rough, the number would provide comfort for buying when HealthSouth's stock became deeply oversold. **Louiswu_2000**'s summary: "Subject to new revelations, HRC still appears to be viable."[7]

Others looked beyond the stock valuation and bankruptcy question to speculate on the fate of Richard Scrushy:

---

lese_majeste2003: Re: Serious Discussion End of HS? #51139

"I have to say that we can expect criminal indictments soon, and not limited just to RS. Expect others to get indicted from the financial side of the business. There are multiple sources. Just trust me on that.

HS will be the poster boy for corporate fraud and RS is about to be linked to Sarbanes-Oxley in future business school textbooks. A final cynical comment, how long before we hear the religious conversion story? That is the standard defense nowadays."[8]

JRM30655: Re: JRM! #51180

You may be right. It appears that Scrushy is a common thief. I didn't see it coming and that will probably cost me money. Isn't the first time, probably not the last. My satisfaction is that I just lost money . . . Schruchy has lost it all."[9]

Immediate problems, however, could sink HealthSouth before a long-range plan could be implemented; cash accounts and its line of credit were frozen. **Marvelmeister2002**, a stock trader, wondered: "Let's say that the credit facility remains frozen. Is that the ballgame?"[10] HealthSouth had drawn down about a third of the funds available to them. **JRM30655** replied: "Probably not (the ball game.) Banks don't like fraud on any scale. On the other hand, they don't like losing money either."[11] Because HealthSouth's debt was unsecured, a bankruptcy filing was dangerous to all creditors.

>>> BOTTOM-FEEDERS' FEAST

Scrushy's digital hospital made news March 25, the day trading resumed. Construction managers issued an ultimatum that work would stop, at 12:00 NOON, without proof that HealthSouth could pay $125 million to finish construction. But, there was also good news: HealthSouth's convertible bonds, trading at $17 (bid) traded upwards to $20, a handsome gain for risk takers and an indication of investor confidence.

CBS Marketwatch reported shortly after noon on March 25 that the New York Stock Exchange (NYSE) found HRC no longer suitable for listing. As a result, HealthSouth would now trade under the listing HLSH.PK, meaning that it would trade as an OTC (over-the-counter) stock, rather than a qualified listing of the NYSE. Pinksheet stocks (so-called because they are often listed on pink paper) are not monitored by or supported by the NYSE or the American Stock Exchange. They often are not as easily traded, and regulatory requirements to report financial data for these stocks are not as stringent. These conditions make pinksheet stocks riskier.

Along with many others on the message board, I didn't have a good grasp of pinksheet trading or what additional risks it entailed. We neophytes were fortunate that many experienced traders exchanged insights and information on the message board after trading resumed, giving us a quick education in OTC stock trading. Poster **The_Dow_Bum,** for example, was straightforward and unwavering in his opinion. In real life, **The_Dow_Bum** was an engineer named Ken. His job had been to evaluate risk in energy plants around the world, working in remote locations in central Asia and Siberia on occasion. His hobby was evaluating and investing in distressed companies. His advice and insights, like those of **JRM30655, The_Emerging_Analyst,** and **iammurfthesurf,** were to be of enormous help to new traders and those on the board whose pensions had been decimated.

Those who had predicted only a dollar drop from the presuspension price of $3.91 had been wildly optimistic. HLSH opened at 36 cents on a shortened, half day of trading. Nearly all of the trading was driven by sellers dumping their shares and day traders churning the repeated bounces. It was a trader's feast. I presumed that aggressive hedge funds were buying along with a contingent of bottom-feeding retail traders who, like **The_Dow_Bum,** traded in distressed companies, with hopes of turning up some hidden value.

In later phone conversations and e-mail correspondence, I learned more about **The_Dow_Bum**'s experience as he traded in the new HLSH stock. His story illustrates how traders swoop in to capitalize on the devaluation of downed companies. Initially, **The_Dow_Bum** bought 10 thousand shares at 15 cents, then watched a bounce go by before buying more—first at 11, then at 7.5 cents per share. The low for the day was recorded at 4.6 cents but there was no real opportunity to get an order filled at that level and few shares traded below 9 cents. At closing, **The_Dow_Bum** owned 100,000 shares at about an 11-cent average price. Few traders would fare better. On the message board, **Bopper63** held claim to the largest cache of shares at 7.5 cents, not including his precrash holdings.

FIGURE 7.1

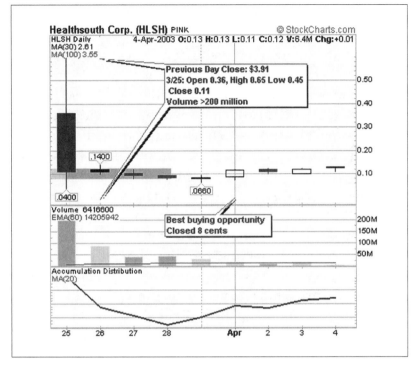

Message chatter on the board on March 25 was typical of any red-hot trading day, and following the trading lingo was like trying to understand hand signals and verbal shorthand at an auction: "Some guy just got a three bagger."[12] "Huge sell at the open . . ." "We are the #3 requested quote on the pinks! WorldCom #1." "Astounding!!!!! We're at 12 cents and someone dumps a million at 6!! Now there's a guy who just wants OUT."[13] "Hundred thousand lots mixed with a few small trades. Sad! I can't remember anything quite this ugly." A post titled "grinding its way back," said: "the 40c down to 6c move was on no volume, but succeeded in shaking out 50 million shares at/near the low . . ."[14]

Translated, the traders were saying that it was possible to buy low and within minutes sell for a profit (or loss) of three-fold. Institutions were dumping millions of shares on a thinly traded market—too few retail buyers buying only small lots—without regard to price. This allowed market makers (sometimes referred to on the board as "MMs") to keep a wide and profitable spread between their offer to buy (the *ask,* or the higher number) and what they would pay (the *bid,* or lower number). Market makers define the market by buying shares as cheaply as possible and selling them at a higher price, the difference being "the spread." They accumulate an inventory of shares. When buying is brisk and share volume high, they run out of shares to sell and must then move the buying price (their bid) higher to dislodge shares from current owners. A danger is that they will hold too much inventory when buying interest wanes and be forced to drop the asking price so low as to lose money. The market makers were building an inventory of HLSH shares at a very low price—as low as 4.6 cents—and selling them to a market that firmed up between 12 and 15 cents.

About 3:00 PM on March 25, Reuters released news that "scandal-ridden" HLSH.PK was now trading at 12 cents on more than 127 million shares of volume (the words "scandal-ridden" would become as fixed to HealthSouth as a birthmark). Someone asked: "MMs make the market? Why are people buying all these shares? Isn't HRC going bankrupt—am I missing something?" **JRM30655** and other posters added their comments throughout the day:

JRM30655: Re: What was the low today? #53717 3/25/03

". . . If it beats bankruptcy it could be worth $5 to 10 in 3 to 5 years. If it goes Chapter 11 and survives, it could be worth $1 in 6 months. Either way it is a good bet at 12 cents."

> **leadtheherd: Re: What was the low today? #53721 3/25/03**
>
> "If Index funds were unloading indiscriminately…why are buyers stepping up?"

> **JRM30655: Re: What was the low today? #53732 3/25/03**
>
> "Because it is probably the cheapest it will ever be unless it hits Chapter 7 BK (bankruptcy.) Here's the deal. S&P 400/500 funds just buy the package of stocks. They don't care if they go up or down, just so they have the right basket … The S&P valued the 'out' at $0. That means that no matter what they sell it for, it doesn't impact the funds numbers … This is a lot like owning a car that suddenly you can't own or drive. Someone's going to pay off your car note. Anything you can get for scrap is gravy … 12 cents is the scrap rate today …"

>>> HEALTH CARE OPERATIONS CONTINUE AS USUAL

During the avalanche of trade on March 25, HealthSouth's acting chairman, Joel Gordon, had taken a thumping; his millions of shares were now worth $1.2 million, a great loss from the previous close of nearly $40 million. As **Bopper63** said: "If anyone has paid a price for inattention and being asleep at the switch, I guess this is a whole new definition."[15] **QuiteRisky** got straight to the point: "If anyone wants to avoid bk [bankruptcy], it's him."[16]

This was an essential point for investors. When a distressed company faces bankruptcy, the stock ownership of the insiders is a key feature to watch. If they have little "skin in the game," they may be neutral to the fate of share prices; in this case, the board of directors shared the same interests as ordinary shareholders, and that might influence the decisions of the crisis manager, Bryan Marsal.

HealthSouth announced that PricewaterhouseCoopers had been hired to carry on a forensic accounting study separate from the necessary restatements of past years' financial statements. Meanwhile, HealthSouth advised investors not to rely on any previous financial statements, as SEC reports indicated the fraud might have begun as early as 1986.

But the new CEO, Robert May, assured us that business was ongoing when he announced that the company's clinical operations were continuing without interruption from the upheaval at corporate headquarters. Message board posters took this assurance to mean that income from operations would continue without harm from the conspiracy. This, too, was valuable investing information.

After the fury of trading, there was time to talk about Scrushy. One fellow said: "I wouldn't put it past him to plead innocent . . ." There were a multitude of "life in jail" comments, but **JRM30655** was on target when he said that Scrushy wouldn't plead guilty, but would claim he knew nothing of the fraud. I posted, under my alias **charon_xxx**, without knowing how accurate my parody would become:

---

charon_xxx: EXTRA, EXTRA, Scrushy betrayed by pals . . . #54587

"I can read it now. Birmingham News: Entrepreneur Richard Scrushy, favorite son of Alabama and philanthropist to hundreds of causes (all with his name on them) was vacationing in Palm Beach when it was discovered that those very employees he trained, befriended and trusted had cooked the company books. Mr. Scrushy stated that he will leave no stone unturned to find and punish the perpetrators and restore HealthSouth, the world's largest provider of out-patient health care services, to a position of trust. Mr. Scrushy said that HRC should soon trade "north of 20 cents" and that he was personally going to buy a million shares on the open market. He advises all employees to put their life savings in the company . . ."[17]

>>> **TRADERS CASH IN**

The marketplace was ready to trade the next morning. **The_Dow_Bum** took time at the beginning of Day 2 of trading to post a hopeful message:

The_Dow_Bum: Any guess on the close for today #53765 3/26/03

"S&P Index funds are out, Institutions are out, Chicken littles are out, . . . Bargain hunters are in. Volume drops off today and we get up to high end of .15 to .20 range. PREMARKET: $0.12 to 0.20 Good luck to all. I'm still buying. -the bum."[18]

Nearly 100 million trades took place on March 26 and, after fluctuating between 10 and 14 cents, the stock closed at 11 cents. This range, given 100 million trades, created paradise for the penny stock crowd. **The_Dow_Bum** had set up several brokerage accounts, including one that involved his stock trading club; altogether, they would hold over a million shares of HLSH.PK. His average purchase price was between 12 and 15 cents.

And so the second day of trading set a pattern that was to continue on the message board, as posters formed a consensus on underlying value. Many independent posters had arrived at the conclusion that HealthSouth was worth more than 12 cents a share and that bankruptcy could be avoided. As posters read the multiple discussions and analyses of HealthSouth's condition, opinions converged to form a consensus of predictable exuberance regarding share value. In opposition to this trend was a negative and unavoidable force: annoying legions of bashers (a term used to describe short traders) trying to drop the share price penny stock style by exaggerating or manufacturing bad news, so as to profit from trading volatility. That conflict would continue for many months.

Over the next two weeks of trading, the stock remained in the range of 11 to 13 cents per share, but the trading volumes continued in the double digits, ranging between 8 and 25 million trades per day. **The_Dow_Bum**'s strategy was clear from the first week and never changed. He urged his fellows not to trade in and out without considering that the stock price might race ahead of them. Volatility with high volume tempted nimble traders to skim profits, and day traders flocked to the message board like buzzards to roadkill. HLSH day after day made the list for high volume on the pinksheets.com Web site.

Activity on the message board was high, too; on some days, the message board registered nearly 500 postings. Perhaps a quarter of messages predicted bankruptcy or some other disaster, enhancing what some posters referred to as FUD—fear, uncertainty, and doubt—the friend of short sellers. **The_Dow_Bum** agreed with **JRM30655**, who said that HLSH was safer than it appeared; these posters suspected that most investors were unaware that the majority of HealthSouth's 2,000 clinics were still making money, and that, as **Bopper63** had noted, Joel Gordon's pride would be a factor in their favor. Gordon would not want to leave a legacy of bankruptcy.

The chief factor depressing price of HealthSouth stock was fear that debt holders would act precipitously. Bonds were actively trading at about 25 percent of face value. On April 1, **The_Emerging_Analyst**, in posting #54731, offered this wise advice:

The_Emerging_Analyst: Patience #54131 4/01/03

"The financial officers have pled guilty and are cooperating. Part of their cooperation is to work with the new auditors to reconstitute the books. This is important . . . they will know what journal entries were real and what are false . . .

The banks and bondholder deals can't be made until there are financials that everyone can agree upon. Market makers can't make a real market until there are reliable numbers. And no registered portfolio manager can risk owning this stock until there are new financials . . . even if the upside is ten times the downside, the brokers, portfolio managers, traders etc will wait for numbers . . . When we get new numbers and if there is a chance of survivability, this stock will pop above .50 immediately. Looking at the situation, I believe the upside far exceeds the downside, but we must be patient until there are numbers and Wall Street can once again become involved in this stock."

The_Dow_Bum replied: "Emerging Analyst, you make more sense than most of the so-called analysts. Good post and good thought process—the bum."[19]

On April 9, **The_Dow_Bum** reiterated: "Folks, if you sell for less than 50 cents, you're really going to hate yourself in a few weeks."[20] **Catsabouncing** agreed: "Patience . . . that is not how these double and triple baggers work. They start with a modest gap up . . . People wondering, is that all there is? Bashers start yapping about return to old lows. Then starts climbing, climbing, climbing. With no room for day trades."[21]

That same day a very significant new alias appeared. **Corstrat** (who gave his real name as Art and his address as Houston, Texas) had bought stock when trading resumed, and joined the board to comment on the market makers. **Corstrat** filled a new slot on the message board; he had been an OTC market trader and had owned a small brokerage. **Corstrat** posted messages nearly every day for a year, giving colleagues his interpretation of the market makers' signals and methods. Despite having a few detractors (who cited his history in the every-man-for-himself world of penny stock wins and losses), **Corstrat** became, for many, a hero during the period of

FIGURE 7.2

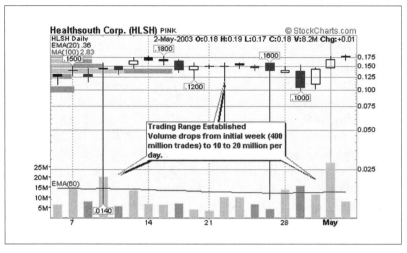

HealthSouth recovery. In my opinion, **The_Dow_Bum**, **JRM30655, The_Emerging_Analyst,** and **Corstrat** topped the list of many whose calm and expert analyses helped firm the resolve of neophytes who agonized over their investment.

Corstrat was able to shed light on the arcane world of market makers, who were playing an active role in HealthSouth's stock volatility. These traders have the advantage of a better view of market demand; they also know their inventory and are able to trade with each other in ways that confuse retail traders. To me, it resembled reading tea leaves; Corstrat's explanations in this post from April 9 were instructive:

---

corstrat: I would suspect the Market Makers will try to . . . #55686 4/09/03

"open this with a large spread between the bid and ask this morning. Probably two or three cents. They know that in spite of the obvious positive nature of the latest news, that many current shareholders won't have a clue why the stock might be going up and will sell first and read later . . .

The only real wild card out there is whether the MM's on balance closed out the day long or short yesterday. If they are long, they will try to make the stock look stronger and will keep the bid a little tighter. If they are short they will really expand the spread by keeping the bid weaker which, psychologically, usually slows down the buying by those who don't want to pay the offer on a large spread . . . I am a retired OTC MM who started playing this stock on the day it opened in the pinks . . . so I have watched the trading closely and can assure you that is the way they have been trading it so far . . . Remember when you are playing the pinks, it's their house so you play by their rules which of course gives them an advantage. About the only way an investor can get some of that advantage back when wanting to buy is to put some of your buy order on the offer and some in at a limit in the middle. This forces them to keep the spread tighter . . ."[22]

>>> HEALTHSOUTH CATCHES A BREAK

A first break came on April 10, when it was announced after market close that HealthSouth had reached a deal with the company's lender. It was only a three-day extension of debt, but it indicated a willingness to talk, and importantly, it was in writing. This deal reassured the message board that bankruptcy was not immediate. By May 9, HLSH had traded 737 million trades (368 million shares, since each buy and sell is counted as a trade on the pink sheets) and now stood 260 percent above its 8 cent low at the end of March 2003. There was but a single down week in the whole month of May. Perhaps best for us all was that favorable impressions of HealthSouth were being confirmed independently by others in the investment community. The message board continued to be a huge plus for small investors. Working by ongoing iteration, errors were corrected by consecutive posters and information was dredged up from remote sources and posted immediately. As **JRM30655** commented to me in a phone conversation: "If I want to know the color of Bryan Marsal's socks today, I can find out in five minutes on the message board."[23]

News media reports about HealthSouth continued to be bad. Most media stories focused on Richard Scrushy or the fraud and continued to refer to the company as "the scandal-plagued, struggling HealthSouth." On the message board, bashers continued to talk of imminent bankruptcy. We were hearing from stragglers, wanting to buy at a lower price, and they were afraid they had missed the last flight.

>>> WEEKEND POSTS OFFER VALUABLE INFORMATION

On message boards, long and serious messages are often posted on Saturdays and Sundays when time is free and market pressures are absent. On May 10, a thread of long posts offered the message board some valuable opinions from knowledgeable traders. It was clear that a consensus group was building regarding the long-term viability of HealthSouth stock; this group would probably hold their shares and not play dips with their core holdings. Appearing only six weeks after trading resumed, these were important messages:

> **corstrat: After 30 years of short-term stock evaluations . . .**
> **#59914 5/10/03**
>
> "I must admit. This is the hardest one I have ever dealt with . . . as a former IPO underwriter, I know how to deal with no, or low numbers in a startup development stage company with a good business plan. But this one has me baffled. From EVERYTHING I have read and researched in the past seven weeks about this company, there is no rational reason to

believe that this company is, or ever was a BK candidate. The industry group is in great shape as compared to WorldCom's, there is no evidence that its operating subs and partnerships are bogus as was the case in Enron, the debt seems to be very manageable for this size and type of company as compared to Kmart or WorldCom, and the 'fat' that this company has been supporting seems so obvious and so easily eliminated that future profits should not only be easily sustainable, but probably accretive. BUT, and I do stress to importance of that 'BUT', all of this means very little at this moment in evaluating a proper share price. Why? Because the future of this company is in the hands of a few individual representatives of factions whose agenda should be obvious (do what is best for the Company), but possibly is not (get my money and run). So, weighing the above, conventional analysis is out the window. So what's left? 'Read the tea leaves? Hunch? Gut Feel? Wild A** Gamble? Probably all of the above. But, IMO, one thing for sure. This is probably not a $1.00 stock . . ."[24]

His comments were followed by remarks from another poster whose investing preferences were distressed companies:

ITSABLOODYFIGHT: Perspective from a BK stock follower #59917 5/10/03

"I come from the perspective of a BK stock trader after having my own food trading company . . . I bought heavily days #1 and #2 following the halt, fully expecting BK— . . . Since the crash, the headlines have been fraud, guilty plea, etc. But behind the scenes, the situation has been far better than expected, just hard for the average investor or even Wall Street Trader to latch onto . . . In my normal analysis, HRC would not be a BK candidate. The reason they got close, seems to be the fraud-shock syndrome and PANIC . . .

> In any event, great risk reward ratios . . . I thought I was buying a bankrupt company; now the darn thing looks highly probable to live. Just another perspective."[25]

The reply from **The_Emerging_Analyst** was unexpected. Of all those who had great experience, he remained the most distant, a mystery man. On this day, he opened his message by revealing that he had been a security analyst for many years—his first and only offer to the board of any personal information. After reiterating the issues that made HealthSouth's situation so unique, he offered some encouragement to the board:

> **The_Emerging_Analyst: Re: After 30 years of stock evaluating #59938 5/10/03**
>
> ". . . The stock went down to almost zero not because bankruptcy was a 100% conclusion but for several reasons: The chance of bankruptcy was substantial but is lessening with time. The need for institutions to get the stock off their books before the March 31 reporting date, the delisting which forced many institutions to sell, S&P dropping it from the 500 index forcing 35 million shares to hit the market on the first day of trading and lastly Blue Sky laws that forced analysts to issue sell recommendations and drop coverage even though the stock was trading at .07 and the upside far exceeded the downside. I look for the company to recover above one dollar with audited numbers and any positive agreements with lenders. Once relisted or on NASDQ we could go substantially higher."[26]

>>> **THE PERFECT STORM**

We were encouraged by word from some on-the-scene posters that HealthSouth's facilities were functioning smoothly. "Tidbits from Birmingham" was posted by **gprewitt**. He reported that he had just returned from Birmingham and saw newly-laid-off employees being interviewed by news media. He also said that a construction crew was completing the exterior of the digital hospital, and that HealthSouth's south side hospital was thriving—some were speculating that it might be purchased by other local hospitals.[27] Finally, he noted that all clinical operations were running "very smoothly." **The_Emerging_Analyst** thanked him for the update on the state of HealthSouth's bread-and-butter operations. "Sometimes with sensational fraud headlines," he wrote, "we lose the concept of an operating company with thousands of hard-working employees providing patients with quality care."[28]

As May drew to a close, the trend in HealthSouth stock value continued upward. Turnaround specialist Bryan Marsal was taking a firm grip on the company. There had been doctor uprisings in clinics, and Marsal was reported to have told doctors who wanted their contracts cancelled (allowing them to work apart from HealthSouth) that he, Marsal, would rather "burn the clinics to the ground, than void the contracts." The clinics continued in operation.

In April, Congress had begun an investigation into the HealthSouth fraud. As part of that effort, Congress investigated the relationship of UBS Warburg to HealthSouth, and in particular questioned a scheme alleged to have been hatched in September of 2002, whereby UBS brokers were said to have advised HealthSouth to split the company as a device to cover the fraud (the congressional hearing on this investigation took place in November of 2003; action is pending in this case).[29] The positive aspect of the story for traders on the message board was that valuation of the project's two resulting halves

FIGURE 7.3

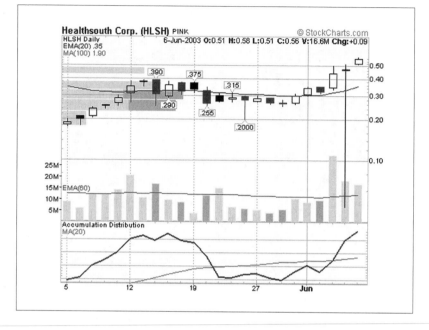

implied a valuation of HealthSouth of several billion dollars more than the market price and, if that were true, it gave credence to hidden value that supported HealthSouth's debt.

After a dip in share price during which bashers pounded away at investor confidence, **Corstrat** posted what is probably the best-known message on the HRC message board: "Perfect Storm, The Sequel." It was a long post, but it served to soothe nervous shareholders who still reacted to every hint that bondholders might dilute the holdings of those who held shares. Here are some excerpts:

---

corstrat: Perfect Storm, The Sequel #68581 6/12/03

"... HRC's becoming HLSH, was the "Perfect Storm"....
Though I bought my first shares on the 25th, I spent that afternoon and night researching what was happing to HLSH.

My research, experience and instincts told me by the next day that this company was NOT a Bankrupt company. Not even close. I knew it . . . Had it not been de-listed and forced to the pinks, just four days before the end of the Institutions reporting quarter's end, while being 80% owned by Institutions, this stock would never have dropped below a dollar, maybe not below two dollars. As all on this board probably know by now, Investment Institutions by covenant, can rarely own 'pink sheet' stocks in their portfolios . . . Had they [the NYSE] held it just a few more days at least it would have given the funds a full quarter to try to 'sort things out' and if delisted, have an orderly liquidation. Instead, they let it trade with only four days left in the quarter forcing a mass dump of up to 300 million shares into a market that can only be supported by 'retail' investors, and in many cases, only retail investors trading with non-wire house brokerages. Yes, this was . . . a terrible paper loss for the old shareholders, but a once in a lifetime opportunity for a select group of new ones and astute old ones.

. . . Some day in the next month or two, after the financials show what IMO is how strong this Industry Leader really is, this stock will be re-listed on some exchange. This will be the day of the next Perfect Storm . . ." (See the list of references at the end of this book for a link to full post)

>>> MARSAL PAVES ROAD TO RECOVERY

The confluence of these problems added to HealthSouth's inability to pay its bond coupons because its bank accounts and lines of credit were frozen. Additionally, a $300 million convertible bond was due payment in ten days, and its lack of financial records breached its covenants and contracts with debtors.

One strong key for investors was that bond prices had firmed and moved upward. New bondholders, those who bought junk bonds at the bottom, now had capital gains in bonds that not only paid favorable rates of interest, but also appeared to be money-safe. Now, the interests of the new bondholders were different from those of the old bondholders. Both groups could believe that HealthSouth assets might eventually be sufficient to cover debt, but forcing bankruptcy as a preferred course of collection was clearly not an interest of those who held capital gains profits. Recovery of bond prices gave Brian Marsal additional negotiating leverage.

At HealthSouth, Marsal was busy identifying and overcoming what he would later describe as "rocks in the road"—obstacles that stood in the path of HealthSouth's recovery. After discovering that over $300 million was missing from a HealthSouth bank account, Marsal froze all expenditures. To help conserve remaining funds, Marsal also had begun a series of employee layoffs (some of the 400 employees in this group were later rehired). Real estate leases were renegotiated at more favorable rates, and land intended for new facilities was sold. Poorly performing clinics also were sold, as well as those located remotely from HealthSouth's main operations.

In early June, prices reached 94 cents only to dip after yet another report on CNBC, this one referencing HealthSouth during a program segment about bankruptcy. Furious investors were certain this adverse publicity had caused the pullback in share price. CNBC was not alone, however; reading the published accounts, one could believe that half the financial world was mistakenly convinced that HealthSouth had already declared Chapter 11:

---

scooterpass: (34/F) CNBC Reiterated what I've always thought #70662 6/16/03

"the average joe on the street thinks HS is done . . . already in bankruptcy. You can't blame them if they haven't kept up with it like we have. All they remember is the bad press and the raids . . . quotes like 'worst case of outright fraud I've ever seen . . . ' I've made my decision. I've got a couple

---

of weeks to increase my position under a buck!!! Lucky me!
A bit of patience will be rewarded. Sorry to gloat, but
things are good in the Scooter household."[30]

>>> THE BASHERS RETURN

Volatility increased again, but now HLSH gyrated between
20 cents and 94 cents. In the trading of such stocks and on
message boards dealing with investments that many would
class as sheer speculation, it is common for touts to lie about
their holdings and urge others to buy as they sell. Duplicity is
so common that seasoned traders never rely on such dialogue
unless it is backed up with reasoning, evidence, and links to
other sources. This kind of touting can be especially effective
in situations where information is scarce—as it often is in the
case of small companies or companies in trouble. HealthSouth
fit this profile—it was troubled, without financial statements,
and now approached a rational valuation. Buying had been
easy at a dime, but at a dollar, new buyers had rabbit ears for
fear, uncertainty, and doubt

Under ordinary circumstances, a claque of bashers and
manipulators cannot depress the price of a company such as
HealthSouth, with a float of 400 million trading shares and a
previous market cap of $12 billion. With media reports nearly
unanimous in predicting disaster, however, and with each pullback of HLSH share price, critics bombarded the message
board, hoping to "buy the dip and play the bounce." The message board became filled with blather, horrid manners, and
foul-mouthed personal attacks—page after page of noise, at the
pace of a new post every 30 seconds. But, there are always
bashers who make valid points, intelligent short sellers, and
they are the most despised even when they make comments
that should be considered.

FIGURE 7.4

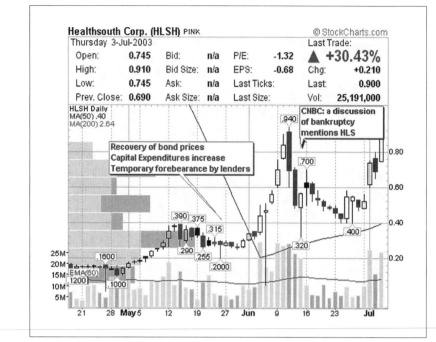

After a message reading "POS [Piece of Shit] is Heading South Again . . . You Lose!!!"[31] another poster advised the message board not to reply to bashers. Many on message boards believe that hedge funds and other mysterious groups pay "by the post" for negative messages, though I've never found evidence to substantiate that belief. The more satisfactory explanation is that most of them are short sellers trying to force share prices down, that others wish to buy at a lower price, and that others are entertaining themselves by creating havoc among the "longs." But the fall of HLSH shares from a dollar to 40 cents followed by another upward spike was perfect for bashers and added to the noise on the board.

A message titled, "My Prediction," suggested that no sane person would hold shares of HealthSouth overnight—bankruptcy was moments away. **DemiWhite** answered: "My call is that your assessment is perfect." The target of many on the board and the sharp-tongued person most despised for bashing, **Demi-White** claimed a home in the "Catskills of Oklahoma." **Corstrat** disagreed with DemiWhite, however, saying the price drop was due to simple profit taking. He asked: "Would the three day drop from 19 cents to 10 cents two months ago be caused by your theory? Or the drop from 39 cents to 25 cents? . . . Simple enough to me."[32] DemiWhite replied:

---

demiwhite: 54 Recs to my post #70856

"Bad examples Corset. The two previous drops in your reference occurred with decreasing volume, whereas this last drop was 2x volume. To put it another way, the two previous drops occurred from lack of interest. The last one from 90 cents to 40 cents because of mass exiting."[33]

An effective basher always uses worrisome facts, creates likely numbers when necessary, and plays on uncertainty. **DemiWhite** was a master and a good trader. He was hated because he was effective, so hated that he was occasionally threatened by others on the message board and took extreme measures to hide his identity and location. He was an archtype and typical of many who trade on the Internet.

---

demiwhite: RE: Opinion on Cash Impact? #71120

"It's a moot point. Even if they are cash flow positive, which is doubtful, they still have too many issues to contend with.

HealthSouth will 'violate its maximum debt to EBITDA covenant requirement of 3.5x for the period ending Dec. 31, 2002. HealthSouth is also contending with the maturity of $344 million of convertible notes on April 1, 2003'. Healthsouth is in violation of its covenants. HS not only needs to

---

be cash flow positive to prove viability, they need to reach 900+m EBITDA. They also must pay a $344m maturity on their convertibles, $200+m in medicare fraud charges, and countless shareholder lawsuits."[34]

>>> INVITATION ONLY MESSAGE BOARD IS CREATED

Noise, clutter, and foul language on the message board became so disruptive that several members established a "private group message board," an option for groups on Yahoo! that was accessible by invitation only. Though it lacked the healthy criticism offered by some of the other posters, the private board was temporarily successful because it offered serious posters the advantage of a friendly forum. An investor, **Instructmba,** posted the results of his private e-mail survey of message board investors:

Instructmba: Private Board Group is now 100 Members Strong! #72336

"Below is a list of the shares owned by posters on this message board. Anonymous: 1.457 million shares. Those who post here on a daily basis own 6.003 million shares. The total of all who emailed their numbers is 14,752,900 shares."[35]

I corrected his numbers by posting that the private board had nearly 210 posters. I added that I assumed that most were shareholders.[36]

>>> MESSAGE BOARD ADVICE ON THE MONEY
FOR MANY

On the first of July, with the holiday approaching, **marvelmeister2002** left a message saying: "The downside is gone. We will jump after the meeting, but we should run up huge before the meeting too."[37] The board was ready for the holiday, but for many, it was not time to leave town; it was time to buy more HLSH. Typical of OTC-traded stock, HLSH charts did not exhibit gradual ups and downs but instead moved jerkily in huge stair-step configurations. On July 3, HLSH shares rose to $0.91 and closed at $0.90 for a weekly appreciation of 84 percent. Volume traded was 76,702,200 shares. From a close at $0.08 the low, the weekly price in March, appreciation was now 1025 percent and message board bulls saw no end in sight.

One poster gave thanks publicly for the advice and information he'd gained from the message board; he was not alone. As time went on, dozens of posters echoed his sentiments. He said, "This is the best darn board I have EVER had the pleasure of being on! Sound reasoning. Totally Professional. If this works out . . . I will be giving some money to my Church and thanking God I had the pleasure of being part of something grand . . . I have had some family health issues and this has lessened the mental load . . .Thanks so much." He signed his note: Lance. [38]

Early in July, a press release announced that Bryan Marsal was about to have a meeting in New York to make an announcement on his crisis management team's progress at HealthSouth. Discussion on the board dissected the prospects. As was often the case, **The_Dow_Bum**'s analysis was thorough; he succinctly summarized every reason that bankruptcy was finally out of the picture, and why those who had not bought should have confidence now. Investors who agreed with **The_Dow_Bum**'s reasoning and bought stock as a result enjoyed a fivefold profit. Here is his message about the importance of Marsal's upcoming meeting:

The_Dow_Bum: In Summary #76592 7/1/03

"... It took me two hours to read through all the posts from last night and it sounds like the party's starting. Even our little HLSH investment group from the second floor of an Albuquerque office building had to stop at the local Costco after work for a celebratory ice cream. We were hashing out each phrase and word in the PR. And here is a summary of you all's posts and our analysis on why this is good for us:

1. The meeting announcement came on 6/30 just like the new management team had proclaimed back in the 5/30 employee letter.

2. "June 30, HLSH today announced that it will hold a meeting for creditors and stockholders" You don't have meetings to announce BK's, you just send out a press release. And you would never think of inviting stockholders to a BK announcement meeting. That's like inviting someone to their own funeral.

3. This is the first time since HRC was halted and possible BK was mentioned that the company acknowledged that stockholders exist. This is a big positive since in BK deliberations a company is only beholden to debt holders.

4. "In New York City on Monday, July 7, 2003, at 3:00 EST" The place and time are significant. If negative news, you'd hide it in a Bham tabloid.

5. The date and time are equally critical. 7/7 is after the July 4th holiday and everyone is back to work. And 3:00 EST is while the markets are still open. If it were a BK announcement, you'd never pick a date and time when the markets are open. BK's are always announced out of hours and for some reason companies like Sundays a lot for their BK proclamations.

6. "To review its preliminary business plan" The Company is calling it a business plan and not a restructuring plan. The fact that they have a business plan implies no BK, since declaring BK as part of your plan for doing business is not normally done – like never.

7. "And to provide current financial projections for the next twelve months" A company could give projections if BK were imminent, since the BK court rulings would totally impact those projections. HLSH is claiming they can make them for the coming year.

8. "The meeting will be hosted by Joel C. Gordon, Interim Chairman of the Board, Robert P. May, Interim Chief Executive Officer, and Bryan Marsal, Chief Restructuring Officer" The big three are going to be there and you sure wouldn't have them attend a BK announcement – they'd be too easy of a target. I wish I could attend to shake there hands after the meeting.

9. "Individuals may access the meeting by phone by dialing 888-913-9967" No company broadcasts their BK announcements.

10. "A live Internet broadcast will also be available at www.healthsouth.com by clicking on an available link. The Web cast will be archived for replay purposes for one week after the live broadcast" And no BK company would ever have their BK announcement available for replay for a week.

I hope this summarizes all the high points of last night's PR. So as we HLSH longs plan our upcoming holiday activities, I think we have a lot more to celebrate than just July 4th. -the bum"

Corstrat had friends at the public meeting in New York City who reported to him by cell phone, and others on the board posted while listening to the conference on computer links. They presented a blow-by-blow from the meeting that read like a ten-reel, B-movie thriller. As we waited anxiously to read definitive news on the fate of our investments, one poster, aliased **The_Freedom_Nebula,** joked: "5 minutes and the wives will either be wearing some Victoria Secret stuff tonight or have the divorce lawyers at the door."[39]

The meeting began at 3:03 PM on July 7, 2003. By 3:09, a message reported that Joel Gordon had introduced everyone on stage and then announced, "Solid and profitable. This is the new HealthSouth." Another message soon lit up the board, reading, "$0.96 and moving up! Watch it trade!" As we read the messages that rapidly filled the board, we saw only good news: HealthSouth board and management were committed to following action plans, restoring trust, and disclosing information to all regulatory bodies.

---

cowardly_long: No Way They File Bankruptcy 3:16 PM #80345

"NO WAY"

The_Freedom_Nebula: I am still waiting for the magic phrase #80355

---

cowardly_long: Just Used Bankruptcy in the PAST tense 3:20 PM #80360

"Brian Marsal . . . No material Medicare Issues ! go Go GO ! Huge Relief!"

At 3:23 PM, this quote from the meeting hit our screens: "We Intend To Pay All Creditors In Full." The message went on to report that HealthSouth had arranged with Credit Suisse/ First Boston to help finance the convertible bond now due. HealthSouth announced sufficient cash flow to make all other debt payments as they came due. They released a pro-forma plan that showed net profits from operations of $650 million from July 2003 to 2004, and expected to have $500 million in cash after selling hospital assets. Finally, we learned that Price-waterhouseCooper's forensic audit was expected to be finished in the third quarter, and that 1999 through 2002 accounts would be restated the following year. The message board read: "250,000 shares just went at $1.25 at 3:38 PM." "Hindsight's great. Should have mortgaged the farm," said another.

To the enjoyment of all, CNBC stated: "One must keep in mind that Healthsouth's disclaimer went far beyond the standard Safe Harbor disclaimer and these figures should not be relied on." From Amsterdam, a basher named **Q** said: "Please sell. Can I have some?"[40] Mike Tomberlin, of the *Birmingham News* posted, using his alias of **L_T_Chickin,** asking to be contacted at the newspaper: "If you'll let your name be used," he said, "we are looking for successful bottom feeders who made big money on HLSH stock."[41] The word of investors' success was spreading.

The message board lit up with thanks and glee. At 4:00 PM, a post read:

"Thank you God for blessing me. Amen and thank you Jesus!!!" [42]

Another message, #81210, said: "Dream Come True!!!! . . . I am in for 8000 shares at 50 cents. I have been sweating the whole time as we are supposed to buy a house in the next couple of months . . . my wife says sell . . ." **Lisagoodman20002000,** a possible play on trans-gender alias, thanked **JRM30655**: ". . . brilliant . . . Miss you."[43]

FIGURE 7.5

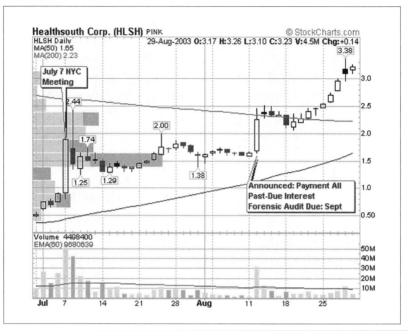

>>> THANKS GIVING COMES EARLY THIS YEAR

The message board had seldom seen messages giving thanks for blessings, and many of the aliases were unfamiliar. These were lurkers who seldom, if ever, posted. It seemed certain that many were among the scores of employees whose funds had been trapped in HealthSouth 401(k)s, which were decimated by the crash. Investors on the message board represented the tip of an iceberg of shattered pensions, for which surging prices meant salvation. The message board was to see more heartfelt testimonials to recovery as HealthSouth's fortunes improved. For many, recovery held out the possibility of an eventual retirement from a daily job at the age of 65. **The_Dow_Bum** took time to thank his colleagues:

> **The_Dow_Bum: Gratitudes and Congratulations #80681**
> **7/07/03**
>
> "This is truly a once-in-a-lifetime moment, and I must thank the people that made it possible.
>
> First and foremost, let me give my sincere appreciation to HealthSouth's new management team and all the HS employees. The management team of Joel Gordon, Robert May and Bryan Marsal had the foresight and professionalism to see this through. The doctors and employees have been the backbone of this company and continued to do their normal great jobs during the last three tense months. The turnaround of HLSH is directly a result of the management and employees – I salute them all. Now let me thank the posters on this board . . ."[44] (Links to those posters are included in the list of references at the end of this book.)

After the conference call, several analysts and brokerages made comments. Jeffrey Dobro, analyst for Trilogy Capital, said: "The projections today were certainly better than what we thought possible a week ago, when some people thought there was no value in the company. If it wasn't for all the rocks in the road, which includes possible federal penalties, I'd give HealthSouth a thumbs up," Dobro continued. "But those are huge unknowns."[45]

Media reports also focused on the remaining unknowns, all things that the message board had discussed for weeks. One article noted that any one of them could force Health-South into bankruptcy-court proceedings. Among the problems Marsal noted were the civil investigation into Medicare fraud at HealthSouth and the penalties it might incur, SEC fines, and the looming shareholder lawsuits. These were among the "rocks in the road," Marsal had outlined in his presentation, which had been placed on screen and later permanently posted on the SEC Web site.[46]

>>> **RECOVERY CONTINUES**

The recovery continued. HLSH shares eventually traded up to $6.24 before falling back into the $5 to $6 range, where they stayed until Richard Scrushy's January 2005 trial. The real work of the message board was complete, and is worthy of note as an example of a complex adaptive organization. Michael Fitzgerald, writing in *Technology Review*, commented on James Surowiecki's book, *The Wisdom of Crowds*, in particular, and what he referred to as Surowiecki's "intuitive theory." Fitzgerald noted that "groups can act as parallel-processing decision engines, pooling disparate knowledge to answer even hard questions in hard areas like public policy." He went on to discuss the power of blogs and Howard Dean's unprecedented use of the power of the Internet in his presidential campaign. Fitzgerald also quoted newspaperman Walter Lippmann as commenting on the communications infrastructure of democracy and the necessity of "creating and organizing a machinery of knowledge." After citing this quote, Fitzgerald wrote: "That machinery may finally have arrived."[47]

CHAPTER *eight*

The Prosecution

On April 19, 2005, the prosecution wrapped up its case in the trial of *The United States of America v Richard M. Scrushy.* U.S. attorney Alice Martin had presented the case for the prosecution before Judge Karon Bowdre, in a trial marked by public clashes between the two women over Bowdre's rulings.

Since the trial's opening on January 25, 2005, the prosecution had made a long and complex case. Jurors had heard admissions of guilt from five former HealthSouth CFOs. In various trials associated with the $2.7 billion HealthSouth fraud, 10 of the 15 company executives who entered guilty pleas received sentencing before Scrushy's trial began; Emery Harris was the only one to receive a jail sentence (five months in prison).[1] On June 22, 2005, it was announced that the 11th U.S. Circuit Court of Appeals overturned the sentences of former HealthSouth CFO Michael Martin and former Vice President Richard Botts, both of whom had pleaded guilty and received home detention and probation. The order from the Court of Appeals requires that the lower court review and give reasons for the sentences, which, according to the higher court, have departed from the federal guidelines in their leniency.[2]

The jury could be certain that there had been intentional fraud; Scrushy agreed that was true. But in 41 days of testimony, had the prosecution proven that Scrushy knew of the fraud as it was taking place? If Scrushy were convicted, he easily could receive what would amount to a life's sentence, so the jury's responsibility was great.

>>> SETTING THE STAGE FOR TRIAL

The trial, thus far, had been long and tiring, with the drama taking place among the legal teams often as sensational as the testimony of those who admitted to the fraud. On October 29, 2003, Richard Scrushy had been indicted in the United States District Court for the Northern District of Alabama, Southern Division.[3] Scrushy was facing multiple counts of corporate corruption; violations listed in the original indictment included conspiracy, mail fraud, wire fraud, securities fraud, false statements, false certification, money laundering, and aiding and abetting.[4] Scrushy was being represented by a team of attorneys, chief among them home-spun Alabama attorney James (Jim) Parkman III and wealthy Birmingham attorney, banker, and entrepreneur Donald V. Watkins—an influential member of Birmingham's African-American community.

If the proceedings themselves had not thus far proven to be "sensational" (the typical term employed for describing high-profile prosecutions), the trial had been accompanied by what the *Wall Street Journal* dubbed a "legal sideshow."[5] Scrushy had gone through four teams of attorneys, first retaining and then dismissing some of the country's most prestigious law firms over reported disagreements regarding both money and strategy.[6] Finally, he chose Watkins to oversee his case, drawing him out of retirement from legal practice. Jim Parkman was partner in a Dothan, Alabama, law firm that employed Scrushy's son-in-law—a determinedly "small-town" legal firm with a hand-lettered sign in its window reading "Hicks That Care."[7]

In two other prosecutions peripherally related to the HealthSouth fraud case, attorney Alice Martin had clashed with federal judges U.W. Clemon and Inge Johnson. According to the *Wall Street Journal,* in 2003, prosecutors had requested a delay in sentencing for five HealthSouth defendants, pending the conclusion of Scrushy's trial. Judge Johnson had refused.[8] In 2004, Martin also had asked Judge Clemon to recuse himself from the trial of former Alabama Governor Don Siegelman, citing prejudice against the government.[9] Judge Clemon had refused to comply with the request, saying he had no such prejudice. In that trial, according to the *Wall Street Journal,* "Immediately after opening statements, he [Clemon] criticized the main charge in the probe, leading prosecutors to drop their case."[10]

And now, there were suspicions among some of Scrushy's critics that Judge Karon Bowdre was lenient on his behalf. This suspicion was bolstered when reporters from the *Birmingham News* obtained the May 2005 release of sealed transcripts of a hearing Bowdre held with prosecutors and defense lawyers in November of 2003, on the day Scrushy's prosecution was announced.[11] In that hearing, as reported in the *Birmingham Business Journal,* Judge Bowdre had admitted to having previous contact with Scrushy, his daughter Melissa, and his ex-wife Karen Brooks. According to the transcripts, Bowdre said she had ridden horses with Melissa and Brooks at Scrushy's estate, where Bowdre made use of the Scrushy's stables. She was quoted as saying: "I am quite fond of Melissa. I think she is a wonderful, wonderful girl." In the same hearing, Bowdre was reported to have said that she didn't think her previous contact with Scrushy or his family would diminish her ability to try the case fairly, but then added: "As you all know, though, I am somewhat of a neophyte to criminal law . . . And so I will rely on all of you to educate me about the legal issues that are involved, and I know that you will do a good job of doing that. But don't expect me to do something just because you say that's the way it needs to be done."[12] After hearing her statements, neither the prosecution nor the defense attorneys requested Bowdre to recuse herself from the case.

>>> WHO'S WHO OF THE SCRUSHY TRIAL

Although stories of corporate scandal were becoming almost commonplace by the time Scrushy's trial began, this case drew special attention from both the public and the media for reasons other than the unfolding drama of the prosecutors, defense lawyers, and judge. Scrushy's trial would be the first prosecution under the Sarbanes-Oxley Act, passed by Congress in 1997, which required top officers personally to attest, under penalty of law, to the validity of company financial reports. Scrushy's lawyers claimed that Sarbanes-Oxley was unconstitutionally vague; but another federal judge upheld the law. Scrushy did not appeal that decision.[13]

While the case held the attention of corporate attorneys around the nation, many of us on the message board were following it with equal attention. The long list of charges the prosecutors had filed was of special concern to some on the message board. Stacked charges seemed to serve no purpose, other than to make Scrushy the object of sympathy. And even with many of the charges dropped, Scrushy faced sentencing that could amount to more than 200 years in prison. The message board was split; though few questioned Scrushy's guilt, many doubted that he would receive severe punishment—or any punishment at all—while others were certain he'd be found guilty. After reading countless messages speculating on just how much time Scrushy would spend behind bars, I posted a message reminding others that a guilty verdict was no certainty. Scrushy had waged a vigorous public relations campaign, I noted, and juries were unpredictable.

Without question, the guilty pleas and testimony against Scrushy of a string of HealthSouth's CFOs were damning. And of the extensive lineup of indicted HealthSouth executives, many had long-term professional and personal connections to Scrushy. Aaron Beam, CFO from 1984 to 1997, was a Health-South founding partner and member of Scrushy's band. William Owens, in addition to his role as HealthSouth CFO, had also served as controller, COO, and CEO, and had been a drummer in Scrushy's band.[14] CFO Weston Smith had entered a guilty plea to charges of conspiracy to commit wire fraud and securities fraud.[15] Treasurer Malcom "Tadd" McVay and CFO Michael Martin were indicted, as well as Controller and Chief Information Officer Ken Livesay (also lead guitar in Scrushy's band). Also among the indicted were Senior Vice President Richard Botts, Vice President of Finance Emery Harris, and Vice Presidents Cathy Edwards, Rebecca Morgan, Angela Ayers, Catherine Fowler, and Tom Carman, along with Assistant Vice President Virginia Valentine and Vice President of Finance Jason Brown.[16]

As the chief prosecutor, attorney Alice Martin was facing a daunting task; to make a case for illegal conspiracy, she would have to prove to the jury that Scrushy and one other defendant had agreed on an illegal plan. She also would have to show that one of them overtly acted to carry out the plan. To prove additional charges, Martin would have to secure testimony and evidence proving false statements, false SEC filings, false certifications, false testimony, knowledge of criminal action, and the purchase of valuable goods for the purpose of laundering stolen money. Most important, she would have to prove beyond a reasonable doubt that Scrushy intentionally performed or asked others to perform those criminal acts, and that he knew at that time that what he was doing was illegal.

In the absence of a confession or signed papers saying, in effect, "I, Richard Scrushy, knew about the fraud and participated in it," Martin had to illustrate each of the above points with exhibits, evidence, and witness statements that supported the prosecution's claim that Scrushy acted specifically and knowingly to break the law. Jurors in the case would be required to sort through esoteric issues of accounting and minute details of weekly ledgers, consolidated ledgers, and capital budget variances—data that might have fascinated a CPA, but would be less than riveting to most laypeople. To prove her case, Martin would have to lead the jury through the process of assessing this minutia, along with the testimony of a string of other witnesses, to arrive at a guilty verdict against Richard Scrushy.

The jury to whom Martin would make this case was not in a technical sense a collection of Scrushy's peers; no one on the jury was a millionaire entrepreneur who yearned to be a stage performer. Most of the seven men and five women, who were chosen from an original jury pool of 600, came from blue-collar backgrounds. Several had previously served on juries, and two had been foreman. Michael Tomberlin and Russell Hubbard gave readers a profile of the jury in an article published in the *Birmingham News*, while the jury was in its ninth day of deliberation on June 2, 2005.[17] To protect their identities in the press, the article referred to the jurors by the numbers they had been assigned by the court:

> The current foreperson was #157; she had served previously on a jury that convicted the accused of drug and weapons charges. Juror #300 was a lineman for Alabama Power Co. and had served in the Army and Army reserves. Juror #467 had served before on a jury; she had a nephew who was a police officer (during the

trial, #467 sent a note to Judge Bowdre asking if the jury's decision had to be unanimous). Two other jurors, #'s 546 and 343, also had served on juries—one that convicted the defendant of child rape, the other a hung jury. Juror #459 lived in the wealthy suburb of Vestavia Hills where Scrushy owned a mansion. Juror #123 was from Birmingham and stated that he continued to read the newspaper while empaneled—but only the headlines. Juror #152 was an Air Force Reservist with five children. Juror #188 was a Shriner, who the reporters quoted as saying "I feel like it's a fact that a wealthy person can afford better attorneys, and I think quite often they have an advantage in that regard." The juror went on to say, however, that he didn't hold Scrushy's wealth against him, and presumed he was innocent until proven guilty.[18]

Martin's task may have been made even tougher by Scrushy's ongoing efforts to get his story out to the Birmingham community, including through the locally broadcast paid-program *Viewpoint*. Scrushy started the program after his indictment because, he said in a statement released by his spokesman Charlie Russell, he had "time on his hands while awaiting trial." The statement went on to say: "He sees the daily television program as a community service, providing uplifting programming while providing access to pastors . . . and others . . . in the community which could not find a voice on ordinary commercial television."[19] In his article "Former HealthSouth CEO Scrushy Turns Televangelist," *USA Today* reporter Greg Farrell stated that "Scrushy books a steady stream of local ministers and pastors as guests." (On his Web site, Scrushy has posted a "News Article" denouncing Farrell's *USA Today* piece as containing "numerous false and misleading statements." As an example, Scrushy points to Farrell's designation of Leslie Scrushy's show-opening "short devotional" as a prayer, citing this as an illustration of the "journalistic liberty Farrell takes in his writing."[20]) Some of these guests and others in the local religious community would partially occupy the two courtroom benches assigned for Scrushy's family and supporters throughout the trial

>>> THE TRIAL OPENS

On January 25, attorney Alice Martin was prepared to deliver her opening statement. Present in the courtroom that day were numerous reporters and attorneys who would be responsible for trying upcoming civil cases involving the HealthSouth fraud. I followed the trial proceedings from afar—reading newspaper and online accounts of daily events. The best reports came, of course, from Birmingham. Online, Marc Thomason's Warliberal blog (http://warliberal.blogspot.com) and Phil Smith's Scrushy-Report.com offered ongoing updates on the trial's events and progress. Smith (who has generously allowed me to use some of his commentary in this account) traveled from his home in Tampa to attend the trial daily, and then chronicled the day's events on his blog. Smith's highlights and keen eye for detail, when supplemented with reports from the *New York Times*, the *Wall Street Journal*, the *Washington Post,* and the *Birmingham News*, provide a good overview of the prosecution's case and of Scrushy's pit-bull defense strategy. Standing before the courtroom that day, Martin thanked the court, then opened her statement by asking jurors to return with her to a conference room at HealthSouth headquarters in March of 2003. She noted that on that day, Richard Scrushy, accompanied by five attorneys and a court reporter, was being deposed by two representatives of the SEC in connection with an investigation into whether Scrushy had signed false financial statements for public release. According to court transcripts, Martin went on to say:

". . . at 8:58 that morning in that conference room, defendant [Scrushy] raised his right hand and he swore to tell the truth, and he was asked about those forms . . . And they said, did you sign those? Yes, I signed those. And was the information contained in those forms that you signed that you gave to the public, was it true and correct? Yes, it was true to the best of my knowledge. Now, that's Friday. I want you to step through the weekend with me. Monday morning, back in that same headquarters building . . . Mr. Scrushy comes to work that morning about 9:00 o'clock, and he goes down into Mr. Owens' office and he says, this didn't happen. Swear to it. He sees another man in the room that he knows, he knows him very well, Ken Livesay . . . and he says you need to hear this because you were sitting under the CFO for a long time.

> They [the federal officials] are on a witch hunt. They don't know blank. They're not looking at the numbers . . . They asked me something about the financial forms I signed. The guy, he didn't know what he was doing . . . The guy from the SEC, he didn't have a clue. He shuffled some papers around on the desk, and he asked did I sign that, and I said, yeah, I signed that; sure, I signed that. He said, was it true? And I said, sure. What else am I going to say? Yeah, it's true to the best of my knowledge. And Bill—because, you see, Bill [Owens] was under subpoena to testify before the SEC, too. And he said, Bill, that's your answers, to the best of my knowledge."[21]

Martin then named and asked jurors to consider some of the many small investors who had lost important sums of money to the fraud and as a result of the conspirators' deception. She said she would present evidence over the next weeks that Richard Scrushy knew about the deception, that he participated in it, and that he profited from it—all elements needed for conviction.[22] She continued:

> "The defense is going to be he didn't know. Yeah, something happened out there, but he just didn't know about it. So, the case is really going to come down to one word, something I predict that you're going to discuss a lot when you go in to deliberate, and it's knowledge. We are going to prove to you that he did know, and the way we're going to prove to you that he did know is we're going to take you inside HealthSouth. You're going to meet the people that he met with, the people he conspired with. And you are going to see the private reports that he was given showing what the true numbers were, and you're going to hear what they told him and you're going to listen to what he said."[23]

To help ground the jury in some of the basic legal and technical issues of her case, Martin explained to the jury the difference between a public and a private company and the rules that demand and govern corporate quarterly financial statements, conference calls that provide facts to analysts and investors, and public interviews conducted by corporate CEOs. "The public, you will learn during this trial," Martin said, "relied on that information. They relied on it to make important investing decisions. You will hear people that say, I looked at that information, and because of that, I bought. And you will hear banks say that I looked at that information, because of that, we lent money."[24] According to the court transcripts, Martin then told the jury that evidence would show that HealthSouth's numbers were phony; the company was not making as much money as its representatives publicly stated it was making. Scrushy knew the budget, she said; it was a big company, in all 50 states, but it had a budget, just like ordinary people have for their households, and the budget is something the CEO knows. She went on to help cement in the jury's mind that Richard Scrushy was the absolute leader of HealthSouth and its operations:

> "Richard Scrushy was the Chief Executive Officer. That means he was the boss. He was the man. There wasn't anybody higher than him. He was also the chairman of the board . . . You are going to hear that he was a hands-on leader. This was his baby . . . he hand-picked all of his top officers . . .
>
> . . . You will hear that he said often, 'HealthSouth is the best managed healthcare company in America.' Why? Because he would tell people 'I manage weekly. I manage by the numbers.' And that's exactly what he did. He managed by the numbers and he demanded a lot of financial information . . ."[25]

Martin next described Scrushy's management style. She explained that he got detailed weekly reports on every clinic and told people proudly that he "took them home to read." Martin characterized Scrushy as a micromanager, who pored over the private financial records presented to him by CFO Aaron Beam. Martin then told the jury that they would hear former HealthSouth CFO Beam testify about an incident that occurred in mid-1996, when Beam and then-controller Bill Owens confronted Scrushy with the news that the next financial report would show that HealthSouth hadn't met their estimated profits for the preceding quarter:

> ". . . they went to Mr. Scrushy's office, and they said, 'Richard, here are the numbers, and we're just not going make it this quarter. We're not going to hit the numbers that we had predicted.' And they said Rich-

ard looked at them and said 'I'm not reporting that. We're not going to do that.' He [Beam] said, 'There's nothing more we can do. There's no techniques that we can use in accounting to make the number.' They were short, you know, a little less than ten million dollars. And they said, 'We can't do anything.' He [Scrushy] said 'Fix it.' They said, 'The only way we can fix it is just to make up numbers, just fake it.' 'Do it; fix it.'"[26]

Scrushy wasn't just smart and demanding, according to Martin, he was also very cunning. Beam, she said, also would testify that, following the meeting, the accountants "fixed" the problem, and the next day, submitted the adjusted account to Scrushy, who then told them they would be 'on their own' if the fraud was ever revealed:

"Came back the next day, and said, '. . . We made the entries.' And you will hear him [Beam] say Richard Scrushy looked at him and said, 'Ever get caught, you're on your own.' But quarter after quarter, year after year—not one, not two, but lots of people showed him those reports, the true numbers, the inside numbers . . . And each time they came up, and after that very first time when he said, 'You're on your own,' there's evidence he signed it. He signed it saying it was true, and that report went out to the public, and that was the beginning of that conspiracy . . . Over time, the conspiracy grew. Not only in the size of people involved, but in the dollar amount. These are the five CFOs that will tell you the story of their involvement in this conspiracy, and they've all pled guilty to their crimes. You will hear the story in detail from each of these people."[27]

Then Martin did a fast-forward to the summer of 2002. The conspiracy was in trouble because the numbers were getting bigger. HealthSouth had been going deeper in the hole, she said, at the rate of $10 million per month. Martin described how Weston Smith, who at the time was CFO of HealthSouth, reviewed the terms and penalties of the Sarbanes-Oxley Act, which had just come into effect, and panicked:

> "In fact, he left the building one day and he said, 'I'm not going to do it. I'm not going to do it.' And, of course, this concerned the Chief Executive Officer, because if your Chief Financial Officer won't sign the form and that information is made known to the public, these people are going to have a lot of questions, aren't they?

> Richard Scrushy was cunning, though. He got him [Smith] back in the fold by saying . . . if you'll come back and sign this, I will promote you. I will put you somewhere where you don't ever have to sign another one of these that's false. And the evidence will show that's what happened. But because of the huge stock sale, SEC had opened an investigation, as we talked about earlier. And the SEC had subpoenaed Richard Scrushy and . . . people that were on that fifth floor, members of the conspiracy, to come and testify."[28]

Finally, Martin explained Scrushy's motive to the jury. She posed the rhetorical question, "Why would a rich guy steal?" Scrushy, indeed, lived very well, Martin said—she had evidence that between 1996 and 2002 Richard Scrushy had spent over $200 million. During that period, according to Martin, Scrushy's salary amounted to around $1 million annually, so the rest had to come from some other source. It was the stock options that supplemented his salary, Martin explained, then went on to outline for the jury the way stock options work and why it would personally benefit Richard Scrushy for Health-South's share prices to climb higher: ". . . between 1996 and 2002," Martin told the jurors, "Richard Scrushy sold stock options and stock that put over a hundred and fifty million dollars in his pocket."[29]

Martin wrapped up her opening comments by telling the jury that they would be able to judge this case based on information the public never received—including the truth of HealthSouth's finances between 1999 and 2002:

> "You're going to hear what Richard Scrushy heard. You're going to hear what Richard Scrushy said. You're going to see what Richard Scrushy saw. And you're going to see that through the evidence.
>
> And you know what? You're the first ones to ever see it. Judge is right, you're going to know more than anybody else, because the public has never seen it. And that's the point of why we're here, because we have laws. Because when you don't show the public the truth, this is where you come, this is where you come."[30]

In her opening comments, Martin had outlined both the means and the motive of the conspiracy, and was ready to begin testimony. But first, the courtroom heard the opening comments for the defense.

After introducing himself to the jury, Scrushy's attorney, Jim Parkman, opened by trotting out a somewhat shopworn homily he had learned from his grandmother:

> "Boy, after listening to all that from the government, it doesn't sound like we stand much of a chance, does it? You know, except for something that my grandmamma used to tell me a long time ago that fits into an opening

statement and what a trial is all about. She used to tell me, she used to look at me and say, you know what, grandson, no matter how thin you make the pancake, it still has two sides to it."[31]

Parkman went on to explain that the case was really "simple"—a term he used time and again throughout his opening comments:

". . . You know, in this case, they tell you that this case is made up of forty-six counts. They showed you up on their board that it involved conspiracy, that it involved mail fraud, it involved wire fraud, it involved money laundering, it involved perjury, it involved obstruction of justice. But you know what, we want to try to make this case as simple as we can for you.

So I am going to tell you right now . . . it's not going to matter who licked the stamp. It's not going to matter who faxed the letter. It's not going to matter who put the envelope in the mail, because if the evidence in this case shows that he, Richard Scrushy, did not know, did not commit, did not participate in the fraud, then the rest of all of these charges go with it, not guilty also.

Fraud, well, it's really simple. All it is is deciding whether or not Richard Scrushy had actual knowledge of what was going on in the fraud, whether he intended for the fraud to continue, whether he knowingly participated in the fraud with others."[32]

The fraud was real, Parkman assured the jury; it did happen, and it happened because Richard Scrushy trusted people—people who deceived him, kept him in the dark. Parkman repeatedly expressed the defense's trust in the wonderful employees of HealthSouth, but pointed out that among these honest citizens had lurked a "family of conspirators."[33] He pointed to an old fashioned cardboard diagram on an easel. The diagram depicted a giant web of rectangles connected by lines of communication and association. The indicted conspirators, except for Scrushy, were connected into a "family"; Scrushy himself was linked to the company by only two lines, one marked "lies" connected to "HealthSouth-paid lawyer," and another line marked "Code Words." "Code Words" was connected to the conspirators, who in turn were connected to a blue circle labeled "Personal Gain" that lay at the heart of the chart.[34] After reminding the jury that many of the conspirators were accountants, he continued:

> "In this corporation, you are going to hear that there was this group of people, they called themselves 'the family.' Oh, this was no ordinary family. Oh, no. This was a family that operated as a unit, as an entity in their own rite. Oh, you couldn't get in this family. Not by blood or not through marriage. Oh, no. This family was by invitation only."[35]

Parkman next described each of the 15 executives, other HealthSouth employees who would testify at the trial, and the accounting firm of Ernst & Young, and explained how all of them had either been the duplicitous masterminds of the HealthSouth fraud conspiracy or unknowing pawns of the "the family." The fraud started, Parkman said, with aggressive accounting—that's like "permissible speed," he explained, where a person is a little over the posted limit, but "the police don't arrest you for that." Parkman went on to explain that aggressive accounting is common—Wall Street does it and the SEC allows it. But, Parkman said, the HealthSouth "family" had dreams. And so, Parkman said, they doctored the books in order to increase earnings. But, he stressed to the jury, the conspirators did not do it for Richard Scrushy; they did it for themselves:

> "They needed the power. They needed larger raises and more money that they got when income started going up and the books started looking better. And they, as a group, were in charge of what we know as obtaining acquisitions. Real simple . . . The problem was . . . this group who did the purchasing of other acquisitions, other businesses, they didn't do it right and it turned out to be bad. So to hide that to hide the fact that they were going to be demoted or fired, they used bad acquisitions to hide this fraud they were committing so no one would ever know . . . You know something, the question ought to come . . . How could they hide it?"[36]

By now, the jury could anticipate the answer: Parkman assured them it was "simple." Owens and other conspirators lied to the board of directors, and that board—not Richard Scrushy—was responsible for overseeing the work of the auditors and accountants:

> "First of all, you are going to find that the board of directors with HealthSouth, it's no ordinary board. These are going to be the smartest, the brightest men and women in the country that are set apart to run HealthSouth and to make sure it's done right. These are not going to be a bunch of dummies they put in. You are going to find some of them on the board of directors are going to be Harvard graduates, MBAs, they are to observe and make sure things are happening . . . through Richard Scrushy's leadership, they developed what was known as a check and balance system in the corporation . . . to prevent people like this from trying to do the fraud."[37]

According to Parkman, the HealthSouth board of directors relied on committees. Board member George Strong (Yale, accounting) ran the audit committee and met with CFO Bill Owens, the controller, the Ernst & Young people, and the compliance people. These individuals did not answer to the CEO, said Parkman. They were responsible for the internal and external audits, and HealthSouth's CFOs were the source of their documents. Further, Scrushy had arranged the Ernst & Young "Pristine Audits" specifically to help ensure the accuracy and compliance of all HealthSouth facilities:

> "What do we mean by that? Listen to this. HealthSouth had employed Ernst & Young, one of the largest accounting firms . . . like I mentioned to you, to audit their books every year. They bring in a team of people, not just one, a team of people and they go through and they look at everything, they dissect everything, they try the best that they can, they are bright people, they are all accountants, they all graduated from great places and they come in and they try to figure out what is going on and how it's working and make sure it is done right. That is not enough. Oh, no. We then have the internal audit group made up of internal people that go behind and go with E&Y, the external people, to check and make sure that E&Y is doing it right and to make sure that they are there to give the answers that they need. So when E&Y needs an answer, who do they go to, they can go to the internal audit committee, they can go to Bill Owens, or any of the CFOs to get their answers."[38]

It was a good thing Richard Scrushy started having those Pristine Audits, Parkman told the jury: That "stopped them, the family, in their tracks" from trying phony business in the clinics. And that wasn't all, Parkman continued. Scrushy even had a fraud hotline. Employees had a card they wore, and they had to carry it, wear it, and hold it up when asked. It had the hotline number on it. "And the unfortunate thing about it was," said Parkman, "nobody called. They weren't calling him. They were calling the compliance committee. Who do they report to? The board of directors."[39]

The family was behind all of it, Parkman explained, and they made a lot of money through their efforts. ". . . Folks, wait until you hear what these people ended up making through the recommendations of these people [indicating] and the compensation committee agreed with it. Not Richard Scrushy. The board of directors agreed with it. Not Richard Scrushy . . . We are going to go inside, but we are not going to go inside HealthSouth to do it, we are going inside the family to do it."

Then, Parkman told the story of HealthSouth and Richard Scrushy's humble beginnings and struggle to start up his company with little money and a small group of friends. Parkman told the jury that HealthSouth became a large and successful company because of Scrushy. He reminded them of Scrushy's gifts and generosity, then went on to say:

". . . Guess who isn't a member of the family? Guess who didn't go to a single family meeting? Richard Scrushy. In this case, what you are going to find out is, is there are a lot of difference between Richard Scrushy and them. You are going to find out that he paid his taxes, he paid his notes. He didn't transfer his property." Parkman continued:

> ". . . The gist of it is going to be this: That these people right here lied to Richard Scrushy. They didn't want to answer the truthful questions to him about the money and about what was going on. This is not going to be a dumb defense. This is not going to be a defense that is built on someone like Richard Scrushy being stupid or oblivious to what's been done, no. This is going to be a defense based on a lied-to defense."[40]

After Parkman, a second Scrushy attorney, Art Leach, addressed the jury, opening his comments with more family wisdom. Leach told the jury that upon returning from World War II, his father ("a United States Marine") told him never to give in to bullies; Leach assured the jury that he and others on Scrushy's legal team were going to fight it out there in the courtroom, taking—and giving—their "licks" as they proved that Richard Scrushy was also a victim—rather than the perpetrator—of this fraud.[41]

>>> TESTIMONY BEGINS

After all opening arguments had been made, Alice Martin was ready to begin questioning witnesses. Each witness Martin called served a necessary purpose. Martin called the first CFO, conspirator Aaron Beam. His testimony continued for three days. As Martin had predicted in her opening statement, Beam testified that they "fixed" the numbers and Scrushy knew it.[42]

On February 1, conspirator Bill Owens began his testimony. At various times, Owens held the positions of CFO, COO, controller, senior vice president, and CEO at HealthSouth.[43] Owens testified that in March of 2003, he had volunteered to help the government's investigation into Scrushy by wearing a "wire" to transmit and record his conversations with Scrushy at HealthSouth headquarters.[44] Owens's testimony was similar to Beam's, as he described the "pixie dust" used to create the phony financial results HealthSouth reported to the public: "Look at any quarter of HealthSouth," he said in court, "and you'll see low month, low month, blow out!"[45] Owens provided an insight into the slippery slope of deception when he remarked: "When it first started, it wasn't a big number and it wasn't meant to last."[46]

In her opening comments, Martin had told the courtroom that when CFO Weston Smith told his bosses he would not sign false documents, and refused additional salary or further involvement, Owens allegedly went to Scrushy to tell him that it was all over.[47] Together, Scrushy and Owens hatched the plan to drop profits by blaming a projected $175 million loss on proposed Medicare cuts. Simultaneously, they launched a plan to split the company into PT (physical therapy) and ASC (ambulatory surgical centers) divisions. In his testimony, Owens said the plan was to hide the fraud in the PT division; the ASC would have clean books. Smith, as enticement to sign the false documents, would be assigned to the newly clean ASC division. If the plan had worked as Owens alleged, the fraud would gradually be offset by losses and deductions from the capital account in the PT company.[48]

Message board members had predicted early on that the split would not take place, and I had agreed with that prediction; the split needed permission from the bondholders who held the large debt and who would need to approve transfer of that obligation. I had talked with **Bopper63,** and we agreed that the ASC division was more valuable; we both doubted that bondholders would agree to the assumption of debt for the lesser company. None of us knew at the time that the company was also significantly short of cash and couldn't produce clean books even in the cash accounts—a cash account shortage overlooked by Ernst & Young.

During the ten days of Owens's testimony, the courtroom heard some of the taped conversations that had been captured through the hidden wire Owens wore during conversations with Scrushy. As the *Washington Post* reported, jurors could clearly hear Scrushy making statements such as "Bill, they— they ain't got nothing . . . They didn't ask me nothing about the numbers."[49] Owens's testimony and tapes made an effective case to the jury, but Owens himself was not a particularly effective witness, according to Phil Smith, who faithfully attended and reported on the trial's proceedings. Smith re-corded in his blog chronicle, Scrushy-Report.com, that Owens often looked overly pleased with himself, sometimes smiling as he described his activities within the HealthSouth fraud. Scrushy's defense portrayed Owens as the mastermind behind the fraud.

Following Owens's testimony, the court heard from Leif Murphy, HealthSouth's treasurer and vice president. Murphy testified that, in 1999, he had been asked to compile a report outlining the financial situation at HealthSouth. In the pro-cess of preparing that report, Murphy said, he had stumbled upon the fraud. He prepared a notebook that included charts displaying HealthSouth's actual earnings and cash flow with those that would have to be reported if the company wanted to appear to meet analysts' forecasts. When Murphy (along with his boss, CFO Michael Martin) took the notebook to Scrushy's office and presented his findings, Murphy testified, Scrushy listened "silently, but intently." According to Murphy, after he had returned to his office following the presentation, Scrushy rushed in and shouted at him for "telling him how to run his company."[50] The *Birmingham News*, in reporting on Murphy's testimony, quoted him as saying that Michael Martin warned Murphy, telling him to "take a copy of the book and, you know, bury it somewhere for my own protection." When Mur-phy resigned a few days later, he—following Michael Martin's advice—took a copy of his notebook with him.[51]

At the close of the trial that day, Smith reported that the defense announced outside on the courthouse steps that Scrushy was a victim of "evidence tampering." But when Mur-phy's testimony ended at the close of the next day's hearing, the jury had much more to ponder than this shallow claim. Smith, in his record of the trial, wrote that Murphy's testimony had been quite powerful because he came across on the stand as an honest, believable guy who found wrongdoing, reported it to his superiors, and then left the company when the fraud was continued. Smith felt that Murphy's testimony may have been especially effective, because he was not indicted, nor was he ever rewarded by his bosses. Smith described the courtroom as Murphy left the witness stand on February 17: grim faces at the defense table; Scrushy taut and pale; Parkman looking tired, head on hands.[52]

Leif Murphy was followed in the witness chair by Diana Henze, HealthSouth's vice president of finance. Henze testified that she had found the fraud while working on documents and, unlike many of her colleagues, reported the matter to her compliance officer. She was told that the matter would be given to Michael Martin. Henze, who at the time of the events she was describing was HealthSouth's compliance auditor, testified that she did not have access to the general ledger. Through that testimony, the jury learned that HealthSouth had never put adequate systems in place for review or to create checks and balances—with those in place a fraud could not have succeeded.[53] The defense team hit hard at Henze, asking complicated accounting questions and confusing the jury with the data, but they did not shake her basic testimony. (Henze, it should be noted, is at the time of this writing still employed by HealthSouth.) Afterward, Henze was transferred to another position, away from the fraudulent accounting activities. Kelly Cullison, director of compliance, backed up Henze's story on Day 18 of the trial.[54]

On the February 23, Ken Livesay took the stand. Livesay testified that, as HealthSouth controller, he was present at meetings where the conspiracy was discussed. Livesay also testified that he had insisted on being transferred to the information technology department, where he did not need to participate in the actual fraud. Livesay reported Scrushy as saying: "Hang in there, we won't have to do this for long, and we are all going to make a lot of money. We'll all retire to the lake."[55]

Livesay was followed on the witness stand by Lee Anne Tyler, Michael Martin's assistant, and then Michael Martin, himself. Michael Martin, one-time HealthSouth CFO, testified that he was at the meeting Murphy had previously described in court, in which Scrushy was presented with a clear outline of the fraud that was taking place at HealthSouth.[56] According to his testimony, Michael Martin had talked with Scrushy, and told him—using the word "fraud"—that bankruptcy or exposure was inevitable. When Scrushy suggested a merger with a smaller company, Michael Martin allegedly advised Scrushy that the merger plan, too, would only lead to exposure. He said he tried to get the fraud stopped and the numbers corrected. According to Michael Martin, he also told Scrushy, during a visit to Scrushy's Lake Martin mansion, that "if we do this transaction, we're all going to jail. The fraud would be disclosed." "And I used that word: fraud," Martin said."[57]

Michael Martin was the third HealthSouth CFO to testify and an important witness because he corroborated testimony of Leif Murphy—perhaps the most important witness to date. According to an Associated Press report of the trial, Michael Martin testified that he punched Murphy at Murphy's going away party. The article quotes Michael Martin as saying in court: "If they hadn't have broken it up, he would have whipped my butt."[58]

Next to testify was Malcom "Tadd" McVay. Another HealthSouth CFO, McVay said he discovered the fraud after being promoted from his position as treasurer of the company.[59] He said he talked about the fraud frequently with Scrushy and Owens. According to coverage of McVay's testimony reported in the *Birmingham News,* McVay stated that Owens assured him that there were plans to correct the balance sheet.[60] McVay testified that he was "surprised but not shocked" to learn of the fraud, but stated he was pleased to go back to the treasurer's job when Owens took back his CFO job at the time a "split" of the company was proposed. McVay also stated that, after discovering the fraud, he was worried about losing his job, but that Scrushy assured him his future with the company was secure. It was then, according to McVay's testimony, that McVay told Scrushy of concerns about the fraud and HealthSouth's cash shortage. McVay testified that Scrushy said that the books would be fixed and that "all public companies fudge their numbers." "That was Scrushy's term," McVay said, "fudge." In cross-examination, the defense made much of the fact that McVay negotiated a bonus in exchange for signing a 10Q, but McVay was able to explain that he needed a contract guarantee or a bonus, similar to those received by the other executives, which may have defused the allegation that he had been bought off.[61]

Weston Smith, took the stand on March 31—the 30th day of the Scrushy trial. Smith had been the last of the HealthSouth CFOs under Scrushy, and among the first of the HealthSouth officers to plead guilty to the fraud.[62] Smith's testimony helped the prosecution a bit, but he was on the witness stand for several sessions as the defense tried to use him to weaken the testimony of other witnesses. Smith, too, admitted to being intimidated by Scrushy:[63] "Richard Scrushy had a reputation for tearing down whoever left or quit or didn't do what he wanted. That's intimidating," Smith said. He began to testify about the guns carried by Scrushy's security force, but the judge sustained the defense objection.[64]

>>> THE PROSECUTION RESTS

Following Weston Smith's testimony, the prosecution presented four more witnesses to confirm dates, then rested on April 19. As I followed the unfolding events of the trial, I recalled an old maxim: Sometimes the prosecution doesn't win the trial, the defense loses it. The corollary is, of course, that the prosecution also can lose the case. During the prosecution's presentation, the defense pressed every advantage and contested every point. Scrushy was waging not only a "lied to" defense, as Parkman had explained, but a "didn't know," "wasn't there," defense as well. Meanwhile, Richard Scrushy demonstrated that the courtroom was not the main focus of his personal defense, and that he was prepared to go down fighting. He was at his best on the courthouse steps, on the pulpit, and on the airwaves.

It was obvious throughout the trial that much of the prosecution's case was made up of very dry, technical data that tested jurors' attention spans. The defense had less of a problem in pressing its strategy, which relied on Jim Parkman's attention-gathering, florid, attack-mode style of courtroom drama. My reading of accounts of the trial made me suspect that Alice Martin would have done better in combating this defense strategy by making a simpler case for the jury. No doubt, there were effective moments in the prosecution's case. Certainly Leif Murphy and Diana Henze must have been effective, because these witnesses were unlikely to have been motivated by greed and neither was branded with the stigma of a plea bargain.

And Scrushy's claim that he knew nothing of the fraud created some questions for the defense to answer. If he truly were ignorant of the financial manipulations, didn't he wonder why no CFO would sign the books? Couldn't Leif Murphy and Weston Smith have been fired, rather than kept on with the incentive of special job arrangements?

Many more witnesses were necessary to confirm to the jury such things as stock market losses and the use of mail for mail fraud—and each charge and witness prolonged the trial. In the end, however, the prosecution's case rested on the testimony of the CFO, Lief Murphy, and Diana Henze.

On May 18, in her closing comments, Martin would tell the jury again what they must consider when arriving at their decision:

"All right. Now, in a moment you're going to hear Mr. Parkman and hear what he calls the other side of the pancake. And, as you do that, I'm going to ask a favor of you. I want you to keep a list, either in your head, write it down if you want, but keep a list of everybody he's going to tell you lied to you in this trial.

And I know who the headlines are. You know who they are. Leif Murphy, he's going to be a liar. All the CFOs, Aaron Beam, Mike Martin, Bill Owens, Tadd McVay, Weston Smith, he's going to say they're all liars. He's going to say Ken Livesay lied. He's going to say Diana Henze lied.

But I want you to remember, you're going to have to find a lot of other people lied to you, too, to believe their side of story.

You're going to have to believe LeAnne Tyler lied to you. LeAnne Tyler said she will never forget the look on Leif Murphy's face when Richard Scrushy stormed out of that room.

You go back and look at her testimony. You remember her sitting here. She doesn't remember much. She remembers the look on Leif Murphy's face.

You're going to have to think that Mary Esclavon lied. Richard Scrushy's own former secretary overheard the call, Weston's left the building. You're going to have to find she lied.

. . . You're going to have to find the pilot lied . . .

. . . You're going to have to find Ms. Pugh, the Verizon operator . . . lied . . .

. . . You're going to find Chuck Newhall lied to you . . .

. . . You're going to have to find Sage Givens lied . . .

. . . You're going to have to find Jim Lamphron, the only Ernst & Young lawyer (sic) they called . . . lied to you . . .

. . . And, finally, you've got to find his old buddy Jim Whitten, who they called to come up and tell you we made T-shirts with HealthSouth, we're branding, we're doing great stuff, well, you're going to have to find he lied, too . . .

I'm sure I left a lot off my list. I just ask you to keep that in mind as you hear their case. And I want to ask you to ask yourselves, has nearly every witness in this case lied to you like they're asking you to believe, or is it just like we told you all along, Richard Scrushy was the commander in chief of this criminal enterprise, and he raked in eighty-three percent of the proceeds from those efforts?

Thank you so much for your time and patience."[65]

But on April 19, 2005, the jury in the Richard Scrushy case had yet to hear these closing arguments. Instead, after Alice Martin declared that the prosecution had rested its case, the jury prepared to hear from the defense.

CHAPTER *nine*

The Defense

If many on the Yahoo! finance HRC message board expected the government's case against Richard Scrushy to be a slam dunk, they had good reason for harboring that opinion. Scrushy had been the subject of critical articles in the *Wall Street Journal* and the *New York Times,* not to mention the thousands of damaging messages posted to the Yahoo! message board. During the first 41 days of the trial, the prosecution had made a compelling case against him. After hearing testimony from a score of witnesses, surely jurors would be pondering questions that couldn't have encouraging answers for Scrushy's defense.

Is it possible, for example, that Richard Scrushy—a man many on the message board had described as a micromanager, a man some nicknamed "The King," a man who concerned himself with even the smallest details of cleanliness in bathrooms and parking lots in his company's far-flung facilities—

was totally unaware of what former prosecutor and SEC enforcement lawyer David Gourevitch described as "the biggest thing going on in the corporation"?[1] Could such a man—the company's founder and CEO—not know why his company's books were reported so late? Is it possible that such a man wouldn't know that $300 million in cash was missing from his business's accounts?[2]

In 1998, when some posters on the Yahoo! financial HRC message board had speculated that something was wrong with the financials that HealthSouth reported, calling the company a "pyramid scheme" and predicting that its billing "scam" would come under rigorous scrutiny one day, Richard Scrushy had sued to silence the posters.[3] Could he have been unaware of—or totally incurious about—the content of their messages? Could he also have been unaware that his founding partner was a crook, as was every CFO he ever chose to come to work for his company—as demonstrated by their guilty pleas and testimony?[4] And most importantly, could every witness who had testified that Scrushy knew about, or even masterminded, the HealthSouth fraud be lying? In the final analysis—as both the defense and Jim Parkman had pointed out in their opening arguments—that was the one essential question the jury must answer in reaching their verdict: Did Scrushy know?

Scrushy's defense would not be able to succeed through a matchup of witnesses. Instead, innuendo and commonsense challenges to prosecution stories would be the most effective weapon in the defense arsenal. The defense would need to show the jury that the facts that at first seem very clear could be muddied if seen from a different perspective; perhaps "this" was actually "that." If the case were too complicated; if the government seemed mean-spirited; if the jury members were outraged or offended by prosecution comments or witnesses, then the jury might well be drawn to Scrushy's defense.

With only one vote needed to hang the jury, the defense had the better odds—the prosecution needed *every* vote. As I read newspaper accounts of the forming of the jury and the legal team, I felt relatively certain that the trial would end in a hung jury. I had lived in the South while in the Army, and grew up in a small midwestern town where provincialism was honored. My guess was that a Birmingham jury cared more about the Alabama Tide football team than the *New York Times* editorials. And Scrushy had made a brilliant move in creating a defense team that eschewed such high-profile players as the well-known Washington, D.C.–based attorney Abbe Lowell in favor of local Alabama attorneys, Jim Parkman and Donald Watkins.

Scrushy had begun his pre-defense with a legion of lawyers chosen for specific tasks. In the months surrounding his indictment, he had gone through teams of lawyers like a tornado in Kansas, picking them up and throwing them out. The *Wall Street Journal* had covered the "revolving door" of Scrushy's legal defense team in a February article titled "Behind Scrushy's Courtroom Defense: Shifting Teams and Feuding Lawyers."[5] According to that article, when questions first began to surface about Scrushy's 2002 $100 million stock sale (immediately followed by a 44 percent decline in stock value due to Health-South's announced billing changes), Scrushy had begun gathering high-powered legal assistance to avoid indictment for insider trading. He met with Michael Deaver, a former deputy chief of staff to President Reagan, and with Jody Powell, a spokesman for the Jimmy Carter Administration, for public relations advice. Lanny Davis, a partner at Patton Boggs in Washington, D.C., and former White House special counsel to President Bill Clinton, signed on to represent Scrushy and HealthSouth. Scrushy already had the services of Haskell, Slaughter, Young and Rediker in Birmingham, who had represented HealthSouth in the past, and an Atlanta firm, Alston & Bird, that had helped HealthSouth with litigation arising out of shareholder suits.[6]

When Scrushy testified before the SEC for nearly eight hours in February of 2003, he was represented by William

Clark, a Birmingham lawyer who did criminal work. The following month, the SEC filed fraud charges against Scrushy and froze $250 million of his assets. Scrushy needed new attorneys to fight the SEC. In February, he dismissed Davis, who speculated that he may have been let go because he pressured Scrushy to cooperate with the SEC investigation. Clark and another attorney representing Scrushy on the SEC matter—Mark White—resigned.[7]

After Scrushy's offices were raided by the FBI in March of 2003, Scrushy made a canny move; he contacted Richard Arrington, former mayor of Birmingham, who in turn put Scrushy in contact with another influential Birmingham leader, attorney Donald Watkins. Arrington, who is African-American, had successfully fought government charges of corruption while in office, waging what Carrick Mollenkamp's *Wall Street Journal* article described as ". . . a provocative and racially charged fight, orchestrated by Mr. Watkins." The article further said that Scrushy had been among a very small group of Birmingham business leaders who publicly supported Arrington during the investigation.[8]

Watkins was a prominent political figure in Birmingham and founder of Alamerica Bank. Watkins admits to being worth millions, and his net worth is rumored to be as high as a billion dollars—a claim he will not confirm or deny. He graduated from Southern Illinois University and was one of the first black graduates at the University of Alabama's law school.[9]

For a retainer of $5 million, Watkins agreed to help Scrushy wage his defense.[10] Watkins proposed a strategy identical to that used by Arrington, namely challenging every allegation and doing it very publicly—that meant radio, television, and newspapers. Watkins put together his old team: Jonathan Rose of Jones Day in Washington (a firm of more than 2,000 lawyers); the Alabama firm of Thomas, Means, Gillis and Seay; and Thomas Sjoblom of Chadbourne & Parke of New York. By the terms of their agreement, if Scrushy's assets were unfrozen by the SEC, each of the three firms would receive $5 million.[11]

Scrushy's legal costs for unfreezing his assets climbed to $21 million spread across four law firms. Judge Inge Johnson released all of his cash, ruling that the SEC had not established his involvement in fraud.[12] After Scrushy turned himself in to the FBI, following his indictment in October of 2003, Scrushy and Watkins took control; they asked all legal firms working on the Scrushy and HealthSouth cases to transfer all files to the downtown Birmington offices of Chadbourne & Parke.[13]

Scrushy's appearance later that month on CBS's *60 Minutes* after refusing to testify before Congress, foreshadowed his defense strategy. Scrushy essentially told Mike Wallace that anyone who said he was involved in the HealthSouth fraud was a liar. Scrushy also said he was "shocked" to learn of the fraud carried out by his trusted friends and associates: "You pay them good salaries and you expect them to do the right thing," he said. "I signed off on the information based on what was provided to me and what I was told."[14]

In November, Scrushy released the Atlanta law firm of Jones Day and hired prominent criminal defense lawyer Abbe Lowell, who had represented President Bill Clinton during his impeachment hearings. But Watkins and Lowell soon clashed over the defense strategy, with Watkins favoring a public relations defense over Lowell's more subdued approach. In March 2004, a battle arose over the government's control of evidence. Watkins led Scrushy to carry the fight to the Birmingham courthouse steps, where Scrushy and his legal team accused the Justice Department of concealing evidence. Lowell remained behind the cameras, and later withdrew from the case.[15] It was to be the Watkins defense—unyielding, aggressive, contentious, and well-crafted to present Scrushy as a victim, rather than as a perpetrator. To carry out such a defense, Scrushy needed homegrown lawyers. And so, after Lowell's departure, he replaced the high-profile Washington, D.C., attorney with Jim Parkman.

James Parkman III was an old shoe from Dothan, Alabama—a town of about 60,000, nestled tight in the southeastern corner of the state in Houston County. In December of 2004, Parkman was profiled in *The Dothan Eagle*. In an article titled "A Hick with a Heart," *Eagle* staff writer Lance Griffin gave the newspaper's readers an accurate preview of the tactics Parkman would use so effectively in the Scrushy trial:

> ". . . Most likely, Parkman will introduce the jury to his country accent, then he will talk about how his mama loved to make pancakes. And, no matter how thin his mama's pancakes were, there were still two sides to every one, just like there are two sides to every story. Then, he will launch into Scrushy's defense."[16]

Griffin quoted Parkman's friend and associate, Houston County District Attorney, Doug Valeska: "I've seen him pull all kinds of stunts with the jury," Valeska said. "This diagram and that, models, getting down on the floor, screaming and yelling, you name it."

In his article, Griffin noted that ". . . Parkman somehow manages to weave an unpretentious, aw-shucks disposition" in the courtroom, but warned that it would be a mistake for others to buy the "hick" persona Parkman sometimes adopts:

> "The feds better get ready," said . . . Valeska, longtime friend and courtroom adversary. "Parkman will punch a hole in them."[17]

In other words, Parkman was well-suited to the task before him as lead trial lawyer in the Scrushy defense. His job was to keep things folksy and act as the hometown counterpoint to the federal "Goliath." He would have to cloud and confuse prosecution arguments by attacking the character and motivation of prosecution witnesses—as he would later do, for example, by referring to Michael Martin's blood pressure medicine as a "mood altering drug."[18] His job was to make sure simple things seemed complex, and that complex things were simple. His job was to attack. In addition to Parkman, the final Scrushy defense team included Martin Adams, a lawyer in his firm. Art Leach, Scrushy's son-in-law and a former assistant U.S. attorney in Georgia, also would serve as a trial attorney. Lewis Gillis of the Thomas Means firm in Birmingham would assist with the case. And Donald V. Watkins would be the team's lead strategist.[19]

>>> CRAFTING A DOWN-HOME DEFENSE

Watkins would help Richard Scrushy craft a defense that was well-tailored to Birmingham and the South. Birmingham is a modern American city today, generating about one-third of the state's payroll. But Birmingham's history of civil rights abuses and unrest—Birmingham is now home to the National Civil Rights Museum—have left their mark on the city and its people. After the 1963 bombing of the Sixteenth Street Baptist Church, which resulted in the deaths of four little girls, and the civil rights marches that followed, the business community grew tired of the burden of segregation and was reluctantly ready to move on. Most in Alabama remember the wounds of that time, and the role of their state in our nation's struggle toward civil rights. On his Web site, Scrushy places his personal history squarely in the context of the civil rights struggle that took place in his Selma, Alabama, birthplace. His online biography declares: "Richard Scrushy is now fighting for his *own* rights and freedoms in the face of false allegations."[20]

In seeking the support of Birmingham's African-American community, Scrushy had a balancing act to carry out. According to *USA Today* reporter Greg Farrell's article, "Former HealthSouth CEO Scrushy Turns Televangelist," prior to his indictment, Scrushy had attended church in Vestavia, an exclusive, wealthy, and predominantly white suburb of Birmingham.[21] Nor did Scrushy's personal lifestyle—his $20 million jets and mansions—place him in intimate contact with the common citizen. But, Scrushy also had been generous to a number of charities; he had given money for scholarships and other causes that had been popular with the community. He also had reached out to the African-American community through gifts to Miles College and Lawson State Community College, and he was known to be someone to call for help with projects.[22]

After the indictment, Scrushy's charitable foundation had placed a number of additional gifts within the community. The predominantly African-American Guiding Light Church, for example, which Scrushy began attending around the time of his indictment, received $1,050,000 from the foundation.[23] The Vestavia Church had received about $600,000 the year before.[24]

A February 17, 2005, *New York Times* article by Simon Romero asked: "Will the Real Richard Scrushy Please Step Forward?" The article noted: "In the months before the start of his trial on Jan. 25, Mr. Scrushy seems not to have missed an opportunity to portray himself as a friend of Birmingham's black community." [25] In the months following his indictment, Scrushy had become quite public about his religious beliefs and habits, and he frequently featured local ministers on his paid-programming talk show *Viewpoint*.[26] On that program, Bishop Jim Lowe, pastor at Guiding Light Church (which, according to reporter Greg Farrell, purchased a year's worth of airtime for *Viewpoint* in 2004), recommended letting a higher power decide whether Scrushy was guilty of fraud. Speaking to the congregation about Scrushy's presence in the Church, Pastor Lowe said: "People will say it's manipulative, and then we see the truth of understanding the lies that people are saying about him. Seeing those lies is an eye-opener. Black people are not the only people that are railroaded by lies, and we see even whites railroad whites."[27]

>>> THE TESTIMONY PARADE CONTINUES

It was against this backdrop of Birmingham's social stratification, religion, and civil rights history that Watkins and his legal team would play out their carefully tailored defense in the Scrushy fraud trial. When Parkman first addressed the jury in the Scrushy trial on January 25, 2005, his opening statements closely followed the pattern Griffin had told readers of *The Dothan Eagle* to expect, as he trotted out the somewhat shopworn tale of his grandmother's thin pancakes. But his opening comments also had established the basis from which Scrushy's defense team would operate—that the government must prove beyond any doubt that Scrushy knew of the fraud being perpetrated at HealthSouth. Parkman told the jury that the defense team intended to prove he did not know, based on a lack of evidence:

> "As we go through this case . . . Look at the evidence. Look at what isn't in evidence, for example. You are going to find there is not one single memo. There is not one single document. There's not one note, email, nothing with Richard Scrushy's fingerprint on it that indicates he was involved in the fraud."[28]

Watkins's courtroom strategy focused on cross-examination. Promoting the truthfulness of Scrushy's defense witnesses was less important than punching holes through the testimony of prosecution witnesses. In particular, the defense spent days cross-examining HealthSouth CFOs Aaron Beam,

Bill Owens, Michael Martin, Tadd McVay, and Weston Smith.[29] During his cross-examination of Aaron Beam, Parkman confirmed that the defense team would attack every possible angle of prosecution-witness testimony. When Beam testified that he and Owens "fixed" the numbers and Scrushy knew it, Parkman attacked his memory, his veracity, and the meaning of "fix."[30] Beam held fast throughout his cross-examination, however: "I was intimidated by Richard. I thought he would pin the crime on me. Richard's not the kind of person you cross. I felt he'd do anything to protect himself." Beam also recalled Scrushy saying: "If we are ever caught, I am going to deny everything, and you guys are on your own."[31]

Parkman also challenged HealthSouth CFO Bill Owens's every word. Owens was a key witness for the prosecution, spending a total of ten days in the witness chair, and Scrushy's defense team grilled him on minute details of his testimony. Owens had testified that he and Scrushy never used certain words at headquarters and that they had a "special way of communicating," but they both knew what was meant. Parkman hammered away at the "code words" used by "the family," asking what was meant by the terms he used in his testimony, including "gap," "hole," "dirt," "pixie dust," "fraudulent number," "fix," and "stop."[32]

The famous tapes, recorded through the "wire" worn by Owens as he assisted in the government's investigation, made it into evidence after challenge, but were attacked from every angle by the defense. In an article reported in the *Washington Post*, jurors are said to have listened to 13 minutes of the taped conversation in which Scrushy could be heard to say that "this conversation did not happen." The article also noted Owens's testimony that Scrushy was very concerned that the HealthSouth offices had been bugged and had the offices "swept" for bugs frequently.[33]

Later in the trial, Parkman presented a specialist who suggested that the tapes had been tampered with by the FBI.

"What was erased? Why don't we hear conversations on the way out of the building and in the car?" Parkman asked.[34] For every explanation given by a prosecution witness, Parkman created an alternative explanation, which had the potential for creating doubt within the minds of the jurors and deniability for Scrushy. The *Washington Post* reported that Judge Bowdre gave a "boost" to the defense when she instructed the jurors that "any gaps or holes or any missing links in the chain of custody go to the weight you must give those tapes."[35]

According to Phil Smith, who carefully followed and reported on the trial, Michael Martin was a strong witness who appeared unshaken by Parkman's cross-examination.[36] When Parkman mentioned Michael Martin's use of Lexapro, an antidepressant, Martin explained that the drug was prescribed for his blood pressure.[37] On the message board, a HealthSouth employee, using the alias **going_to_niceville**, commented: "I think we've hit a new low—Half the Corporate office was on some type of anxiety medication—Richard even discussed it in a Monday Morning Meeting once . . ."[38]

Parkman also commented on Michael Martin's net worth of nearly $10 million, and he noted that Martin paid about $2.4 million in forfeitures and fines for his role in the fraud. Michael Martin responded that he owned over half of another health care company worth millions.[39] Owens had testified that Scrushy told him he (Martin) would be the "fall guy" for the fraud. Parkman reminded him of that testimony, then asked: "Did Scrushy do that?" "What made me the fall guy was the truth," Martin said. "I committed fraud. I'm not going to run from that."[40]

Leif Murphy was the strongest prosecution witness, and the defense team appeared to have little luck in weakening his testimony. Murphy had testified that when he had presented an outline of HealthSouth's financial fraud to Scrushy in 1999, Scrushy showed no surprise at the variance between HealthSouth's real and reported earnings. According to Phil

Smith, who attended the trial, Murphy was a strong, believable witness, and the defense appeared unable to rattle him or alter his testimony.

It was ironic that one of the defense's own witnesses caused them more trouble than most of the prosecution's. During the week of April 27, the defense called former HealthSouth Marketing Director Jim Whitten as a character witness. Whitten took the stand and, under friendly defense questioning, lauded Scrushy as his friend and colleague, calling him "Richard."[41] In cross-examination, the prosecution was able to show that Whitten had been less generous toward Scrushy in his remarks to FBI investigators just two years earlier—remarks that had been duly recorded by the FBI on the agency's reports. Prosecution attorney Richard Smith asked Whitten if he had told the investigators that Scrushy had made false statements about his stock during an appearance on CNBC. Smith went on to remind Whitten that he (Whitten) had not only stated that Scrushy had lied on CNBC, but also told the FBI that "nothing goes on at HealthSouth without Richard Scrushy's approval." "So," asked Attorney Smith of Jim Whitten, "does this mean the FBI made a mistake?" According to Kyle Whitmire, writing for the *Birmingham Weekly*, Whitten ". . . fell apart on the stand after prosecutors asked him if he told the FBI that Scrushy had treated HealthSouth 'as his personal piggybank.'"[42]

>>> THE DEFENSE RESTS

At the time of closing arguments, the major problems for the defense continued to be the testimony of Leif Murphy and Diana Henze. In the case of Diana Henze, Jim Parkman admitted to the jury that she found the fraud, but denied that the message ever reached Scrushy:

"We come now to Diana Henze. First of all, I want to clear this up. The government told you that I'm going to call everybody in this case a liar. Absolutely not. I have got six people I'm calling liars, that is the rodent and the pack of mice. I say to you the rest of them they told the truth, Diana Henze included. Do you know what is strange about her testimony? You still don't get the story right. You still get two people giving two different things.

. . . Diana Henze told you the truth. She did. I'm telling you. Do you know what she told you? I was in Mike Martin's office talking to him about what was going on and why they were transferring—why they were transferring me, not Richard Scrushy. Do you remember? Even Martin and Owens said that they are the ones that put her over in IT to get rid of her.

Here comes the other lies, folks. Richard Scrushy opens the door, steps in and sees her sitting there. Got it. Mike Martin said that Diana was sitting there crying, upset. Diana Henze told you the truth, I wasn't crying. I was upset. But I wasn't crying. And what happened, Ms. Henze, when Richard stuck his head in the door? She said, all I did is look around and see him, and I said, I've got to get up, so I got up and left. I had enough of Mike Martin. Listen to this: If a fraud was going on and they're going to cover this up, right then and there would have been the time for Mike Martin to say, oh, Richard, I'm glad you're here. Come on. Diana Henze has uncovered this fraud. We need to do something about this. Didn't happen."[43]

The defense then tackled Leif Murphy's story. The defense found reason to believe that because a word was changed in one place but not another in the Murphy notebook that there may have been more than one book. Perhaps Scrushy saw another book, another chart? Were the charts the same? The episode became confusing. And Leif Murphy? Parkman suggested that he could have been guilty of serious crimes for which he was let off to secure his cooperation.[44] And, according to an article in the *Wall Street Journal,* Parkman also raised questions about the FBI's evidence-gathering techniques when he pulled on rubber gloves and waved a plastic bag about as he asked questions about why the FBI hadn't checked "Murphy's book" for fingerprints.[45]

As he summed up all of these points in his closing arguments, Parkman also tried to re-raise the specter of evidence tampering:

> "Are you ready? Watch. The government comes out with a notebook that's got 'fabricated' written on it. And then it's kind of marked out, and they give you this story about how Mike Martin did this. Are you ready for this? And all of a sudden, folks, another notebook appears. One coming from Bill Owens. And you know what? You know what Jim Parkman said when he sat over there and heard that? Same thing you did, I smell a rat. And you're right. We did. All of a sudden, two books change 'fabricated' to 'blue sky.' And let me tell you something, the story about it is even more contradictory than the books are.
>
> . . . Leif Murphy says, I talked to Richard Scrushy about the notebook one time in his office sitting on the sofa . . . Mike Martin says, no, no. He talked to him three times.
>
> . . . And if that wasn't enough, the FBI knew about the problems. They knew there were two books all along. And they never . . . went back to Bill Owens or Mike or

Leif Murphy and said, explain to me how these two came about. You know why they didn't do that? Because it's like life, folks, it's common sense, you don't ask a question that you don't want the answer to, because you're afraid or you know it's going to hurt you. There it is.

And then we get to the bottom line of Leif Murphy. Are you ready? Yeah, the defense sent in some material to the government they were going to use in their case. And lo and behold, I done found out I have committed bank fraud. I didn't know I had done that. I forgot I signed that thing for five hundred million dollars. He knew it. The government knew it. But, you see, they don't want to throw no dirt on their Winn-Dixie chitlin (Murphy).[46] They have got to have that baby clean when it gets in here to y'all."[47]

Toward the end of his closing statement, Parkman treated the jury to another bit of advice from his grandmamma and a tribute to the hardworking generosity (and innocence) of his client, Richard Scrushy:

". . . Every one of these guys get up on the stand and they say to you, crying, well, except for no more tears over here, Mr. Weston Smith, sit up here and tell you, I'm sorry, I did it, I didn't mean to. Richard Scrushy made me do it. I'm a good guy. Y'all believe me, please.

And it's something my grand mama use to tell me, you know about the pancakes, here we go. The more they talk of honor, the quicker we count the silverware . . .

It starts with LifeMark back with Beam. Beam admitted back then, Richard Scrushy was a division president. He never asked Beam to do anything illegal. That is where it all starts . . . And then you come on down—no slip ups, fingerprints, letters. You come on down to no salary or bonuses that he didn't take. You come down to how much money he had. And the kicker is, let me tell you something, folks, thieves don't give away twenty-one point five million dollars in charitable contributions during the time of a fraud, thieves keep the money.

Then we come down here to stock options. They give you that. We know what happened. We know about the executive loan. Guess who paid his executive loan? Richard Scrushy did. Guess who didn't? Bill Owens. Guess who paid his taxes? Richard Scrushy. Guess who didn't? Bill Owens.

Let me tell you something, it wasn't just Richard Scrushy that didn't know what happened, every one of these didn't know what happened. We put on the division presidents, legal counsel, Fulbright & Jaworski, board of directors, Ernst & Young, audit committee, they didn't figure it out either, because it was so well hidden and so well done. Why didn't Richard Scrushy know it was going on? Because Richard Scrushy is not just in accounting, he's into sales. That was his name when he got into the group . . . Let me tell you what he spent his time doing, are you ready? He spent his time with things like, the auto ambulator, trying to help people in this country, that is what he spent his time doing. He spent his time trying to build a company that these people tore up.

. . . In closing, I hope I hadn't done anything to embarrass me with any of y'all during this trial. If you don't know where Dothan is, it's a great town, great city. It's where you stop to get gas on the way to the beach.

Proud of my people, proud of this case and proud of what my team has done.

I ask you, please, please bring in a verdict of not guilty on every count for Richard Scrushy in this case . . ."[48]

And at last, Donald Watkins gave a closing statement that included a tribute of sorts to the struggle for equality among all Americans and the American judicial system.[49] Watkins's closing argument began with his expressions of admiration for Judge Bowdre, his devotion to the American flag, and his gratitude for the men and women serving in Afghanistan and Iraq. After being admonished by the judge to get on with his closing argument, Watkins went on to tell about his own childhood, explaining to the jury that he had grown up in a pre–civil rights South where he and other blacks couldn't use whites-only drinking fountains or eat at whites-only lunch counters. But because of the efforts of men and women just like them, Watkins told the jury, he was able to get an education and become a success. In describing himself as "Mrs. Watkins's little boy," the attorney told the room:

> "Ultimately, thirty-two years later, he (Watkins) can represent Richard. I don't—they use all these titles in here, defendant, and Mr. Scrushy. He is Richard to me. The man who grew up on the other side of the Edmund Pettus Bridge.[50]
>
> One of the reasons I'm here, they tell me, is I'm his lawyer. The real reason I'm here is I'm his friend.
>
> I love the jury system. I love it. Let me tell you about it.
>
> When you have to climb in the protection of the flag, case by case, it has a special and personal meaning to you."[51]

Watkins then reminded the jury that the burden of proof in this case lay solely with the prosecution:

"... the judge has instructed you on burden of proof and beyond a reasonable doubt, that means that every time, in every case, on every charge, on every element you must make sure that they carry the burden. He doesn't have any burden. They must carry it.

... And when they don't carry it, your job is not to be a wheelchair for them, not for this crowd. It's not to be a crutch to help him limp on over to the other side when the evidence just is not there. That is not your job.

That is not why eight hundred six thousand American service men and women have died. That is not your job."[52]

Watkins also reminded the jury that in the taped conversations they had heard—those taped by Bill Owens when he was wearing a hidden wire—that Richard Scrushy is never heard to say that he will sign false financial reports. Watkins then waged a final attack on Bill Owens:

"So what does Scrushy do? What does he do? The man [Owens] doesn't even come direct with him. He comes with this weird conversation. I have got problems. I have got marital problems. Wife is all crying and throwing a fit, weird.

What is his head space? It ain't hard to figure out. Bill Owens, November 2002, sitting around a room with Tadd McVay; Bill Horton, they are out there planning the coup, they are out there planning on how to ouster Richard from his own company."[53]

And then, after questioning the quality of the FBI tapes, the government's failure to take fingerprints from Leif Murphy's notebooks, and the lack of a recorded declaration of guilt from Richard Scrushy, Watkins reminded the jury that they had the ultimate power in this case, and that a "not guilty" verdict would teach many people in the government and the FBI to be more careful in their work:

> "Right now, in Birmingham, the eyes of the nation are on you. They know you're here. They know what you're doing. They are here. They are watching. The folks up in D.C., the big shots, the ones who call the plays, who make the decisions for the group here, I am talking about that bourbon-sipping, martini-drinking, cigar-smoking crowd, the ones who gather at 7:00 o'clock out at the club. They say, I wonder what the folks in Birmingham are going to do, the ones that just, oh, they don't think we have got any sense at all down here? I tell you what you can do, you can have more power doing this, and the best use of power than any congressman, any senator, any legislator, any lobbyist that I know of, you can use your power.
>
> . . . You know, so many times Birmingham, Alabama, people look at us and say, you know, what's going on with these people down there, how come they can't get it together.
>
> Well, we have got a chance to set a standard for justice and excellence in this country. We have got a chance to get America off of her knees and never let her go there again in this kind of situation.
>
> . . . Know that the U.S. Senate can't filibuster your decision. Know that nobody can stop a change in an idea

whose time has come. And you, you know, I will forever remember this jury. I will forever remember this
case. Long after we are all gone, we will look back and
remember what was done here in this courtroom and
how the country was better off for it, and how this
country was off its knees and these twelve people will
be the Hiroshima of Birmingham and it will be
watched all over the world.

And I thank you for that contribution. Because right
now, you can get more done than any politician, any
political figure, any public officer, any celebrity that I
know and I'm proud of you. And thank you for your
time, your attention. And know that we want to get up
again, but we cannot because we respect the system
and that is the way the founding fathers wanted it.

Thank you very much."[54]

That was the defense. Scrushy had waged a community-
wide public relations blitz, donated a million dollars to the
Guiding Light Church, starred in a paid-programming television show, and compiled a defense team that remained on constant attack. After spending millions of dollars on his defense,
Scrushy had opted for a courtroom strategy that focused on attacking prosecution witnesses and a personal defense aimed
directly at the Birmingham community.

>>> THE VERDICT IS IN

Jurors retired to deliberate a 37-page verdict form that, according to one account, included four pages of questions that
dealt just with the conspiracy.[55] The jury also asked for "lay-
man's terms" explanations, and at one point asked that Judge

Bowdre "circle one—yes or no" to answer a question about whether the jury needed to agree unanimously. On June 3, the jury returned to the courtroom to tell Judge Bowdre that they were unable to reach a verdict. Judge Bowdre told the jury to go back and try again, encouraging them with what is called an "Allen Charge" to renew their efforts.[56]

Jurors' vacations and a juror's illness allowed the jury to meet only four times between June 9 and June 22, causing Judge Bowdre to call the attorneys into her chambers for consultation to discuss removing a juror who had suffered from illness during the trial. Judge Bowdre announced that she would replace the sick juror, an elderly white man suffering from migraine headaches, with one of the alternate jurors who had followed the case. Her directions to the jury were to start the deliberations process from scratch.[57]

No one was prepared for the jury to return in only five working days with a verdict. On June 28, 2005, the jury spokesperson stood before Judge Karon Bowdre and, one by one, declared that the jury had found Scrushy innocent of all charges—36 criminal charges of fraud including a single charge under the Sarbanes-Oxley Act. Judge Bowdre read a statement prepared by the jurors that explained that the reason behind the verdict was the lack of substantial evidence and witness credibility.[58]

Alice Martin was "shocked."[59] Jim Parkman wept, and said he was "scared to death" before the verdict was read: "I almost passed out in the middle of it. I had to ask someone what the verdict was after it was all over."[60] However, after coming out of the courthouse, Parkman said: "I'm just elated. Thank goodness it's over . . . Not bad for a bunch of hicks."[61]

Immediately after the verdict was announced, Robert May, chairman of HealthSouth, issued a statement: "The new board and new management team remain appalled by the multibillion-dollar fraud that took place under Mr. Scrushy's management and the environment under which such fraud could occur. Under no circumstances will Mr. Scrushy be offered any position within the company by this management team or by this board of directors."[62]

Richard Scrushy, however, seemed to feel vindicated by the verdict, saying: "God is good." Scrushy thanked his "prayer partners" who had prayed at the courthouse and occupied spectator benches in the courtroom, and told reporters: "Jesus taught us how to love each other . . . We've got to have compassion, folks, because you don't know who's going to be attacked next."[63]

>>> QUESTIONS UNANSWERED

The verdict was in, reporters were off to file their stories, and the time for second-guessing had begun. After a trial that had plodded along for months, the final verdict seemed like an explosion that left many people asking the same questions: "What happened?" and "What does it mean?"

Epilogue

The events surrounding Richard Scrushy's tenure at Health-South—including the fraud perpetrated there under his reign, the resulting first court test of legislation aimed at curbing corporate corruption, and the incredible recovery of Health-South and some of its investors from the devastating results of just such corruption—will have a far-reaching impact on many facets of our nation's culture. As the story continues to unfold, we can expect to gain an even greater understanding of the impact of these events on corporate practices and ethics, investment strategies, and the workings of our legal system.

Among this story's most sensational elements, of course, is the outcome of Richard Scrushy's federal trial. In the aftermath of Scrushy's acquittal, experts were quick to give their assessment of the trial, and to lay on criticism of nearly every aspect of it, including the verdict, the venue, the judge, the lawyers—and even the law itself.

I had expected a hung jury, but like many observers, I was shocked by the acquittal on all counts. "It's a stunner, given how strong the government's case seemed to be," said Gregory J. Wallance, a former prosecutor, now a partner at Kaye Scholer in New York.[1] "I think most people thought there would be some conviction," said Arthur Gross-Schaefer, a business-law professor at Loyola Marymount University in Los Angeles. "A clean slate? It does raise some concerns."[2] Comparing the "I didn't know" defense to the stammering of a character from the old 1960s sitcom *Hogan's Heroes*, former U.S. Attorney for Connecticut Stanley Twardy said: "This may be the first time that the Sergeant Schultz defense has worked."[3]

Some legal experts interviewed in the wake of the verdict believed that the trial's location played a role in the outcome. "It was the venue," said George B. Newhouse, Jr., a former federal prosecutor at Thelan Reid & Priest in Los Angeles, "as in the O. J. Simpson trial, the key mistake was where they brought the case." James D. Wareham, a defense lawyer at Paul, Hastings, Janofsky & Walker in Washington, agreed: ". . . a Southern case tried in a Southern manner."[4] Scrushy's lead attorney, Donald Watkins, agreed that the prosecution had chosen the wrong venue: "That was a strategic mistake," he said after the victory. "Given a chance to indict him in New York, why would you indict him in Birmingham? That's our home turf." Watkins added that, after serving as an attorney in Birmingham for 32 years, he never doubted that the jury would find his client innocent.[5]

Many commentators agreed that Scrushy's popularity and strenuous public relations efforts also were important factors in his acquittal, and may have contributed to the jury's elevated demand for absolute and irrefutable proof. Rick Fuentes, an expert in jury psychology from R & D Strategic Solutions in Atlanta, was quoted in a post-trial interview with the *Birmingham Post-Herald*: "They liked the defendant, and they raised the standard of proof to absolute certainty rather than beyond a reasonable doubt." Paul Lapides, director of Corporate Governance Center at Kennesaw State University in Marietta, Georgia, agreed: "It's the CSI effect," Lapides said (referencing the popular TV crime-procedural drama). "They want a lot more evidence, things that sometimes aren't even possible."[6]

The jury was torn on the verdict for weeks, only arriving at a decision after the replacement of one juror. Prior to that event, according to postverdict interviews, the jury had been hung with only two voting guilty. Mr. Willis Vest, who was dismissed from the jury by Judge Bowdre, said that he had been one of two holdouts (Vest declined to name the other holdout juror).[7] "To me there was more than ample evidence that [Scrushy] knew of the fraud," Vest told reporters. He also stated that he had wanted to stay on the jury, but was dismissed by Bowdre after he missed one day of testimony and three days of deliberations.[8]

Other jurors, however, were critical of the government nearly from the start of deliberations. In an interview reported by the *Wall Street Journal*, Juror Debra Williams questioned why there was no physical evidence tying Scrushy to documents related to the fraud. "They should have gotten fingerprints on those records," she said.[9] Jurors also reported that they were disturbed by the behavior of the cooperating CFOs, naming such things as Bill Owens not filing income taxes and hiding his money—issues that the defense emphasized in court.[10] Jurors specifically denied any racial or religious influence in post-trial interviews, although one juror said he was impressed by Scrushy's supporters, who appeared each day in court, that included pastors and congregants from several predominantly black churches.[11]

Edward Iwata, writing in *USA Today*, commented on how tough it can be to nail executives in white-collar fraud cases, listing several reasons: prosecutors must prove criminal intent; the defendants are likely to be pillars of their communities—

churchgoers who are generous to charity; defendants typically hire "elite" defense attorneys; and, finally, the cases are complex, involving facts that are difficult to understand without specialized knowledge of corporate accounting practices. Iwata also notes that jurors don't see accounting violations hurting people in the same way as, for example, do street muggings and other violent crimes. As a result, the juries may fall back on lesser charges; Iwata gives the example of Martha Stewart's conviction for lying to investigators—an offense easier to understand than a securities violation.[12]

Defending such cases takes time and makes great demands on everyone involved with the trial. I thought that the defense, through their dogged objections and relentless cross–examinations, controlled the pace throughout Scrushy's trial, and ultimately exhausted all of the participants. I also agreed with columnist John Helyar, of *Fortune* magazine, who wrote of Judge Karon Bowdre's role in allowing the trial to drag on: "She was the other reason for a pace that was languid as a drawl. Judge Bowdre held long and frequent conferences with the two sides' lawyers, both in court and in chambers. She allowed many weeks of the trial to go by with only two or three days of testimony, separated by long inactive interregnums."[13]

In an article written for *USA Today*, by Greg Farrell, former SEC associate David Gourevitch, now a white-collar-crime attorney in New York, notes: "There's deep skepticism toward the federal government down there, not just from the jury but from the bench, which is unusual." The article goes on to note that Judge Bowdre frequently sided with defense lawyers and had dismissed several perjury charges against Scrushy. In his article, Farrell writes: "Perhaps most damaging to the prosecution were Bowdre's repeated instructions to the jury that no one could declare with absolute certainty what was in Scrushy's mind, and that they, the jurors, would ultimately decide if they thought Scrushy was aware of the fraud and took part in it. Prosecutor Alice Martin said several jurors cited that instruction in their decision to acquit."[14]

Judge Bowdre defended her performance in an interview published in the *Birmingham News*, saying she never wanted the case but had a duty to make sure that the defendant was treated fairly: "My obligation is to ensure the defendant—any defendant—receives the constitutional protections he or she is entitled to," she said. "It makes no difference to me who that defendant is or what the charges are. I am committed to that."[15]

The prosecution's tactics in the Scrushy trial also came under consideration by legal experts weighing the implications of his acquittal for future prosecutions under Sarbanes-Oxley. In an article for the *Wall Street Journal*, journalist Anne Marie Squeo noted the reactions of some of those experts: "Prosecutors may take notice that to pile on charges may not always be in their best interest," the article quotes former SEC enforcement attorney Derek M. Meisner (now with Kirkpatrick & Lockhart Nicholson Graham). Ted Sonde, another former SEC enforcement officer now in practice with the Washington firm Hogan & Hartson, is also quoted in the article as saying: "The government took a very complicated case and made it more complicated." Attorney Alice Martin, lead prosecutor in Scrushy's federal trial, commented: "Just because you have a not guilty on Sarbanes-Oxley, it doesn't mean the statute loses any of its teeth."[16]

Still, the law under which Scrushy was prosecuted came under scrutiny following his acquittal. Senator Orin Hatch, Republican from Utah, spoke of Sarbanes-Oxley as "an overreach by Congress." Of Scrushy, he said: "Yeah, there were some people at HealthSouth who did some rotten things. I just don't think he was one of them." Senator Richard Shelby, Republican from Alabama, heads the Senate Banking Committee and plans hearings later this year: "We've been building a record and listening," he said. He added, "I never second-guess juries."[17]

>>> ACQUITTAL DOES NOT END SCRUSHY'S TROUBLES

For Richard Scrushy, the legal fallout from the Health-South fraud has not ended with his acquittal in this federal trial. While Scrushy dodged what nearly everyone thought was an easy prosecutorial shot at conviction, his legal battles in association with the HealthSouth fraud are far from over. He remains surrounded by attackers—the Department of Justice, shareholders, tax-men—and still faces civil charges. The U.S. Court of Appeals in Atlanta was to rule on Alice Martin's plea to remand criminal charges of perjury arising out of his testimony before the SEC (dismissed by Judge Bowdre) back for possible trial. Before a ruling could be delivered, U.S. attorney Alice Martin issued a one-sentence statement: "Based on legal considerations, the United States has filed a motion with the 11th Circuit Court of Appeals today to drop its appeal of perjury counts which were dismissed by the lower court against Mr. Scrushy,"[18]

The three perjury counts had been based on testimony given by Scrushy to SEC investigators just days before FBI agents raided HealthSouth's Birmingham headquarters.[19] Of the SEC perjury dismissal, a media report said: "U.S. District Judge Karon Bowdre told jurors to disregard testimony that Scrushy claimed he was 'unaware of any fraud' at HealthSouth during an SEC investigation. The judge ruled that separate SEC and DOJ fraud investigations had improperly overlapped and violated Scrushy's constitutional rights."[20]

Judge Bowdre at the time of dismissal commented: "Our justice system cannot function properly in the face of such cloak and dagger activities by those charged with upholding the integrity of the justice system."[21] At question for future policy is whether the SEC has an affirmative obligation to disclose parallel investigations in progress or whether merely instructing opposing counsel and their clients that they should "assume the worst—that other criminal investigations may be in progress."[22] The Scrushy legal team claimed that the jury has already decided that he was misled. But, because the dismissal was not based on the sufficiency of the evidence, the government had the right to appeal.

Scrushy's legal team was elated. "This is the end of Richard Scrushy's criminal issue once and for all," said Scrushy spokesman Charlie Russell. "We are free to turn our attention to resolving the civil issues." Scrushy is still named in dozens of civil lawsuits over the HealthSouth fraud, including one filed by the SEC accusing him of leading the accounting scheme. Martin said the decision to skip the appeal wasn't connected to the SEC's suit.[23]

On August 18, Federal Judge Inge Johnson, gave the SEC until September 7, 2005, to file an amended suit against Scrushy who continues to deny complicity in the HealthSouth fraud. Following the filing, Scrushy will have time to respond to the SEC's suit that seeks from him $785 million, plus interest, in civil fines and restitution to shareholders.[24]

When defending civil charges for insider trading Scrushy can be deposed and required to testify at trial.[25]

Other civil suits against Scrushy and HealthSouth had been on hold, awaiting the decision in the criminal case. The victims of the fraud can now proceed with their own actions. And, in addition to the lawsuit filed by the Securities and Exchange Commission, Scrushy is named in at least 61 other federal lawsuits.[26]

Neither Scrushy's acquittal nor his local popularity seem to hold much sway with his former employer; HealthSouth's public statements indicate that Scrushy is part of the company's past, not its future. Current HealthSouth CEO, Jay Grinney, issued this statement: "As we have said many times, HealthSouth was not on trial in this case and the outcome has no direct impact on the company. With the support and dedication of our employees, we have a vision for the future of HealthSouth characterized by quality, integrity, compliance, cost-effectiveness and open communication. We are glad to be putting the past behind us and moving forward with a new board of directors, new leadership team, new compliance and governance programs, new business processes and standards, and a new focus on our core businesses."[27]

Scrushy, according to his attorney, Donald Watkins, is readying a fight to regain his CEO post and board role, as well as back pay and legal fees. Says Watkins: "He's entitled to have his job back."[28] Outside the courthouse, Scrushy told reporters: "There are a lot of wrongs that need to be made right," he said. "Thank God for this."[29]

The jury's freeing of Scrushy on all charges, left many observers feeling that less-than-adequate punishment had been delivered to wrong-doers. Commenting on the sentencing of CFO, Abraham Beam, who was given three months in prison, a $10,000 fine, plus restitution of $275,000 in cash, *The Birmingham News* noted: "The people who carried out this sham deserve to pay the price for their crimes, and that price should include jail time. Indeed, the real question is not why Beam got jail time, but why some of the defendants who were previously sentenced did not . . . (the guilty) . . . need to be held accountable for their misconduct, regardless of what happened with Scrushy. Sadly, the message emanating from too many of the HealthSouth sentences is that crime may not pay, but it doesn't cost too much, either. That's a dangerous message to send."[30]

>>> AT ISSUE WERE FIRST AMENDMENT RIGHTS

I watched for seven years as the story of HealthSouth changed from the one of a growing health care company to calamity—at best a soap opera and at worst pure tragedy. For all of us who participated on the Yahoo! message board, our entertaining spoofs of the kookiness of unfolding events surrounding HealthSouth and its leader sometimes masked the more serious issues involved in those events. This certainly was true of the 1998 lawsuits against some posters to the board, and the serious financial losses many of us faced in the wake of the HealthSouth accounting fraud.

It is likely that should the same circumstances prevail today, at least some of the lawsuits brought by HealthSouth and Richard Scrushy against posters to the Yahoo! message board would not succeed. Historically, corporate SLAPP (Strategic Lawsuit Against Public Participation) actions—lawsuits by developers and police departments against public remonstrators—seldom succeed in court because of the First Amendment. But those who initiate such lawsuits often succeed in their purpose anyway, by chasing away critics who fear the high costs of defense. Defendants are overwhelmed by requests for paperwork and depositions until they become quiet; then, settlement was offered.[31]

Under state anti-SLAPP laws, the judge in such a case must rule on the likelihood of its success against First Amendment criteria before allowing discovery (and subpoenas) to take place. If the judge's ruling favors the defendant, in most states with anti-SLAPP laws on the books, the plaintiff must pay costs and legal fees. Today, 25 states have anti-SLAPP laws and 10 states have bills pending.[32]

Newspapers have relied on expanding coverage and lower defense costs arising from state anti-SLAPP laws in defending rights to speech in the public arena. The newest arena for change in application of these laws is, of course, the Internet. To date, many message board posters and blog reporters on the Internet have been given the same protection as their print counterparts, but the law and its application to Internet "speech" remain a source of debate.[33] The ongoing challenges to attempts to stifle free speech are encouraging to all of us on the message board who unexpectedly found ourselves contemplating the potential loss of those rights back in 1998.

>>> CRUSHING THE "ROCKS IN THE ROAD"

As investors, we've also been encouraged by the continuing favorable news about HealthSouth's financial stability and ongoing recovery. Although the company has not yet been able to shake the adjective "scandal-ridden," those familiar with the company have not changed their minds about its upward trajectory. CEO Jay Grinney has kept to the path set by the board of directors under retired chairman Joel Gordon and crisis manager Bryan Marsal. HealthSouth has settled several legal liabilities. According to a report from Reuters posted to CNN Headline news, HealthSouth agreed to pay $100 million to settle charges brought by the SEC against the company and Richard Scrushy (the settlement only applies to action against the company). The report went on to state that, when added to HealthSouth's $80 million settlement of a dispute with bondholders and $325 million settlement in response to charges of improper Medicare billing, the company has made progress in its efforts to eliminate overhanging litigation.[34]

In other words, HealthSouth is a much "healthier" company than it was back in 2003. This news is great for those of us on the message board, and for HealthSouth investors everywhere. In an article in *USA Today*, columnist Matt Krantz noted that "investors looking for scandal-stock bargains may be making room for HealthSouth." Frank Morgan, analyst at Jeffries, estimated HealthSouth would generate $630 million in cash flow this year.[35] His hold rating reflects the remaining rocks in the road: HealthSouth's financial reports are not fully current, the company continues to be traded on the Pinksheets, Scrushy remains on the company's board of directors, and the company still faces risks posed by government health regulations.[36]

>>> HEALTHSOUTH LOYALISTS WAIT FOR RECOVERY

And so, what began as a story of fraud and deception, heroes and villains, may, in fact, be ending as a story of recovery. For many of the HealthSouth investors who participated in the Yahoo! message board, the story of their experience focuses not on betrayal and loss, but the recovery of retirement dreams they thought they'd lost; the comfort of being able to extinguish debt and enjoy financial security and a comfortable lifestyle. Here is a brief catch-up on only a few of the hundred or more long-time posters you've read about in this book:[37]

- **Bopper63** from the far north owned shares in NSCI when it was acquired by HealthSouth: 100,000 shares at $30. "Never saw $3 million disappear so fast in my life," he said. "I held because the accountants for NSCI could find nothing wrong with the books when they did due diligence." Immediately at the crash, he was a leader in buying and accumulating 325,000 shares. His wife, whose job at one point was threatened by HealthSouth attorneys, continues to work at their local surgical center.
- **The_Dow_Bum,** a risk-analysis engineer at a national nuclear laboratory and one of the first to recommend "buy and hold," has retired after accumulating (along with his stock club) 1.5 million shares. But there is another story. A fellow employee, Judy, dreading retirement with little cash, bought 300,000 shares below 12 cents. She left to visit her brother in California when the stock hit $5.
- **The_Emerging_Analyst,** a key strategist on the message board who shared his 30 years of experience in stock analysis, seeks no outside contact; he prefers to be known as a modern-day Ayn Rand character.
- **Going_to_niceville,** a former HRC vice president, left HealthSouth for reasons of health just before the crash

when the stock traded at $4. She had once been a 35-year-old millionaire. "It was scary to be starting over with retirement savings. When it crashed, I knew in my gut it would be back one day and I held and borrowed $2,500 and bought all I could. When it hit $6, I sold 6,500 shares and paid off all my debt but my house mortgage. The message board was a tremendous help."

- **OmahaBeach** (Tom), who left the Army in 1963 after fighting in the Battle of the Bulge at age 19, easily survived the turmoil at HealthSouth. He was stuck with nearly 34,000 shares at the crash, but followed message board deliberations and bought another 80,000 shares under a dollar. "I'm still holding and I'll see you all in Las Vegas," he said.

- **QuiteRisky,** the New York girl, bought HealthSouth at $8 on advice of a friend and, following Richard Scrushy's lead to buy at $5, ended up with 45 percent of her net worth in the company when the stock fell. "I woke up with a stomach ache on March 19." She studied the stock and the message board, invested more, and recovered. "I can't say enough how this experience changed me. Not just from the financial gains, but the amount I learned about valuing companies, bonds, health care. Thanks everybody, even you Richard, for a great learning experience."

- **Scooterpass** was an employee who left—angry at company financial manipulations, disappointed in his idol, Scrushy, and ultimately disgusted by the fraud. "When I saw it trading on the Pink sheets, I thought people were crazy, but I respected a few of the posters and applying all that I had learned in six years with the company, I went for broke and invested most of my savings . . . and now have 420,000 shares and am still holding. Initially, I thought I was a genius for making that risky decision. On reflection, it was all just dumb luck."

I talked by cell phone with Kim Landry, **rehab1KL**. She was represented in her lawsuit by attorney Jill Craft, who helped her to arrange a settlement that cost Landry nothing. She did not countersue and felt no need for reprisal, saying that she felt vindicated by events and at peace with her decision. She is remarried and has fashioned a life without the stresses of HealthSouth. Landry no longer uses message boards. Her many friends on the message board wish her well.

Many other traders have departed and can be found at such sites as the more exciting NFLD (Northfield Labs) or troubled KKD (Krispy Kreme Doughnuts) message boards. **JRM30655** left Atlanta and retired to the Western desert to continue day-trading. **Corstrat** is working with OMOG, a sub-penny oil drilling company. **Iammurfthesurf** and **cmnae** are likely to be following companies where volatility is greatest or where the latest crash has left a smoking ruin.

Many of the Yahoo! HRC message board posters have committed to one last great party. Those who profited from the message board will gather in Las Vegas "at stock relisting" to talk about the adrenalin days. By then, HealthSouth should be just another health care provider, a textbook case for business schools. And talk at the party is likely to turn to Richard Scrushy, the company he founded and led throughout one of the nation's most spectacular corporate accounting frauds, and the bizarre series of shared events that changed our lives.

Appendix

IN THE UNITED STATES DISTRICT COURT
FOR THE NORTHERN DISTRICT OF ALABAMA
<u>SOUTHERN DIVISION</u>

UNITED STATES OF AMERICA,	)
	) **Case No.** _____
	)
v.	) **Violations:**
	) **18 U.S.C. § 371 Conspiracy;**
RICHARD M. SCRUSHY,	) **18 U.S.C. § 1341 Mail Fraud;**
Defendant.	) **18 U.S.C. § 1343 Wire Fraud;**
	) **18 U.S.C. § 1348 Securities Fraud;**
	) **18 U.S.C. § 1001 False Statements;**
	) **18 U.S.C. §§ 1350, 1349 False**
	) **Certification & False Certification**
	) **Attempt;**
	) **18 U.S.C. § 1957 Money Laundering;**
	) **18 U.S.C. §§ 981 and 982 Forfeiture;**
	) **18 U.S.C. § 2 Aiding & Abetting;**
	) **15 U.S.C. §§ 78j(b) and 78ff; 17 C.F.R.**
	) **§ 240.10b-5 Securities Fraud**

INDICTMENT

THE GRAND JURY CHARGES:

<u>**COUNT 1**</u>
<u>Conspiracy</u>
<u>**Title 18, United States Code, Section 371**</u>

At all times material to this Indictment:

<u>INTRODUCTION</u>

1.   HealthSouth Corporation (hereinafter "HealthSouth") was engaged in the business of providing various healthcare services to the public. HealthSouth was organized as a corporation under the laws of the State of Delaware in 1984, and headquartered in Birmingham, Alabama. It was founded by defendant **RICHARD M. SCRUSHY** and four other persons. By 2002, HealthSouth had grown to what defendant **RICHARD M. SCRUSHY** described as the

nation's largest provider of outpatient surgery, diagnostic imaging, and rehabilitative healthcare services, with approximately 1,800 locations in all 50 states, Puerto Rico, the United Kingdom, Australia, and Canada.

2.   From 1984 through early 2003, defendant **RICHARD M. SCRUSHY** was Chairman of the Board of Directors for HealthSouth. He was also the Chief Executive Officer (CEO) for all but a short time in late 2002 and early January, 2003, when a co-conspirator and aider and abetter was Chief Executive Officer. As CEO, **RICHARD M. SCRUSHY** was the highest ranking corporate officer responsible for the overall management of the company, and he owed a fiduciary duty to render honest services to HealthSouth, its shareholders, and its Board of Directors.

3.   From 1996 through March 2003, defendant **RICHARD M. SCRUSHY** directly and indirectly controlled HealthSouth through his control over a small group of senior officers, including all of the corporate President and Chief Operating Officers, the Chief Financial Officers (CFOs), Controllers, and certain other officers, who, along with some members of the corporate accounting staff were co-conspirators and aiders and abetters. Defendant **RICHARD M. SCRUSHY** and these individuals received salaries, bonuses, stock options, and other benefits some of which were tied, directly and indirectly, to the financial performance of HealthSouth.

Compensation of the Defendant

4.   From 1996 through 2002, defendant **RICHARD M. SCRUSHY** received approximately $267 million in compensation from HealthSouth, including more than $7.5 million in base salary, more than $53 million in bonuses, and stock options valued at more than $206 million when exercised. Additionally, defendant **RICHARD M. SCRUSHY** received valuable benefits including company loans, and the use of automobiles, aircraft, and other HealthSouth assets. Defendant **RICHARD M. SCRUSHY** also caused HealthSouth to invest in, and do business with, other companies and ventures in which he had a personal interest, including entertainment ventures such as singing groups.

5.   The stock options that defendant **RICHARD M. SCRUSHY** received allowed him to purchase shares directly from the company at a pre-set price or "strike price." If the market price of HealthSouth's stock increased above the strike price, defendant **RICHARD M. SCRUSHY** could "exercise" the options to purchase the stock, and then immediately sell the stock at a profit.

2

HealthSouth's Sale of Securities

6.   To expand its operations, HealthSouth raised millions of dollars in a variety of ways, including issuing and selling shares of stock which became available for trading on various public markets, selling bonds, and borrowing money from banks. Stocks and bonds are known as "securities."

7.   HealthSouth used the funds that it raised, in part, to acquire other healthcare providers, to expand into new markets, to pay operating expenses, and to pay down debt.

8.   Thousands of individuals from all over the United States and many institutions, mutual funds, insurance companies and retirement systems, including the Retirement System of Alabama, purchased HealthSouth's securities.

Regulation of the Sale of Securities

9.   The United States Securities and Exchange Commission (the SEC), headquartered in Washington, D.C., was an agency responsible for enforcing federal securities laws. SEC regulations protected members of the investing public by, among other things, requiring that a company's financial information was accurately recorded and disclosed to the public.

10.   In order to sell securities to the public and to permit public trading of its securities, HealthSouth was required to "register" its securities with the SEC. HealthSouth was also required to comply with certain laws and SEC regulations designed to ensure that a company's financial information was accurately recorded and fairly disclosed to the investing public. HealthSouth was further required to make and keep books, records, and accounts that accurately and fairly reflected its income, expenses and assets, and to devise and maintain a system of internal accounting controls which would reasonably assure that these objectives were satisfied.

11.   HealthSouth was required to and did file various periodic reports and other documents with the SEC, which included representations concerning its revenues, net income and losses, earnings, the value of its assets and the amount of its liabilities. These documents included:

        a.   Forms S-3, S-4, and S-8 registration statements filed in connection with the registration of HealthSouth's stocks and bonds;

        b.   Forms 8-K detailing material events;

          c.   Forms 10-Q, which included the quarterly report
of its financial condition and the results of its operations; and

    d.   Forms 10-K, which included the annual report of its financial
condition and the results of its operations.

12.   HealthSouth filed its Forms 10-K, 10-Q, 8-K, S-3, S-4, and S-8 with the SEC in
Washington, D.C. These documents were available for public review.

13.   Beginning on or about July 30, 2002, a law, commonly referred to as the
Sarbanes-Oxley Act, required, among other things, that each Form 10-K and 10-Q filed
periodically with the SEC be accompanied by a written certification ("1350 certification") by the
CEO and the CFO stating that information contained in the periodic reports fairly presented, in
all material respects, the financial condition and results of operations of the issuer.

Accounting Principles and Practices

14.   Financial statements produced by HealthSouth included both an Income
Statement and a Balance Sheet.

An Income Statement reported, among other things, the company's
revenue and expenses incurred during a stated period of time, i.e.,
usually a three-month period or quarter, or a twelve-month period
or year. A company's earnings per share (EPS) is generally
calculated by dividing its net income by the number of its
outstanding shares of stock.

A Balance Sheet reported, among other things, the value of the
company's assets and amount of its liabilities at the end of a
reporting period, i.e., usually the last day of a quarter or the last
day of a year.

15.   As is customary in the healthcare industry, HealthSouth billed "third party
payors," such as insurance companies, Medicare, and Medicaid, for healthcare services at
amounts greater than it expected to collect. The total amount billed was entered into gross
revenue accounts. The amount HealthSouth did not expect to collect was entered into separate
"contractual adjustment" accounts. The amount in the contractual adjustment accounts was
subtracted from the amount in the gross revenue accounts to help calculate net income.

Dissemination Of Financial Information

4

16.   Income Statements and Balance Sheets, which reflected the results of its operations and financial condition, were included in and with various documents HealthSouth filed with the SEC. HealthSouth and defendant **RICHARD M. SCRUSHY** also distributed Income Statements, Balance Sheets, and other financial information reflecting income and assets to HealthSouth's Board of Directors, employees, stockholders and bondholders, potential stockholders and bondholders, bond underwriters, market analysts, bankers, the media, and other interested parties, by a variety of means including conference calls, media interviews, press releases, internet web sites, conventions, investor meetings and corporate meetings.

17.   The Board of Directors, employees, stockholders and bondholders, potential stockholders and bondholders, bond underwriters, market analysts, bankers, the media, and other interested parties relied on the information distributed by HealthSouth and defendant **RICHARD M. SCRUSHY** in making investments and other decisions.

18.   HealthSouth and defendant **RICHARD M. SCRUSHY** at times also provided "guidance" to the investing public regarding its anticipated earnings, revenues, net income, earnings per share, cash flow, and assets. Relying in part on the company's "guidance," many professional securities analysts disseminated to their clients and the public their estimates of the company's expected performance. These estimates were often called "earnings estimates" or "analyst expectations." These "earnings estimates" and "analyst expectations" were reviewed by many investors who relied on the information to make investment decisions.

Internal Financial Reports

19.   The corporate accounting staff at the company's headquarters building in Birmingham, Alabama, maintained HealthSouth's corporate books and records, including its general ledger and supporting databases. The staff used the general ledger and databases to capture the company's financial information. They also used the general ledger and databases to generate internal monthly, quarterly and annual reports which showed HealthSouth's current financial information, particularly its revenue, expenses, and net income and losses. These reports were delivered to, and reviewed by, defendant **RICHARD M. SCRUSHY** and other senior officers. Various components of HealthSouth also generated weekly revenue reports which were provided to defendant **RICHARD M. SCRUSHY,** and other senior officers, on a weekly basis. Defendant **RICHARD M. SCRUSHY** often referred to these reports during the Monday morning meetings he conducted with corporate officers.

5

20.   During the period between 1996 and 2003, these internal reports showed that HealthSouth often failed to produce sufficient net income to meet its quarterly and annual "guidance," the consensus of Wall Street, or market expectations, and HealthSouth's internal budgets. Defendant **RICHARD M. SCRUSHY** and other senior officers of HealthSouth would refer to such failure as "not making the numbers," and they believed that revealing the company's actual performance and shortfalls to the investing public and analysts would adversely effect the market price of HealthSouth's stock.

The Conspiracy

21.   From in or about 1996, the exact date being unknown to the Grand Jury, to on or about March 19, 2003, within Jefferson County in the Northern District of Alabama, and elsewhere, defendant

RICHARD M. SCRUSHY

knowingly and willfully conspired with other persons, known and unknown to the Grand Jury, to commit offenses against the United States, that is to:

(a)   devise and intend to devise a scheme and artifice to defraud and to obtain money and property by means of materially false and fraudulent pretenses, representations and promises, and to execute and attempt to execute the scheme and artifice by placing and causing to be placed in a post office and an authorized depository for mail matter to be sent and to be delivered by the United States Postal Service, and to deposit and cause to be deposited matter to be sent and delivered by a private and commercial interstate carrier, in violation of Title 18, United States Code, Sections 1341, 1346 and 2;

(b)   devise and intend to devise a scheme and artifice to defraud and to obtain money and property by means of materially false and fraudulent pretenses, representations and promises, and to execute the scheme and artifice by transmitting and causing to be transmitted by means of wire communication in interstate and foreign commerce, writings, signs, signals, pictures and sounds, in violation of Title 18, United States Code, Sections 1343, 1346 and 2;

(c)   knowingly execute and attempt to execute a scheme and artifice to defraud and to obtain, by means of materially false and fraudulent pretenses, representations and promises, money, funds and credits owned by and under the custody and control of federally insured financial institutions, in violation of Title 18, United States Code, Sections 1344 and 2;

(d)   knowingly and willfully make and cause to be made materially false, fictitious and fraudulent representations in a matter within the jurisdiction of the

6

executive branch of the Government of the United States, in violation of Title 18, United States Code, Sections 1001 and 2;

(e)   willfully certify and cause to be certified a statement required to be filed by Title 18, United States Code, Section 1350, with the SEC, knowing that the periodic report accompanying the statement did not comport with all the requirements set forth in that section, and attempt to do so, in violation of Title 18, United States Code, Sections 1349, 1350 and 2;

(f)   knowingly execute and attempt to execute a scheme and artifice to defraud in connection with securities of HealthSouth, an issuer with a class of securities registered under Section 12 of the Securities Exchange Act of 1934 and required to file reports under Section 15(d) of said Act, in violation of Title 18, United States Code, Sections 1348 and 2;

(g)   willfully and knowingly make and cause to be made false and misleading statements of material fact in applications, reports and documents required to be filed under the Securities and Exchange Act of 1934 and the rules and regulations thereunder in violation of Title 15, United States Code, Sections 78m(a) and 78ff; Title 17, Code of Federal Regulations, Sections 240.13a-1, 13a-13 and 13b2-2; and Title 18, United States Code, Section 2;

(h)   willfully and knowingly falsify books, records and accounts of HealthSouth in violation of Title 15, United States Code, Sections 78m(b)(2)(A) & (B), 78m(b)(5) and 78ff; Title 17, Code of Federal Regulations, Section 240.13b2-1; and Title 18; United States Code, Section 2;

(i)   willfully and knowingly make and cause to be made false and misleading statements to accountants and to omit to state, and cause others to omit to state, material facts necessary in order to make the statements made, in light of the circumstances under which the statements were made, not misleading to an accountant in connection with an audit of HealthSouth's financial statements in violation of Title 15, United States Code, Section 78ff; Title 17, Code of Federal Regulations, Section 240.13b2-2; and Title 18, United States Code, Section 2;

(j)   willfully, directly and indirectly, by use of the means and instrumentalities of interstate commerce, the mails, and the facilities of national securities exchanges, use and employ manipulative and deceptive devices and contrivances, in violation of Title 15, United States Code, Sections 78j(b) and 78ff; Title 17, Code of Federal Regulations, Section 240.10b-5; and Title 18, United States Code, Section 2;

Purpose Of The Conspiracy

22.   A purpose of the conspiracy was to unjustly enrich and benefit defendant
RICHARD M. SCRUSHY and others by fraudulently inflating the results of operations and the
financial condition that HealthSouth reported to others.

Manner and Means of the Conspiracy

23.   It was part of the conspiracy that defendant **RICHARD M. SCRUSHY** and other
co-conspirator HealthSouth officers and employees would and did participate in a scheme to
fraudulently inflate the company's operating results and financial condition, including the net
income and earnings per share that HealthSouth reported to its Board of Directors, employees,
the SEC, bond underwriters, market analysts, bankers, the media, and the investing public.

24.   It was further part of the conspiracy that defendant **RICHARD M. SCRUSHY**
and other co-conspirators would and did cause false and fraudulent entries to be made to
HealthSouth's books and records, which added approximately $2.7 billion in fictitious income to
the books and records during the course of the conspiracy.

25.   It was further part of the conspiracy that defendant **RICHARD M. SCRUSHY**
and other co-conspirators would and did fraudulently induce HealthSouth to pay salaries,
bonuses, and stock options, and otherwise confer benefits upon themselves as a result of the
fraudulently inflated results.

26.   It was further part of the conspiracy that defendant **RICHARD M. SCRUSHY**
and other co-conspirators would and did fraudulently inflate HealthSouth's financial results in
order to increase HealthSouth's stock price and thereby increase the value of their own
HealthSouth stock and options.

27.   It was further part of the conspiracy that defendant **RICHARD M. SCRUSHY**
and other co-conspirators would and did cause HealthSouth to issue fraudulently inflated
financial reports to induce stock and bond investors, bank lenders and businesses to invest in
HealthSouth's securities and to provide funds and other assets to HealthSouth.

28.   It was further part of the conspiracy that defendant **RICHARD M. SCRUSHY**
and other co-conspirators would and did meet and discuss HealthSouth's actual financial
performance, the actual results of its operations, and the need to falsify those results before they
were publicly reported.

29.   It was further part of the conspiracy that after reviewing reports which showed
that HealthSouth's actual financial results had failed to meet quarterly and annual income

"guidance" and the consensus of Wall Street analyst expectations, defendant **RICHARD M. SCRUSHY** would and did cause co-conspirator senior officers to fraudulently inflate HealthSouth's reported income, operating results and financial condition.

30.   It was further part of the conspiracy that one or more co-conspirator senior officers would and did convey defendant **RICHARD M. SCRUSHY's** orders to members of the corporate accounting staff and discuss with them specific methods for falsifying HealthSouth's books, records and financial reports in order to fraudulently inflate its operating results and financial condition.

31.   It was further part of the conspiracy that the defendant **RICHARD M. SCRUSHY** and other co-conspirators, including members of the corporate accounting staff, would and did make and cause to be made, false entries to income statement accounts, including the contractual adjustment accounts, without supporting documentation, in HealthSouth's books and records for the purpose of artificially and materially inflating net income and earnings per share on the publicly reported Income Statements. Certain co-conspirators would and did refer to the false entries as "filling the hole" or "filling the gap."

32.   It was further part of the conspiracy that once false entries were made to various accounts to increase income, one or more co-conspirators, including members of the corporate accounting staff, in order to "balance" the books, would and did make and cause to be made, corresponding false entries to balance sheet accounts in HealthSouth's books and records, including (a) Property, Plant and Equipment ("PP&E") accounts; (b) cash accounts; (c) inventory accounts; (d) accounts receivable; (e) intangible asset (goodwill) accounts, (f) suspense accounts; and (g) the investment portfolio.

33.   It was further part of the conspiracy that the defendant **RICHARD M. SCRUSHY** and other co-conspirators would and did publicize and disseminate the fraudulently inflated financial information.

34.   It was further part of the conspiracy that defendant **RICHARD M. SCRUSHY** and certain co-conspirators would and did sign, and caused to be filed with the SEC in Washington, D.C., Forms 10-Q, 10-K, 8-K, and other documents which contained materially false and fraudulent information about HealthSouth's income, operating results, financial condition, and earnings per share.

35.   It was further part of the conspiracy that in order to avoid detection and exposure, the co-conspirators would and did make few if any fraudulent entries to accounts associated with facilities located in certain states, where state regulators required separate audits for certain facilities, and to certain accounts associated with facilities operated in partnership with physicians.

36.   It was further part of the conspiracy that defendant **RICHARD M. SCRUSHY** and co-conspirators would and did cover up, conceal, and keep secret the fraud, by: (a) controlling and limiting access to HealthSouth's financial information; (b) controlling the internal distribution of financial results; (c) providing fraudulent documentation and false information to its auditors; (d) providing false information to Federal and State taxing authorities; and (e) fraudulently using the acquisition of other companies to conceal fraudulent assets on HealthSouth's books and in its reports.

37.   It was further part of the conspiracy that defendant **RICHARD M. SCRUSHY** would and did seek to control his co-conspirators, HealthSouth employees and the Board of Directors by: (a) threats; (b) intimidation; (c) taking various steps to monitor the activities of said persons, including obtaining and reading their e-mails, placing them under surveillance, and installing equipment that permitted him to eavesdrop on electronic and telephonic communications; (d) obtaining large compensation packages for co-conspirators; and (e) recommending the forgiveness of HealthSouth loans to co-conspirators.

38.   It was further part of the conspiracy that defendant **RICHARD M. SCRUSHY** would and did cause co-conspirator senior officers to continue to sign and file false certifications and periodic reports by: (a) offering them financial and other inducements; (b) appealing to their loyalty to defendant **RICHARD M. SCRUSHY**, to HealthSouth and to its employees; (c) reminding them that they had already committed illegal acts; (d) stating that the company was making money and had a bright future; (e) suggesting that the falsity in the reports could be reduced over time; (f) suggesting that there was a "plan" to take care of the fraud; (g) suggesting that they could get away with it; (h) reminding them of the adverse consequences they and others might suffer if they abandoned the scheme; (i) reminding them of the benefits that would accrue if they continued the scheme; and (j) suggesting that continuing with the scheme was the "right" thing to do.

Overt Acts

In furtherance of the conspiracy and to achieve the objects thereof, the conspirators committed and caused to be committed the following acts, among others, in the Northern District of Alabama and elsewhere:

39.　　From in or about 1996 to on or about March 19, 2003, defendant **RICHARD M. SCRUSHY** and others reviewed internal financial statements setting forth the actual financial condition and results of operations at HealthSouth.

40.　　From in or about 1996 to on or about March 19, 2003, defendant **RICHARD M. SCRUSHY** and co-conspirator senior officers periodically discussed the falsification of HealthSouth's financial statements.

41.　　Co-conspirators, including members of the corporate accounting staff, made and caused to be made entries in the books and records of HealthSouth, which caused the following approximate amounts of fictitious income to be included in the annual reports to stockholders and SEC filings for the years 1996 through 2001, and intended to be included in the annual reports to stockholders and SEC filings for the year 2002, the total amount for each year being a separate overt act:

Year	Amount of Fictitious Income
1996	$　70 million
1997	$　700 million
1998	$　550 million
1999	$　390 million
2000	$　350 million
2001	$　450 million
2002	$　230 million
Total	$ 2.740 billion

42.　　Co-conspirator corporate accounting staff members added and caused to be added fictitious assets to the books and records of HealthSouth which by December 21. 2002, totaled approximately $2.7 billion and included the following amounts, each inclusion being a separate overt act:

(a) Approximately $370 million in cash;

(b) Approximately $27 million in the stock of a publicly traded company;

(c) Approximately $13 million investment in an assisted living facility;

(d) More than $1 billion of fictitious assets classified as "AP SUMMARY"; and

(e) More than $740 million in goodwill.

43. Co-conspirator corporate accounting staff members misclassified assets, including aircraft and medical equipment, for the purpose of fraudulently inflating HealthSouth's balance sheet.

44. On or about each date set forth below, defendant **RICHARD M. SCRUSHY** signed a letter addressed to HealthSouth's outside auditors in which he represented in substance that he recognized that obtaining representations from management was a significant step for auditors to form an opinion as to whether the consolidated financial statements presented fairly in all material respects the financial position and results of operations of HealthSouth and in which he falsely represented that there were no material transactions that had not been properly recorded in the accounting records underlying the consolidated financial statements, each representation letter signing being a separate overt act:

DATE

a. February 24, 1997

b. March 25, 1997

c. August 21, 1997

d. August 29, 1997

e. September 18, 1997

f. February 25, 1998

g. March 26, 1999

h. March 28, 2000

i. November 14, 2000

j. March 23, 2001

12

k. March 20, 2002
l. May 10, 2002
m. August 13, 2002

45.   In or about May, August, and November of each year from 1996 through 2001, and in or about May and August of 2002, defendant **RICHARD M. SCRUSHY** signed a Form 10-Q and caused it to be filed with the SEC, each signing and each filing constituting a separate overt act.

46.   In or about March of each year from 1996 through 2002, defendant **RICHARD M. SCRUSHY** signed a Form 10-K and caused it to be filed with the SEC, each signing and each filing constituting a separate overt act. 47.   On or about November 14, 2002, co-conspirators signed HealthSouth's Form 10-Q for the third quarter of 2002 and caused it to be filed with the SEC.

48.   In or about April 1997, defendant **RICHARD M. SCRUSHY** falsely represented in the HealthSouth 1996 Annual Report sent to stockholders that:

> "Fully diluted income per share, excluding non-recurring expenses related to acquisitions, showed continued strong growth as we posted $0.75 per share for the year, a 38% increase over 1995."

49.   In or about April 1998, defendant **RICHARD M. SCRUSHY** falsely represented in the HealthSouth 1997 Annual Report sent to stockholders that:

> "This year, we extended our record to 46 quarters of meeting market expectations, with a revenue increase of 17% over 1996."

50.   In or about April 1999, defendant **RICHARD M. SCRUSHY** falsely represented in the HealthSouth 1998 Annual Report sent to stockholders that:

> "For the year, we completed 50 quarters of meeting market expectations, with revenue increasing 28% over 1997. Income excluding one-time expenses grew by 34%, while corresponding income per share increased by 18%."

51.   In or about April 2000, co-conspirators caused HealthSouth to send to stockholders the 1999 Annual Report falsely reporting that earnings per share for the year exceeded $0.85, excluding effects of one-time expenses.

13

52.   In or about April 2001, defendant **RICHARD M. SCRUSHY** falsely asserted in the HealthSouth 2000 Annual Report sent to stockholders that:

> "In 2000, our stock rose to promising heights, closing up 203 percent for the year and earning HealthSouth recognition as a top–five performer in the S&P 500. We also fulfilled Wall Street expectations for another year, maintaining our position as the *Fortune 500* company with the second-longest streak for meeting or exceeding analysts' expectations."

53.   In or about April 2002, defendant **RICHARD M. SCRUSHY** falsely represented in the HealthSouth 2001 Annual Report sent to stockholders that:

> "In 2001, we set new records as we pushed our revenues well over $4.3 billion and celebrated another year of fulfilling Wall Street expectations, maintaining our record as the second-longest streak for meeting or exceeding analysts' expectations."

54.   On or about February 27, 1997, HealthSouth issued a press release in which defendant **RICHARD M. SCRUSHY** falsely represented that HealthSouth had its tenth consecutive year of meeting or exceeding analyst expectations.

55.   On or about October 30, 1997, HealthSouth issued a press release in which defendant **RICHARD M. SCRUSHY** falsely represented that HealthSouth had achieved record profitability.

56.   On or about November 3, 1997, HealthSouth issued a press release in which defendant **RICHARD M. SCRUSHY** falsely represented that HealthSouth had its 45th consecutive quarter of meeting or exceeding analysts' expectations.

57.   On or about September 30, 1998, HealthSouth issued a press release in which defendant **RICHARD M. SCRUSHY** falsely represented that HealthSouth's balance sheet was among the strongest in the industry.

58.   On or about March 7, 2000, HealthSouth issued a press release in which defendant **RICHARD M. SCRUSHY** falsely represented that HealthSouth continued to maintain earnings before interest, taxes, depreciation and amortization (EBITDA) margins well in excess of competitors.

59.   In or about April 2002, HealthSouth's 2001 Annual Report was mailed to approximately 7,000 stockholders.

60.   On or about July 11, 2002, HealthSouth issued a press release reporting that it was comfortable with consensus Wall Street estimates for the remainder of the year, and had strong operating results through the first half of the year.

61.   On or about July 8, 2002, upon being told that a government agency communication regarding reimbursements for Medicare patients might reduce income, defendant **RICHARD M. SCRUSHY** told other co-conspirators that they could not reduce earnings projections.

62.   In or about the summer of 1999, defendant **RICHARD M. SCRUSHY** reviewed a binder containing financial data which compared HealthSouth's true pre-tax income and EPS to HealthSouth's reported and projected pre-tax income and EPS and which demonstrated that HealthSouth's true pre-tax income and EPS was less than what HealthSouth had previously reported and was about to report. Afterwards, defendant **RICHARD M. SCRUSHY** confronted the officer who had prepared the binder and told the officer that he could not tell defendant **SCRUSHY** how to run the company.

63.   In or about March 1999, defendant **RICHARD M. SCRUSHY** appeared in a HealthSouth Corporate Show videotape which was distributed to employees, and touted the company's balance sheet and cash flow, and encouraged employees to buy HealthSouth stock.

64.   In or about June 2000, defendant **RICHARD M. SCRUSHY** appeared in a HealthSouth State of the Company videotape which was distributed to employees, and stated that "we have remained committed to prudent fiscal policy and the integrity of our balance sheet," and touted that HealthSouth had an "outstanding balance sheet."

65.   In or about October, 2000, defendant **RICHARD M. SCRUSHY** appeared on "Moneycast" in a televised interview and stated that HealthSouth had a "good strong balance sheet" and had "plenty of available cash."

66.   In or about early 2003, defendant **RICHARD M. SCRUSHY** appeared at a HealthSouth 2003 managers meeting and told the company's employees that HealthSouth did not have the same type of problems as WorldCom and Tyco.

67.   In or about August 2002, after some co-conspirator corporate accounting staff members had advised their supervisors that they would no longer make false entries, and after one of the senior officers who was required to sign the Form 10-Q to be filed that month balked

at signing the report because it contained materially false information, defendant **RICHARD M. SCRUSHY** agreed to, and helped devise a plan to:

    (a)   Cease making phony entries to inflate net income;

    (b)   Publicly blame the resulting reduction in reported net income on the purported effect of an announcement by the government concerning Medicare reimbursements;

    (c)   Maintain the more than $1 billion in previously reported phony assets on the reported Balance Sheets, and look for ways to reduce this inflation over time without provoking undue attention;

    (d)   Solicit potential buyers to conduct a leveraged buy-out of HealthSouth, or parts of HealthSouth, whereby the company or certain parts would be privately owned, therefore reducing public and governmental scrutiny; and

    (e)   Offer the senior officer who had balked at signing the Form 10-Q the position of CFO of a part of the company that was to be spun off from HealthSouth and which was believed "clean," that is, which was largely unaffected by the fraudulent entries, and promise the senior officer that they would "not play games anymore," to induce the senior officer to sign the form.

    68.   On or about August 27, 2002, defendant **RICHARD M. SCRUSHY** announced: (a) that anticipated revenues would be reduced due to the purported effect of a directive known as Transmittal 1753 concerning reimbursement for certain therapies for Medicare patients; (b) that HealthSouth would spin off a portion of the company; and (c) that the aforementioned co-conspirator senior officer would become CFO of the new spin-off company.

    69.   In 2002, defendant **RICHARD M. SCRUSHY** exercised stock options, sold stock on the open market, and transferred stock to HealthSouth in satisfaction of an executive loan.

    70.   On or about November 13, 2002, defendant **RICHARD M. SCRUSHY** and other co-conspirators caused a statement falsely certifying that HealthSouth's Form 10-Q for the third quarter of 2002 fairly presented, in all material respects, the financial condition and results of operations of HealthSouth, to be transmitted and delivered from Birmingham, Alabama, to a publishing and filing company, for filing with the SEC in Washington, D.C.

16

71.   In or about the Fall of 2002, defendant **RICHARD M. SCRUSHY** met with two co-conspirator senior officers and discussed that HealthSouth's balance sheet overstated cash by hundreds of millions of dollars.

72.   In or about January 2003, defendant **RICHARD M. SCRUSHY** asked a co-conspirator how long it would take to fix the cash on the balance sheet.

73.   In or about March 2003, when an investment bank proposed a leveraged buy-out (LBO) plan that included using approximately $249.6 million in cash that appeared on HealthSouth's books and records to help finance the LBO, defendant **RICHARD M. SCRUSHY** ordered a co-conspirator to request that company to propose a plan that did not include the use of such cash.

74.   In or about early 2003, defendant **RICHARD M. SCRUSHY** offered to "take care of" a co-conspirator's family if he would take the blame for the overstatements.

75.   On or about the morning of March 17, 2003, defendant **RICHARD M. SCRUSHY** made statements to a co-conspirator senior officer, who was then cooperating with the government, that a federal investigation of insider trading did not include an investigation of the accounting fraud.

76.   During a series of meetings and telephone conversations on or about March 17 and 18, 2003, between defendant **RICHARD M. SCRUSHY** and the above-referenced senior officer, defendant **SCRUSHY** attempted to persuade the senior officer to continue the scheme, not reveal it to others, and to sign an amended Form 10-Q.

77.   On or about the dates set forth below, in response to an e-mail received at HealthSouth as described below from the person described below, HealthSouth sent and caused to be sent to that person false financial information, each sending being a separate overt act:

Date	Requesting E-mail
(a) September 10, 2002	An e-mail from a person with the initials JB, in Carlsbad, California, to HealthSouth headquarters in the Northern District of Alabama, requesting that HealthSouth send him HealthSouth's annual report and Form 10-K;

(b) October 2, 2002	An e-mail from a person with the initials RC, in Tallahassee, Florida, to HealthSouth headquarters in the Northern District of Alabama, requesting that HealthSouth send him a Form 10-K and annual report;
(c) November 19, 2002	An e-mail from a person with the initials MS, in New York, New York, to HealthSouth headquarters in the Northern District of Alabama, requesting that HealthSouth send him a proxy statement, Form 10-K, Form 10-Q, annual reports, and press releases; and
(d) January 3, 2003	An e-mail from a person with the initials MK, in Marietta, Georgia, to HealthSouth headquarters in the Northern District of Alabama, requesting that HealthSouth send him a Form 10-K, Form 10-Q, annual report, and proxy.

78. The Grand Jury incorporates herein by reference the allegations as set forth in Counts 2 through 50 as overt acts committed by defendant **RICHARD M. SCRUSHY** and other co-conspirators in furtherance of this conspiracy.

All in violation of Title 18, United States Code, Section 371.

COUNT 2
Securities Fraud
Title 18, United States Code, Sections 1348(1) and 2

1. The Grand Jury repeats and re-alleges the allegations contained in paragraphs 1 through 20 of Count 1 of this Indictment as though fully set out herein.

2. The Grand Jury repeats and re-alleges the allegations contained in paragraphs 23 through 38 of Count 1 of this Indictment as describing the scheme and artifice to defraud stockholders, bondholders, potential stockholders and bondholders, bond underwriters, HealthSouth, and others in connection with securities of HealthSouth, an issuer with a class of securities registered under Section 12 of the Securities Exchange Act of 1934 ("Act") that was required to file reports under Section 15(d) of said Act.

3. From in or about 1996, the exact date being unknown to the Grand Jury, to on or about March 19, 2003, within Jefferson County in the

Northern District of Alabama, and elsewhere, defendant

RICHARD M. SCRUSHY

and others known and unknown to the Grand Jury, knowingly executed and attempted to execute the above-described scheme and artifice.

4. On or about August 14, 2002, within Jefferson County in the Northern District of Alabama, and elsewhere, defendant **RICHARD M. SCRUSHY**, and others, for the purpose of executing and attempting to execute the above-described scheme and artifice to defraud, filed and caused to be filed with the SEC a Form10-Q and other documents for the three-month and six-month periods ending June 30, 2002, which contained HealthSouth's fraudulently inflated financial statements.

All in violation of Title 18, United States Code, Sections 1348(1) and 2.

COUNT 3
Securities Fraud
Title 15, United States Code, Sections 78j(b) and 78ff;
Title 17, Code of Federal Regulations, Section 240.10b-5;
Title 18, United States Code, Section 2

1. The Grand Jury repeats and re-alleges the allegations contained in paragraphs 1 through 20 of Count 1 of this Indictment as though fully set out herein.

2. The Grand Jury repeats and re-alleges the allegations contained in paragraphs 23 through 38 of Count 1 of this Indictment as describing the manipulative and deceptive devices and contrivances used and employed by defendant **RICHARD M. SCRUSHY** and others in contravention of Title 17, Code of Federal Regulations, Section 240.10b-5.

3. From in or about 1996, the exact date being unknown to the Grand Jury, to on or about March 19, 2003, within Jefferson County in the Northern District of Alabama, and elsewhere, defendant

RICHARD M. SCRUSHY

and others known and unknown to the Grand Jury, wilfuly, directly and indirectly, by use of the means and instrumentalities of interstate commerce, the mails, and the facilities of national securities exchanges, did use and employ manipulative and deceptive devices and contrivances, by: (a) employing devices, schemes, and artifices to defraud; (b) making and causing

HealthSouth to make untrue statements of material facts and omitting to state and causing HealthSouth to omit to state material facts necessary in order to make the statements made, in light of the circumstances under which they were made, not misleading; and (c) engaging in acts, practices and courses of business that operated and would operate as a fraud and deceit upon purchasers and sellers of HealthSouth securities; to wit, defendant **SCRUSHY** and others caused the dissemination of false financial information into the marketplace in a HealthSouth Form 10-K filed on or about March 27, 2002, with the SEC that materially overstated the operating results and financial condition of HealthSouth by inflating net income and the value of assets at the end of the reporting period, in connection with the sale by defendant **SCRUSHY** of 5,275,360 shares of HealthSouth common stock for total proceeds of approximately $74,118,808.00 on May 14, 2002.

All in violation of Title 15, United States Code, Sections 78j(b) and 78ff; Title 17, Code of Federal Regulations, Section 240.10b-5; and Title 18, United States Code, Section 2.

COUNTS 4 - 21
Wire Fraud
Title 18, United States Code, Sections 1343, 1346 and 2

1.   The Grand Jury repeats and re-alleges the allegations contained in paragraphs 1 through 20 of Count 1 of this Indictment as though fully set out herein.

The Scheme to Defraud
2.   The Grand Jury repeats and re-alleges the allegations contained in paragraphs 23 through 38 of Count 1 of this Indictment as describing a scheme and artifice to defraud stockholders, bondholders, potential stockholders and bondholders, bond underwriters, HealthSouth, and others and to obtain money and property by means of materially false and fraudulent pretenses, representations and promises.

3.   From in or about 1996, the exact date being unknown to the Grand Jury, to on or about March 19, 2003, within Jefferson County in the Northern District of Alabama, and elsewhere, defendant

RICHARD M. SCRUSHY

and others known and unknown to the Grand Jury, devised and intended to devise the above-described scheme and artifice.

20

Execution of the Scheme

4.   On or about the dates set forth below for each of Counts 4 through 21, within Jefferson County in the Northern District of Alabama, and elsewhere, defendant **RICHARD M. SCRUSHY**, aided and abetted by others, knowingly and willfully, for the purpose of executing the above-described scheme and artifice, transmitted and caused to be transmitted by means of wire communications in interstate commerce writings, signs, signals, pictures and sounds, as described for each of said counts.

5.   The allegations of paragraphs 1 though 4 above are re-alleged for each of Counts 4 through 21 below as through fully set out therein.

Count	Date	Transmission
4	April 27, 1999	A conference call hosted by HealthSouth, in the Northern District of Alabama, for the benefit of stockholders, investors, and other interested persons in Alabama and other states, to discuss HealthSouth's performance.
5	August 3, 1999	A conference call hosted by HealthSouth, in the Northern District of Alabama, for the benefit of stockholders, investors, and other interested persons in Alabama and other states, to discuss HealthSouth's performance.
6	April 25, 2000	A conference call hosted by HealthSouth, in the Northern District of Alabama, for the benefit of stockholders, investors, and other interested persons in Alabama and other states, to discuss HealthSouth's performance.
7	July 18, 2000	A conference call hosted by HealthSouth, in the Northern District of Alabama, for the benefit of stockholders, investors, and other interested persons in Alabama and other states, to discuss HealthSouth's performance.
8	October 31, 2000	A conference call hosted by HealthSouth, in the Northern District of Alabama, for the benefit of stockholders, investors, and other interested persons in Alabama and other states, to discuss HealthSouth's performance.
9	March 6, 2001	A conference call hosted by HealthSouth, in the Northern District of Alabama, for the benefit of stockholders, investors, and other interested persons in Alabama and other states, to discuss HealthSouth's performance.

21

10	April 26, 2001	A conference call hosted by HealthSouth, in the Northern District of Alabama, for the benefit of stockholders, investors, and other interested persons in Alabama and other states, to discuss HealthSouth's performance.
11	July 31, 2001	A conference call hosted by HealthSouth, in the Northern District of Alabama, for the benefit of stockholders, investors, and other interested persons in Alabama and other states, to discuss HealthSouth's performance.
12	October 25, 2001	A conference call hosted by HealthSouth, in the Northern District of Alabama, for the benefit of stockholders, investors, and other interested persons in Alabama and other states, to discuss HealthSouth's performance.
13	March 12, 2002	A conference call hosted by HealthSouth, in the Northern District of Alabama, for the benefit of stockholders, investors, and other interested persons in Alabama and other states, to discuss HealthSouth's performance.
14	May 2, 2002	A conference call hosted by HealthSouth, in the Northern District of Alabama, for the benefit of stockholders, investors, and other interested persons in Alabama and other states, to discuss HealthSouth's performance.
15	August 7, 2002	A conference call hosted by HealthSouth, in the Northern District of Alabama, for the benefit of stockholders, investors, and other interested persons in Alabama and other states, to discuss HealthSouth's performance.
16	August 7, 2002	The transmission of an August 7, 2002 press release from Birmingham, Alabama, to a computer server in Atlanta, Georgia, for posting to internet web site www.healthsouth.com.
17	September 19, 2002	A conference call hosted by HealthSouth, in the Northern District of Alabama, for the benefit of stockholders, investors, and other interested persons in Alabama and other states, to discuss HealthSouth's performance.
18	October 1, 2002	A conference call hosted by an individual, New York, for the benefit of stockholders, investors, and other interested persons in Alabama and other states, to discuss HealthSouth's performance.
19	November 5, 2002	A conference call hosted by HealthSouth, in the Northern District of Alabama, for the benefit of stockholders, investors, and other interested persons in Alabama and other states, to discuss HealthSouth's performance.

22

| 20 | November 5, 2002 | The transmission of a November 5, 2002 press release from Birmingham, Alabama, to a computer server in Atlanta, Georgia, for posting to internet web site www.healthsouth.com. |
| 21 | March 3, 2003 | The transmission of a March 3, 2003 press release from Birmingham, Alabama, to a computer server in Atlanta, Georgia, for posting to internet web site www.healthsouth.com. |

All in violation of Title 18, United States Code, Sections 1343, 1346 and 2.

COUNTS 22 THROUGH 25
Mail Fraud
Title 18, United States Code, Sections 1341, 1346 and 2

1.   The Grand Jury repeats and re-alleges the allegations contained in paragraphs 1 through 20 of Count 1 of this Indictment as though fully set out herein.

The Scheme to Defraud

2.   The Grand Jury repeats and re-alleges the allegations contained in paragraphs 23 through 38 of Count 1 of this Indictment as describing a scheme and artifice to defraud stockholders, bondholders, potential stockholders and bondholders, bond underwriters, HealthSouth, and others and to obtain money and property by means of materially false and fraudulent pretenses, representations and promises.

3.   From in or about 1996, the exact date being unknown to the Grand Jury, to on or about March 19, 2003, within Jefferson County in the Northern District of Alabama, and elsewhere, defendant

RICHARD M. SCRUSHY

and others known and unknown to the Grand Jury, devised and intended to devise the above-described scheme and artifice.

Execution of the Scheme

4.   On or about the dates set forth below for each of Counts 22 through 25, within Jefferson County in the Northern District of Alabama, and elsewhere, defendant **RICHARD M. SCRUSHY**, aided and abetted by others, knowingly and willfully, for the purpose of executing the above-described scheme and artifice and attempting to do so, deposited and caused to be

deposited the matters and things listed below, to be sent and delivered by the private and commercial interstate carrier listed below for each such Count.

     5.   The allegations of paragraphs 1 though 4 above are re-alleged for each of Counts 22 through 25 below as though fully set out therein.

Count	Date	Material
22	April 11, 1999	Approximately 22,000 lbs of annual reports for the year 1998, shipped by Roadway Express, Inc., from the Northern District of Alabama, to Jersey City, New Jersey, for distribution to stockholders.
23	April 7, 2000	Approximately 34,346 lbs of annual reports for the year 1999, shipped by Eagle Global Logistics, Inc., formerly known as EagleUSA, from the Northern District of Alabama, to Jersey City, New Jersey, for distribution to stockholders.
24	April 10, 2001	Approximately 15,750 lbs of annual reports for the year 2000, shipped by Eagle Global Logistics, Inc., formerly known as EagleUSA, from the Northern District of Alabama, to Jersey City, New Jersey, for distribution to stockholders.
25	April 5, 2002	Approximately 27,500 lbs of annual reports for the year 2001, shipped by Wright Transportation, Inc., from the Northern District of Alabama, to Edgewood, New York, for distribution to stockholders.

All in violation of Title 18, United States Code, Sections 1341, 1346 and 2.

COUNTS 26 THROUGH 41
Mail Fraud
Title 18, United States Code, Sections 1341, 1346 and 2

     1.   The Grand Jury repeats and re-alleges the allegations contained in paragraphs 1 through 20 of Count 1 of this Indictment as though fully set out herein.

The Scheme to Defraud
     2.   The Grand Jury repeats and re-alleges the allegations contained in paragraphs 23 through 38 of Count 1 of this Indictment as describing a scheme and artifice to defraud

stockholders, bondholders, potential stockholders and bondholders, bond underwriters, HealthSouth, and others and to obtain money and property by means of materially false and fraudulent pretenses, representations and promises.

    3.   From in or about 1996, the exact date being unknown to the Grand Jury, to on or about March 19, 2003, in Jefferson County in the Northern District of Alabama, and elsewhere, defendant

RICHARD M. SCRUSHY

and others known and unknown to the Grand Jury, devised and intended to devise the above-described scheme and artifice.

Execution of the Scheme

    4.   On or about April 12, 2002, within Jefferson County in the Northern District of Alabama, and elsewhere, defendant **RICHARD M. SCRUSHY**, aided and abetted by others, knowingly and willfully, for the purpose of executing the above-described scheme and artifice and attempting to do so, caused a proxy card, a notice of stockholders meeting, an annual report, and the Form 10-K for the year 2001 to be delivered by mail according to the directions thereon to the person described below for each of said counts, each delivery being within the Northern District of Alabama.

    5.   The allegations of paragraphs 1 though 4 above are re-alleged for each of Counts 26 through 41 below as though fully set out therein.

Count	Person
26	A person with the initials WDH, who lived in Birmingham, Alabama
27	A person with the initials MAD, who lived in Shelby County, Alabama
28	A person with the initials LDH, who lived in Shelby County, Alabama
29	A person with the initials JGH, who lived in Ashville, Alabama
30	A person with the initials ARB, who lived in Birmingham, Alabama
31	A person with the initials GHT, who lived in Birmingham, Alabama
32	A person with the initials SLP, who lived in Birmingham, Alabama
33	A person with the initials DRP, who lived in Birmingham, Alabama

34	A person with the initials TRB, who lived in Bessemer, Alabama
35	A person with the initials NAH, who lived in Sterrett, Alabama
36	A person with the initials CFH, who lived in Trinity, Alabama
37	A person with the initials MGH, who lived in Birmingham, Alabama
38	A person with the initials CRK, who lived in Birmingham, Alabama
39	A person with the initials OEV, who lived in Birmingham, Alabama
40	A person with the initials MPM, who lived in Birmingham, Alabama
41	A person with the initials ALT, who lived in Birmingham, Alabama

All in violation of Title 18, United States Code, Sections 1341, 1346 and 2.

COUNTS 42 through 47
False Statements
Title 18, United States Code, Sections 1001 and 2

1.   The Grand Jury repeats and re-alleges the allegations contained in paragraphs 1 through 20 of Count 1 this Indictment as though fully set out herein.

2.   On or about the dates set forth below for each of Counts 42 through 47, within Jefferson County in the Northern District of Alabama, and elsewhere, defendant

RICHARD M. SCRUSHY

knowingly and willfully caused a materially false, fictitious and fraudulent statement and representation to be made in a matter within the jurisdiction of the executive branch of the government of the United States, that is, the amounts reported for net income for certain periods of time and the value of assets at the end of those periods, in documents filed with the SEC and incorporated statements and representations as described below for each of Counts 42 through 47, in connection with the registration of HealthSouth bonds, were materially overstated as defendant **RICHARD M. SCRUSHY** then and there well knew and believed.

3.   The allegations of paragraphs 1 and 2 above are re-alleged for each of Counts 42 through 47 as though fully set out therein:

Count	Date	Report
42	November 9, 2000	HealthSouth's Form S-4, filed to register bonds with a face value of approximately $350 million
43	December 15, 2000	HealthSouth's amended Form S-4, filed in connection with the registration of the bonds on November 9, 2000
44	March 30, 2001	HealthSouth's Form S-4, filed to register bonds with a face value of approximately $375 million.
45	November 19, 2001	HealthSouth's Form S-4, filed to register bonds with a face value of approximately $600 million
46	June 28, 2002	HealthSouth's Form S-4, filed to register bonds with a face value of approximately $1 billion
47	August 22, 2002	HealthSouth's amended Form S-4, filed in connection with the registration of the bonds on June 28, 2002

All in violation of Title 18, United States Code, Sections 1001 and 2.

COUNT 48
False Certification
Title 18, United States Code, Sections 1350(c)(2) and 2

1.   The Grand Jury repeats and re-alleges the allegations contained in paragraphs 1 through 20 of Count 1 of this Indictment as though fully set out herein.

2.   On or about August 14, 2002, within Jefferson County in the Northern District of Alabama, and elsewhere, defendant

RICHARD M. SCRUSHY

did willfully certify and cause to be certified a statement required by Title 18, United States Code, Section 1350, to be filed with the SEC, that is,

> a statement certifying that the periodic report accompanying the statement, namely, a HealthSouth Form 10-Q (1) fully complied with the requirements of Section 13(a) or 15(d) of the Securities Exchange Act of 1934 and (2) that the information contained therein fairly presented, in all material respects, the financial condition and results of operations of the company,

while knowing that the periodic report so filed did not comport with all of the requirements of Title 18, United States Code, Section 1350, in that as defendant **SCRUSHY** then and there well knew and believed, the information therein did not fairly present, in all material respects, the financial condition and results of operations of HealthSouth because said information materially overstated HealthSouth's net income for each of the periods set forth in the report, and materially overstated the value of HealthSouth's assets at the end of each of said periods.

All in violation of Title 18, United States Code, Sections 1350(c)(2) and 2.

COUNT 49
False Certification
Title 18, United States Code, Sections 1350(c)(2) and 2

1.   The Grand Jury repeats and re-alleges the allegations contained in paragraphs 1 through 20 of Count 1 of this Indictment as though fully set out herein.

2.   On or about November 14, 2002, within Jefferson County in the Northern District of Alabama, and elsewhere, defendant

RICHARD M. SCRUSHY

did cause HealthSouth's chief executive officer and HealthSouth's chief financial officer to willfully certify a statement required by Title 18, United States Code, Section 1350, to be filed with the SEC, that is,

> a statement certifying that the periodic report accompanying the statement, namely, a HealthSouth Form 10-Q (1) fully complied with the requirements of Section 13(a) or 15(d) of the Securities Exchange Act of 1934 and (2) that the information contained therein fairly presented, in all material respects, the financial condition and results of operations of the company,

while knowing that the periodic report so filed did not comport with all of the requirements of Title 18, United States Code, Section 1350, in that as defendant **SCRUSHY** and said officers then and there well knew and believed, the information therein did not fairly present, in all material respects, the financial condition and results of operations of HealthSouth because said information materially overstated HealthSouth's net income for each of the periods set forth in the report, except for the third quarter of 2002, and materially overstated the value of HealthSouth's assets at the end of each of said periods.

28

All in violation of Title 18, United States Code, Sections 1350(c)(2) and 2.

COUNT 50
False Certification, Attempt
Title 18, United States Code, Sections, 1350, 1349, and 2

1.   The Grand Jury repeats and re-alleges the allegations contained in paragraphs 1 through 20 of Count 1 of this Indictment as though fully set out herein.

2.   On or about March 18, 2003, within Jefferson County in the Northern District of Alabama, and elsewhere, defendant

RICHARD M. SCRUSHY,

attempted to cause HealthSouth's chief financial officer to willfully certify a statement required by Title 18, United States Code, Section 1350, to be filed with the SEC, that is,

> a statement certifying that the periodic report accompanying the statement, namely, a HealthSouth Amended Form 10-Q (1) fully complied with the requirements of Section 13(a) or 15(d) of the Securities Exchange Act of 1934 and (2) that the information contained therein fairly presented, in all material respects, the financial condition and results of operations of the company,

while knowing that the periodic report so filed would not comport with all of the requirements of Title 18, United States Code, Section 1350, in that as defendant **SCRUSHY** and said officer then and there well knew and believed, the information therein did not fairly present, in all material respects, the financial condition and results of operations of HealthSouth, in that said information materially overstated HealthSouth's net income for each of the periods set forth in the report, except for the third quarter of 2002, and materially overstated the value of HealthSouth's assets at the end of each of said periods.

All in violation of Title 18, United States Code, Sections 1350(c)(2), 1349 and 2.

COUNT 51-70
Money Laundering
Title 18, United States Code, Sections 1957 and 2

1.   On or about the dates set forth below, within Jefferson County in the Northern District of Alabama, and elsewhere, defendant

RICHARD M. SCRUSHY

did knowingly engage in a monetary transaction by, through, and to a financial institution, affecting interstate and foreign commerce, in criminally derived property of a value greater than $10,000.00, that is, the transfer of funds by wire and monetary instrument as listed below in the amounts listed below, such property having been derived from specified unlawful activity, that is, a scheme and artifice to defraud stockholders, bondholders, potential stockholders and bondholders, bond underwriters, HealthSouth, and others, in violation of Title 18, United States Code, Sections 371, 1341, and 1343, and Title 15, United States Code, Sections 78j(b) and 78ff, as alleged in Counts 1 and 3 through 41 of this Indictment.

2. The allegations set out in paragraph 1 above are re-alleged and incorporated in each Count as though fully set out therein:

Count	Date	Amount	Method of Transfer	Purpose
51	February 1, 2000	$90,000.00	Cashier's Check (1st of 4)	Purchase of 360 acres of real property in Wilcox County, AL
52	February 1, 2000	$90,000.00	Cashier's Check (2nd of 4)	Purchase of 360 acres of real property in Wilcox County, AL
53	February 1, 2000	$90,000.00	Cashier's Check (3rd of 4)	Purchase of 360 acres of real property in Wilcox County, AL
54	February 1, 2000	$90,000.00	Cashier's Check (4th of 4)	Purchase of 360 acres of real property in Wilcox County, AL
55	March 30, 2000	$290,808.00	Wire Transfer	Purchase of 2002 Skater 40-foot racing boat "Monopoly"
56	February 7, 2000	$30,775.00	Check	Design and art work on 2002 Skater 40-foot racing boat "Monopoly"
57	August 29, 2000	$79,000.00	Wire Transfer	Purchase of 2000 GMC Yukon and 2000 GMC Denali
58	September 8, 2000	$45,000.00	Wire Transfer	Purchase of armoring package for 2000 GMC Yukon

59	November 22, 2000	$45,000.00	Wire Transfer	Purchase of armoring package for 2000 GMC Denali
60	October 30, 2000	$302,950.75	Wire Transfer	Purchase of four (4) bronze statutes and seven (7) classic automobiles, including a 1929 Cadillac Dual Cowl Phaeton
61	January 9, 2001	$329,062.53	Check	Purchase of 2000 Rolls-Royce Corniche
62	February 16, 2001	$340,000.00	Check	Purchase of four (4) paintings, including works by Picasso, Renoir, Miro, and Wilson
63	November 15, 2001	$120,300.00	Check	Purchase of four (4) antique Persian-style rugs
64	January 7, 2002	$108,087.00	Check	Purchase of two (2) 2002 Cadillac Escalades
65	May 1, 2002	$214,223.00	Wire Transfer	Purchase of 2002 38-foot Intrepid Walkaround boat
66	June 28, 2002	$266,323.00	Wire Transfer	Purchase of 2003 42-foot Lightning boat, with motor and trailer
67	October 28, 2002	$2,811,524.48	Wire Transfer	Purchase of thirty (30) acres of real property in Gulf Shores, AL
68	December 27, 2002	$370,000.00	Check	Purchase of 21.81 carat emerald-cut diamond platinum ring
69	January 27, 2003	$400,000.00	Check	Purchase of seven (7) paintings, including works by Picasso, Chagall, Miro, and Wilson
70	July 29, 2003	$3,225,000.00	Wire Transfer	Purchase of 2001 Cessna Citation 525 aircraft

All in violation of Title 18, United States Code, Sections 1957 and 2.

COUNT 71
Criminal Forfeiture
Title 18, United States Code, Section 981(a)(1)(C)
and Title 28, United States Code, Section 2461(c)

1.   Counts 1 and 3 through 41 of this Indictment are incorporated by reference herein
for the purpose of alleging forfeiture pursuant to Title 18, United States Code, Section
981(a)(1)(C) and Title 28, United State Code, Section 2461(c).

Forfeiture
2.   As a result of the foregoing offenses alleged in Counts 1 and 3 through 41 of this
Indictment, defendant

RICHARD M. SCRUSHY

shall forfeit to the United States any property, real or personal, which constitutes or is derived
from proceeds traceable to said offenses. Such forfeitable interests include, but are not limited
to the aggregate sum of $278,727,674.35 and all interest and proceeds derived therefrom,
including but not limited to:

xxx.   Residence and compound located at 2406 Longleaf Street, Birmingham, Alabama 35243,
including adjoining real properties located at 2410 Longleaf Street, 2320 Longleaf Way, and
2300 Marin Drive, Birmingham, Alabama, together with all improvements, fixtures, and
appurtenances thereon;

yyy.   Residence and real property located at 1470 Willows End, Alexander City, Alabama 35010,
more particularly described as Lots 19, 20, and 21, Willow Point Phase XII, Tallapoosa County,
Alabama;

zzz.   Residence and real property located at 30524 River Road, Orange Beach, Alabama 36561, more
particularly described as Lot 101, Unit 1, Ono Island Subdivision, Baldwin County, Alabama,
together with all improvements, fixtures, and appurtenances thereon;

aaaa.   Residence and real property located at 1000 N. Lake Way, Palm Beach, Palm Beach County,
Florida 33480, together with all improvements, fixtures, and appurtenances thereon;

bbbb.   One (1) 1992 92-foot Tarrab yacht, "Chez Soiree," Hull No. XED09219D102;

cccc.   One (1) 1998 Cessna Caravan 675 aircraft, FAA Reg. No. N208MM, together with amphibious
floats, and other equipment;

dddd.   Certain real property and commercial building located at 415 Fifth Street, West Palm Beach,
Florida 33401, together with all improvements, fixtures, and appurtenances thereon;

32

eeee.   Four items of diamond jewelry:

(lxxvi) One (1) diamond bracelet, with 30 emerald-cut stones (totaling 48.71 carats);
(lxxvii)One (1) fancy yellow radian-cut diamond ring (9.69 carats), with two (2) white trillions (1.40 car
(lxxviii)One pair of round-cut diamond stud earrings (6.08 carats); and
(lxxix) One (1) fancy yellow diamond bracelet with 48 diamonds (14.06 carats);

   i.   Certain real property known as the "Bissell property," located on Highway 180, Gulf Shores,
           Baldwin County, Alabama;

   j.   Certain real property known as Walker Marina, Orange Beach, Baldwin County, Alabama
           36561, together with all improvements, fixtures, and appurtenances thereon; and

      k.   One (1) 2003 Lamborghini Murcielago, VIN ZA9BC10U33LA12454.

3.   If any of the property described above as being subject to forfeiture pursuant to

Title 18, United States Code, Section 981(a)(1)(C) and Title 28, United States Code, Section

2461(c), as a result of any act or omission of the defendant **RICHARD M. SCRUSHY**

   (1) cannot be located upon the exercise of due diligence;

   (2) has been transferred or sold to, or deposited with, a third person;

   (3) has been placed beyond the jurisdiction of the Court;

   (4) has been substantially diminished in value; or

   (5) has been commingled with other property that cannot be subdivided without

   difficulty;

it is the intent of the United States, pursuant to Title 21, United States Code, Section 853(p), to

seek forfeiture of any other property of said defendant **RICHARD M. SCRUSHY** up to the

value of the above forfeitable property.

All pursuant to Title 18, United States Code, Section 981and Title 28, United States

Code, Section 2461.

COUNTS 72-85
Criminal Forfeiture
Title 18, United States Code, Section 982(a)(1)

1. Counts 1 and 3 through 41 of this Indictment are incorporated by reference herein for the purpose of alleging forfeiture pursuant to Title 18, United States Code, Section 982(a)(1).

Forfeiture

2. As a result of the foregoing offenses alleged in Counts 51 through 70 of this Indictment, as identified below, defendant

RICHARD M. SCRUSHY

shall forfeit to the United States any property, real and personal, involved in such offenses, or any property traceable to such property; to-wit:

Count	Property Involved in Offense, or Traceable to Offense	Offense Count
72	360 acres of real property located near Highway 21, Wilcox County, Alabama (known as "Marin Plantation"), together with all fixtures, improvements, and appurtenances thereon	51, 52, 53, 54
73	One (1) 2002 Skater 40-foot racing boat, "Monopoly," Hull No. DUX00665C004042, Alabama Decal No. AL2185SP	55, 56
74	(a) One (1) 2000 GMC Yukon, VIN 3GKGK26U0YG219700, Alabama license number 1C5968M (b) One (1) 2000 GMC Denali, VIN 1GKEK63R6YR216069, Alabama license number 1B5906W	57, 58, 59
75	One (1) 1929 Cadillac Dual Cowl Phaeton, VIN 334647	60
76	One (1) 2000 Rolls-Royce Corniche, VIN SCAZK29E3YCX68035	61
77	Four Paintings: (a) *Profil de Femme,* by Pablo Picasso (b) *Enfants Jouant a la Balle,* by Pierre-August Renoir (c) *Le Visage S'invente,* by Joan Miro (d) *Carrie's and Don's Uncle Ezra's Birthday Dinner,* by Donald Roller Wilson.	62

78	(a) One (1) antique rug from Persia (b) One (1) antique rug from India (c) One (1) antique rug from Turkey (d) One rug from Egypt.	63
79	(a) One (1) 2002 Cadillac Escalade, VIN GYEK63N52R143755 (b) One (1) 2002 Cadillac Escalade, VIN YEK63NX2G225769	64
80	One (1) 2002 38-foot Intrepid Walkaround water craft, Hull No. 1BW37075B202, Alabama Decal No. 1389AV	65
81	One (1) 2003 42-foot Lightning boat, Hull No. FGQ42518DD203, with 2003 Mercruiser motor, Serial No. 0M053088, and 2001 Vanguard trailer, Serial No. 45JC2H93311000879	66
82	Thirty (30) acres of real property located along Highway 182 (also known as Perdido Beach Boulevard), Gulf Shores, Baldwin County, Alabama	67
83	One (1) 21.81 carat emerald-cut diamond platinum ring	68
84	Seven Paintings: (a) *Tete de Femme I*, by Pablo Picasso (b) *L'echelle au Ciel*, by Marc Chagall (c) *Grande Corniche*, by Marc Chagall (d) *Neat Piet*, by Patrick Hughes (e) *L'ogre Enjou*, by Joan Miro (f) *L'oiseau Mongol*, by Joan Miro (g) *Cookie...She Had Seen It*, by Donald Roller Wilson	69
85	One (1) 2001 Cessna Citation 525 aircraft, FAA Reg. No. N525BR or N525WS, together with two (2) Williams FJ441A engines, bearing serial numbers 1901 and 1902, respectively	70

If any of the property described above in Counts 72-85 as being subject to forfeiture pursuant to Title 18, United States Code, Section 982, as a result of any act or omission of the defendant, **RICHARD M. SCRUSHY,**

(1) cannot be located upon the exercise of due diligence;

(2) has been transferred or sold to, or deposited with, a third person;

(3) has been placed beyond the jurisdiction of the Court;

(4) has been substantially diminished in value; or

(5) has been commingled with other property that cannot be subdivided without difficulty;

it is the intent of the United States, pursuant to Title 18, United States Code, Section 982(b)(1), to seek forfeiture of any other property of said defendant

RICHARD M. SCRUSHY

up to the value of the above forfeitable property.

All pursuant to Title 18, United States Code, Section 982.

A TRUE BILL.

_____
Foreperson

_____ _____
ALICE H. MARTIN   JOSHUA R. HOCHBERG
United States Attorney   Chief, Fraud Section
Northern District of Alabama   Criminal Division
                                       United States Department of Justice

_____ _____
MICHAEL V. RASMUSSEN   RICHARD C. SMITH
Assistant United States Attorney   Deputy Chief, Fraud Section
Northern District of Alabama   Criminal Division
                                       United States Department of Justice

_____ _____
JAMES D. INGRAM   RICHARD N. WIEDIS
Assistant United States Attorney   Senior Trial Attorney, Fraud Section
Northern District of Alabama   Criminal Division
                                       United States Department of Justice

Notes

Introduction

1. In June of 2005, HealthSouth announced that it would pay $100 million to resolve SEC claims against the company (see "Healthsouth Reaches Agreement with the Securities and Exchange Commission," press release, HealthSouth.com, 9 June 2005). At the time of this writing, Richard Scrushy still faces civil charges by the SEC (see Marcy Gordon, "Scrushy Still Faces SEC Civil Charges," The Associated Press, 29 June 2005).

2. The SEC's charges can be read in full online at http://www.sec.gov/litigation/complaints/comphealths.htm. Securities and Exhange Commission, Plaintiff, v HealthSouth Corporation and Richard M. Scrushy, Defendants, Civil Action no. CV-03-J-0615-5.

Chapter 1

1. Yahoo! Finance HRC Message Board, Message #52, dated (incorrectly) 31 December 1969, Message #52 (#4342 responds to #52 from 22 January 1998).

2. Ibid., Message #82, 16 February 1998.

3. John Helyar, "The Insatiable King Richard," *Fortune*, 23 June 2003.

Chapter 2

1. "A Biographical Sketch: Richard Scrushy and HealthSouth," http://www.richardmscrushy.com.

2. Carrick Mollenkamp, "Behind Scrushy's Courtroom Defense, Shifting Teams and Feuding Lawyers." *The Wall Street Journal*, 2 February 2005.

3. United States of America v. Richard M. Scrushy, CR-03-BE-530-S, Birmingham, Alabama, 25 January 2005. Transcript of Trial before The Honorable Karon O. Bowdre, U.S. District Judge, and jury, opening statements.

4. John Helyar, "The Insatiable King Richard," *Fortune*, 23 June 2003.

5. Ibid.

6. Ibid.

7. Jeffrey L. Rodengen, *The Story of HealthSouth*. The Write Stuff Enterprises, 2002.

8. Ibid.

9. Ibid.

10. Ibid.

11. Ibid.

12. Helyar, "The Insatiable King Richard."

13. Rodengen, *The Story of HealthSouth*.

14. Ibid., pp. 68, 73.

15. Ibid., p. 87.

16. Helyar, "The Insatiable King Richard."

17. Rodengen, *The Story of HealthSouth*.

18. Ibid.

19. Helyar, "The Insatiable King Richard."

20. Personal communication with Bryan Marsal, July 2005.

21. Helyar, "The Insatiable King Richard."

22. Kyle Whitmire, "Scrushy Watch: All the King's Lawyers; A Short History of the Long Trial of Richard Scrushy," *Birmingham Weekly*, 19–26 May 2005.

23. Department of Justice press release, "Government Seeks More Than $278 Million in Forfeiture," 4 November 2003.

24. Whitmire, "Scrushy Watch: All the King's Lawyers."

25. Helyar, "The Insatiable King Richard."

26. Ibid.

27. Greg Farrell, "From Emperor to Outcast," *USA Today*, 7 July 2004.

28. Rodengen, *The Story of HealthSouth*.

29. Helyar, "The Insatiable King Richard."

30. Interview with former HealthSouth Area Manager, Becky Trimber, June 2005.

31. Personal e-mail communication with Scooterpass, 2 July 2005.

Chapter 3

1. Jonathan Carson and James Felton, *International Corporate Governance*, 2nd Edition, Euromoney Institutional Investor, January 2004.

2. Debt, Yahoo! Enron Message Board, Message #11460, 1 March 2000.

3. Yahoo! Finance HRC Message Board, Message #98, 1 March 1998.

4. Ibid., Message #127, 11 March 1998.

5. Ibid., Message #128, 11 March 1998.

6. Ibid., Message #64, 26 January 1998.

7. Ibid., Message #248, 22 July 1998.

8. Ibid., Message #527, 28 August 1998.

9. Ibid., Message #250, 22 July 1998.

10. Ibid., Message #251, 22 July 1998.

11. Ibid., Message #354, 6 August 1998.

12. Ibid., Message #839, 2 October 1998.

13. Ibid., Message #607, 21 September 1998.

14. Ibid., Message #1265, 28 October 1998.

15. Ibid., Message #1275, 24 October 1998.

16. Ibid., Message #1246, 23 October 1998.

17. Ibid., Message #723, 30 September 1998.

18. James Surowiecki, *The Wisdom of Crowds*, Doubleday, June 2004.

19. Ibid.

20. Personal communication with Bryan Marsal, July 2005.

21. Yahoo! Finance HRC Message Board, Message #1224, 21 October 1998.

Chapter 4

1. John Helyar, "The Insatiable King Richard," *Fortune*, June 23, 2003.

2. "Complaint for Injunction and Relief," Security and Exchange Commission v HealthSouth Corporation and Richard M. Scrushy, U.S. District Court, Northern District of Alabama, Civil Action no. CV-03-J-0615-S, March 2003.

3. Peter Elkind, "Vulgarians at the Gate," *Fortune*, 21 June 1999.

4. Ibid.

5. Helyar, "The Insatiable King Richard."

6. Jerry Underwood. William Owens's Testimony as reported in "Loss of Soul Sad Legacy of HealthSouth," *The Birmingham News*, Sunday, 20 February 2005.

7. United States of America v Richard M. Scrushy, Case no. CR-03-BE 0530-S, 29 October 2003, U.S. District Court N.D. of Alabama, Southern Division.

8. Reed Abelson and Milt Freudenheim, "The Scrushy Mix: Strict and So Lenient," *The New York Times*, 20 April 2003.

9. Yahoo! Finance HRC Message Board, Message #354, 6 August 1998.

10. Ibid., Message #518, 26 August 1998.

11. Ibid., Message #503, 22 August 1998.

12. Ibid., Message #501, 21 August 1998.

13. Ibid., Message #991, 9 October 1998.

14. Ibid., Message #924, 9 October 1998.

15. Ibid., Message #963, 9 October 1998.

16. United States Department of Justice press release, "Health-South Corporation Pays Nearly $8 Million for Overcharging U.S. Health Care Programs," 22 May 2001, www.usdoj.gov. According to the DOJ's press release, "HealthSouth Corporation . . . has agreed to pay $7.9 million to settle allegations of health care fraud . . . The settlement resolves allegations that the Birmingham, Alabama-based company overcharged Medicare and the Defense Department's TRICARE program for equipment and supplies purchased from G.G. Enterprises, a corporation owned by the parents of HealthSouth's CEO, Richard Scrushy. The government alleged that HealthSouth improperly billed these items at a price above G.G. Enterprises' costs, in violation of Medicare's and TRICARE's rules for transactions with related entities. The settlement also resolves allegations that HealthSouth overbilled the health care programs for rental payments and the costs of an abandoned computer system."

17. Yahoo! Finance HRC Message Board, Message #1235, 22 October 1998.

18. Ibid., Message #1292, 25 October 1998.

19. Ibid., Message #1394, 28 October 1998.

20. Ibid., Message #1285, 24 October 1998.

21. Ibid., Message #1268, 24 October 1998.

22. Michael Moss, "HealthSouth CEO Exposes, Sues Anonymous Online Critics," *The Wall Street Journal*, 7 July 1999.

23. Yahoo! Finance HRC Message Board, Message #1096, 16 October 1998.

24. Moss, "HealthSouth CEO Exposes, Sues Anonymous Online Critics."

25. Yahoo! Finance HRC Message Board, Message #1495, 31 October 1998.

26. Ibid., Message #1514, 2 November 1998.

27. Ibid., Message #1418, 29 October 1998.

28. Ibid., Message #1499, 1 November 1998.

29. Ibid., Message #1503, 1 November 1998.

30. Ibid., Message #2481, 15 February 1999.

31. Moss, "HealthSouth CEO Exposes, Sues Anonymous Online Critics."

32. Yahoo! Finance HRC Message Board, Message #544, 2 September 1998.

33. Ibid., Message #547, 3 September 1998.

34. Ibid., Message #904, 6 October 1998.

35. Ibid., Message #914, 6 October 1998.

36. Ibid., Message #1027, 12 October 1998.

37. Ibid., Message #1072, 15 October 1998.

38. Ibid., Message #1361, 28 October 1998.

39. Moss, "HealthSouth CEO Exposes, Sues Anonymous Online Critics."

40. Michael Tomberlin, "HealthSouth Pursues Suit over Attacks on Internet," *The Birmingham News*, 8 July 1999.

41. Yahoo! Finance HRC Message Board, Message #3975, 7 July 1999.

42. Ibid., Message #3997, 7 July 1999.

43. Ibid., Message #4045, 9 July 1999.

44. *The Wall Street Journal* Interactive Edition, 27 July 1999.

45. Robert Lemos, "Online Privacy Shoved to Forefront," ZDNet News, 18 July 1999; http://news.zdnet.com/21009595_22515172 .html?legacy=zdnn.

46. Yahoo! Finance HRC Message Board, Message #12198, 22 February 2000.

47. Elkind, "Vulgarians at the Gate."

48. Yahoo! Finance HRC Message Board, Message #12198, 22 February 2000.

49. Personal e-mail communication with Bopper63, June 2005.

50. Personal telephone communication with Kim Landry, November 2004.

51. Yahoo! Finance HRC Message Board, 20 March 2003. Landry's case never came to court. Landry, represented by pro bono attorney Jill Craft of Baton Rouge, later met with HealthSouth's new management. She was happy with her settlement, which, she said, did not require her to recant her posts, and she remained steadfast that she had told the truth. When I reached Landry by phone, she said that she had decided to put the entire episode behind her and no longer had even an e-mail address, in essence starting a new life.

Chapter 5

1. Trial testimony of CFOs Owens, Martin & Ken Livesay: http://www.scrushy-report.com/wordpress/index.php?m=200502.

2. Bob Johnson and Marcy Gordon, "Scrushy Acquitted of Fraud at HealthSouth," Associated Press, 28 June 2005.

3. http://www.smartmoney.com/search/Jan 1999.

4. Jerry Underwood, "HealthSouth Will Divide," *The Birmingham News*, Business 15 June 1999.

5. Yahoo! Finance HRC Message Board, Message #4308, 3 August 1999.

6. Ibid., Message #3618, 18 May 1999.

7. Ibid., Message #3619, 18 May 1999.

8. Ibid., Message #7131, 14 October 1999.

9. Susan Strickland, "Scrushy Party Merrily Combines Folks from Many Walks of Life," *The Birmingham News*, Lifestyle, 16 December 1999.

10. Yahoo! Finance HRC Message Board, Message #9920, 29 December 1999.

11. Ibid., Message #9923, 29 December 1999.

12. Ibid., Message #9927, 30 December 1999.

13. Michael Tomberlin, "After 15 Rocky Months, Scrushy Upbeat on 2000," *The Birmingham News*, Business, 9 January 2000.

14. Ibid.

15. Yahoo! Finance HRC Message Board, Message #10123, 3 January 2000.

16. "Money Briefs," *The Birmingham News*, 7 March 2000.

17. Yahoo! Finance HRC Message Board, Message #15690, 6 July 2000.

18. Ibid., Message #13556, 10 March 2000.

19. "Scrushy Takes a Pay Cut," *The Birmingham News*, 20 April 2000.

20. Ibid.

21. Yahoo! Finance HRC Message Board, Message #15910, 18 July 2000.

22. Ibid., Message #16570, 5 September 2000.

23. Ibid., Message #16573, 16 November 2000.

24. Ibid., Message #17576, 18 November 2000.

25. Ibid., Message #17907, 28 December 2000.

26. "Update 6: Witness: Scrushy Advised 'Hang in There,'" Associated Press, Forbes.com, 25 February 2005.

27. "Scrushy: 'We've Turned the Corner!!'" *The Birmingham News*, 28 January 2001.

28. Yahoo! Finance HRC Message Board, Message #17998, 1 January 2001.

29. "UBS Warburg Analyst Likes HealthSouth: Howard Capek Interview, The Wall Street Transcript," TWST.com, 7 February 2001.

30. "UBS Analyst Forced Out for Remark," *The New York Times*, 3 July 2003.

31. Jeffrey L. Rodengen, *The Story of HealthSouth*, The Write Stuff Enterprises, Inc., 2002.

32. Yahoo! Finance HRC Message Board, Message #18682, 28 March 2001.

33. "HealthSouth Settles Case: Company Pays $8 Million in Medicare Overbilling Lawsuit," *The Birmingham News*, 23 May 2001.

34. Yahoo! Finance HRC Message Board, Message #18968, 24 May 2001.

35. Ibid., Message #19023, 9 June 2001.

36. Ibid., Message #19049, 14 June 2001.

37. Ibid., Message #19053, 16 June 2001.

38. Ibid., Message #19193, 8 August 2001.

39. Ibid., Message #19294, 1 September 2001.

40. Ibid., Message #19282, 28 August 2001.

41. Ibid., Message #19296, 3 September 2001.

42. Ibid., Message #19297, 3 September 2001.

43. Ibid., Message #19317, 7 September 2001.

44. Ibid., Message #19386, 28 October 2001.

45. Monte Burke, "Back to Life," *Forbes*, 21 January 2002.

46. *The Birmingham News*, 17 January 2002.

47. John Helyar, "The Insatiable King Richard," *Fortune*, 23 June 2003.

48. Department of Justice press release, "HealthSouth to Pay United States $325 Million to Resolve Medicare Fraud Allegations," 30 December 2004, http://www.usdoj.gov.

49. Yahoo! Finance HRC Message Board, Message #20124, 5 February 2002

50. Ibid., Message #20224, 6 March 2002.

51. Department of Justice press release, 30 December 2004.

52. "Scrushy Wants James to Retract Comments," *The Birmingham News*, 21 March 2002.

53. Yahoo! Finance HRC Message Board, Message #20343, 13 March 2002.

54. Ibid., Message #20202, 28 February 2002.

55. Scott DeCarlo, "Pay vs. Performance," *Forbes*, 13 May 2002.

56. HealthSouth press release, "HealthSouth Defends CEO Scrushy," *Birmingham Business Journal*, 2 May 2002.

57. Yahoo! Finance HRC Message Board, Message #20570, 26 April 2002.

58. "Smith Testifies about Final Days," *The Birmingham News*, 21 March 2005.

59. Yahoo! Finance HRC Message Board, Message #20597, 29 April 2002.

60. Ibid., Message #20777, 17 May 2002.

61. Ibid., Message #20824, 25 May 2002.

62. Ibid., Message #20827, 27 May 2002.

63. HealthSouth press release, "HealthSouth Defends Scrushy's Sale of 5.27 Million Shares," *The Birmingham News*, 14 May 2002.

64. Yahoo! Finance HRC Message Board, Message #20637, 2 May 2002.

65. Department of Justice press release, 30 December 2004.

66. "Group Backs Lawsuit against New HealthSouth Hospital," *Birmingham Business Journal*, 27 June 2002, http://www.bizjol.com/Birmingham/stories/2002/06/24/daily32/html.

67. Michel Tomberlin, "HealthSouth Hit, Rebounds: Scrushy Blames Unfounded Rumors about Accounting," *The Birmingham News*, Business, 12 July 2002.

68. Russell Hubbard, "Scrushy Operated Net of Private Firms," *The Birmingham News*, 24 March 2003.

69. Helyar, "The Insatiable King Richard."

70. Ibid.

Chapter 6

1. Russell Hubbard, "Scrushy's Troubles Reach Personal Firms," *The Birmingham News*, 28 March 2003.

2. John Helyar, "The Insatiable King Richard," *Fortune*, 23 June 2003.

3. Tom Bassing, "HealthSouth Lawsuit Is Now in Judge's Hands," *Birmingham Business Journal*, 1 November 2002.

4. Yahoo! Finance HRC Message Board, Message #22087, 27 August 2002.

5. United States of America v Richard M. Scrushy, Case no. CR O# BE 0530-S, U.S. District Court, No. District Alabama, Southern Division, 29 October 2003.

6. Andy Serwer, "HealthSouth's Go-to Guy," *Fortune*, 28 April 2003.

7. Ann Carrns and Nicole Harris, "HealthSouth Stock Falls 44% on Sharp Cuts to Its Forecast," *The Wall Street Journal*, 28 August 2002.

8. Ibid.

9. Yahoo! Finance HRC Message Board, Message #24256, 29 August 2002.

10. Ibid., Message #24231, 29 August 2002.

11. William Borden, "HRC Shares Drop 57%," Reuters, 28 August 2002.

12. Ibid.

13. "HealthSouth Gave Heavily to Campaigns." *The Birmingham News*, 31 August 2002.

14. "Ala. Looks at Political Donations by HealthSouth," Associated Press, *USA Today*, 11 August 2004.

15. "Probe of Siegelman's Administration May Go into Summer," *The Birmingham News*, 18 May 2005.

16. Ibid., *The Birmingham News*, 31 August 2002.

17. Yahoo! Finance HRC Message Board, Message #22880, 28 August 2002.

18. Ibid., Message #24683, 30 August 2002.

19. Russel Hubbard, "Surgery Centers Face 14 Lawsuits," *The Birmingham News*, Business, 15 September 2002.

20. "HealthSouth Shares Dive 36% During Week," *The Birmingham News*, Business, 22 September 2002.

21. Russell Hubbard, "Scrushy's Job Appears Stable at Health-South," *The Birmingham News*, Business, 29 September 2002.

22. "Diagnosis of Fraud," *Financial Times*, 15 April 2003.

23. Russell Hubbard, "Scrushy Open to Changes on Board at HealthSouth," *The Birmingham News*, 3 October 2002.

24. Yahoo! Finance HRC Message Board, Message #36557, 16 October 2002.

25. Russell Hubbard, "Board Member Striplin Wins $5 Million Healthsouth Construction Contract," *The Birmingham News*, 6 October 2002.

26. Russell Hubbard, "Director Resigns from HealthSouth Litigation Panel," *The Birmingham News*, 15 October 2002.

27. Yahoo! Finance HRC Message Board, Message #36195, 14 October 2002.

28. "Lawyers Probe Clears Scrushy," *The Birmingham News*, 31 October 2002.

29. Ibid.

30. Yahoo! Finance HRC Message Board, Message #38555, 31 October 2002.

31. Ibid., Message #38552, 31 October 2002.

32. Ann Carrns, "HealthSouth Swings to Loss on Restructuring Charges," *The Wall Street Journal*, 4 March 2003.

33. Betsy Atkins, "My 16 Days on the HealthSouth Board," *The Corporate Board Member*, November/December 2003.

34. Ibid.

35. Yahoo! Finance HRC Message Board, Message #50106, 18 March 2003.

36. Ibid., Message #50121, 18 March 2003.

37. Ibid., Message #50115, 18 March 2003.

38. Ibid., Message #50228, 19 March 2003.

39. Ibid., Message #50879, 19 March 2003.

40. Ibid., Message #50227, 19 March 2003.

41. "HealthSouth Raided by the FBI," SRiForum Limited, Corporate Governance, 19 March 2003, 11:24.

42. Yahoo! Finance HRC Message Board, Message #51353, 20 March 2003.

43. Ibid., Message #50343, 19 March 2003.

44. Atkins, "My 16 Days on the HealthSouth Board."

45. Ibid.

46. Ibid.

47. Ibid.

48. Yahoo! Finance HRC Message Board, Message #53447, 25 March 2003.

49. Ibid., Message #51224, 20 March 2003.

50. Simon Romero and Reed Abelson, "HealthSouth Officials Seek to Cut Deals with the U.S.," *The New York Times*, 24 March 2003.

51. Department of Justice press release, "Government Seeks More Than $278 M in Forfeiture," 4 November 2003, http://www.fbi.gov/dojpressrel/health110403.htm.

52. Department of Justice press release, "HealthSouth Executive William Owens Charged in Corporate Fraud Conspiracy," 26 March 2003, http://www.usdoj.gov/opa/pr/2003/March/03_crm_180.htm.

53. Greg Farrell, "Former HealthSouth CEO Scrushy Turns Televangelist," *USA Today*, 25 October 2004.

54. Dan Ackman, "For Years, HealthSouth Could Do No Wrong," Forbes.com, 31 March 2003, http://www.forbes.com/2003/03/31/ox_da_0331topnews.html.

55. "The Trader," *Barron's*, 24 March 2003.

56. Russell Hubbard, "HRC Shares at Risk, Dow Jones Says Banks Blocked Line of Credit," *The Birmingham News*, 21 March 2003.

57. Ibid.

58. Romero and Abelson, "HealthSouth Officials Seek to Cut Deals with the U.S." *The New York Times.*

59. "Audit Firm, Banks Face Scrutiny," *The Birmingham News*, 27 March 2003.

60. House Committee on Energy and Commerce, W.J. Tauzin, Chairman, Mr. James Lamphron, Former HealthSouth Engagement Partner for Ernst & Young, The Financial Collapse of HealthSouth, 5 November 2003, http://energycommerce.house.gov/108/Hearings/11052003hearing1123/hearing.htm.

61. Russell Hubbard, "Scrushy Operated Net of Private Firms," *The Birmingham News*, 24 March 2003.

62. Ibid.

63. Simon Romero and Riva Atlas, "New Charges Expected at HealthSouth," *The New York Times*, 25 March 2003.

64. House Committee on Energy and Commerce, The Financial Collapse of HealthSouth.

65. "NYSE Suspends Trading in HRC and Will Apply to SEC to Delist the Company," press release, 25 March 2003. http://www.nyse.com/Frameset.html?displayPage=/press/1048903219735.html.

66. Yahoo! Finance HRC Message Board, Message #53428, 25 March 2003.

67. Ibid., Message #32423, 19 October 2003.

68. Personal communication, Bryan Marsal, July 2005.

69. Ibid.

70. "From Emperor to Outcast," *USA Today*, 29 May 2003.

71. Laura Santini, "On the Mend," *Investment Dealer's Digest*, 23 February 2004.

72. Ibid.

Chapter 7

1. Yahoo! Finance HRC Message Board, Message #50265, 19 March 2003.

2. Ibid., Message #50823, 19 March 2003.

3. Ibid., Message #53049, 24 March 2003.

4. Ibid., Message #50944, 19 March 2003.

5. Ibid., Message #50922, 19 March 2003.

6. Ibid., Message #51009, 19 March 2003.

7. Ibid., Message #51372, 20 March 2003.

8. Ibid., Message #51139, 19 March 2003.

9. Ibid., Message #51180, 19 March 2003.

10. Ibid., Message #51469, 20 March 2003.

11. Ibid., Message #51564, 20 March 2003.

12. Ibid., Message #53479, 25 March 2003.

13. Ibid., Message #53497, 25 March 2003.

14. Ibid., Message #53522, 22 March 2003.

15. Ibid., Message #51569, 20 March 2003.

16. Ibid., Message #52818, 23 March 2003.

17. Ibid., Message #54587, 31 March 2003.

18. Ibid., Message #53765, 26 March 2003.

19. Ibid., Message #54732, 1 April 2003.

20. Ibid., Message #55669, 9 April 2003.

21. Ibid., Message #55714, 9 April 2003.

22. Ibid., Message #55686, 9 April 2003.

23. Personal communication with JRM30655.

24. Yahoo! Finance HRC Message Board, Message #59914, 10 May 2003.

25. Ibid., Message #59917, 10 May 2003.

26. Ibid., Message #59938, 10 May 2003.

27. Ibid., Message #60857, 15 May 2003.

28. Ibid., Message #60917, 15 May 2003.

29. House Committee on Energy and Commerce, The Financial Collapse of HealthSouth, W.J. Tauzin, Chairman, Mr. James Lamphron, Former HealthSouth Engagement Partner for Ernst & Young, 5 November 2003, http://energycommerce.house.gov/108/Hearings/11052003hearing1123/hearing.htm.

30. Yahoo! Finance HRC Message Board, Message #70662, 16 June 2003.

31. Ibid., Message #71852, 19 June 2003.

32. Ibid., Message #70843, 17 June 2003.

33. Ibid., Message #70856, 17 June 2003.

34. Ibid., Message #71120, 18 March 2003.

35. Ibid., Message #72336, 20 June 2003.

36. Ibid., Message #72345, 20 June 2003.

37. Ibid., Message #76543, 1 July 2003.

38. Ibid., Message #78845, 4 July 2003.

39. Ibid., Message #80245, 7 July 2003.

40. Ibid., Message #80545, 7 July 2003.

41. Ibid., Message #50585, 19 March 2003.

42. Ibid., Message #80661, 7 July 2003.

43. Ibid., Message #81306, 7 July 2003.

44. Ibid., Message #80681, 7 July 2003.

45. William Borden and Randell Piersen, "HealthSouth May Avoid Bankruptcy," Reuters, 7 July 2003.

46. http://www.sec.gov/Archives/edgar/data/785161/000100515003001110/ex99.txt.

47. Michael Fitzgerald, "Group Rethink: Can Technology Raise Society's IQ," *Technology Review*, Massachusetts's Institute of Technology, June 2005.

Chapter 8

1. Dan Morse and Evan Perez, "Legal Sideshow at Scrushy Trial Takes New Turn," *The Wall Street Journal*, 18 May 2005.

2. "Court Rules Two HealthSouth Sentences Oddly Lenient," Associated Press report, 22 June 2005.

3. United States of America v Richard M. Scrushy, Case no. CR-03-BE-0530-S.

4. Ibid.

5. Morse and Perez, "Legal Sideshow at Scrushy Trial Takes New Turn."

6. Carrick Mollenkamp, "Behind Scrushy's Courtroom Defense, Shifting Strategies and Feuding Lawyers," *The Wall Street Journal*, 2 February 2005.

7. Lance Griffin, "A Hick with a Heart," *The Dothan Eagle*, 21 December 2004.

8. Morse and Perez, "Legal Sideshow at Scrushy Trial Takes New Turn."

9. Clemon dismissed the charges against Siegelman the day after the trial began (John Davis and Jannell McGrew, "Rulings Displease Federal Prosecutor," *The Montgomery Advertiser*, 6 October 2004). As of this writing, a grand jury investigation into other corruption charges against Siegelman continues (Phillip Rawls, "Grand Jury Probes Siegelman Transportation Dealings," *The Decatur Daily*, 13 May 2005).

10. Morse and Perez, "Legal Sideshow at Scrushy Trial Takes New Turn."

11. "Scrushy Judge Reveals Friendship with Defendant's Daughter," *Birmingham Business Journal*, 16 May 2005.

12. Ibid.

13. "Highlights of Arguments Challenging the Constitutionality of Sarbanes-Oxley and Multiplicity of Counts," News Service Web site, http://richardmscrushy.com.

14. Jeffrey L. Rodengen, *The Story of HealthSouth*, The Write Stuff Enterprises, Chapter 2 , 2002.

15. CRS Report for Congress, "Criminal Charges in Corporate Scandals," Congressional Research Service, The Library of Congress, 16 July 2004.

16. Ibid.

17. Michael Tomberlin and Russell Hubbard, "Variety of Interests Found in Jurors' Backgrounds," *The Birmingham News*, 2 June 2005.

18. Ibid.

19. Greg Farrell, "Former HealthSouth CEO Scrushy Turns Evangelist," *USA Today*, 25 October 2004.

20. "Farrell's USA Today Article Incorrect," News Service, http://richardmscrushy.com, 5 November 2004.

21. United States of America v Richard M. Scrushy, CR-03-BE-530-S, Transcript, Opening comments. Transcripts are also available for purchase from the court: Court Reporter Teresa Roberson, 1-205-492-2483, 1729 North 5th Avenue, Birmingham, Alabama 35203.

22. Ibid.

23. Ibid.

24. Ibid.

25. Ibid.

26. Ibid.

27. Ibid.

28. Ibid.

29. Ibid.

30. Ibid.

31. Ibid.

32. Ibid.

33. Ibid.

34. Phil Smith, "Parkman's Web," Scrushy-Report.com, 15 February 2005.

35. United States of America v Richard M. Scrushy, Transcript, Opening Comments

36. Ibid.

37. Ibid.

38. Ibid.

39. Ibid.

40. Ibid.

41. Ibid.

42. United States of America v Richard M. Scrushy, Court Transcripts, Day 1.

43. Rodengen, *The Story of HealthSouth*.

44. Kyle Whitmire, "When the Wheels Fell Off the Wagon," *The Birmingham Weekly*, Scrushy Watch, Volume 8 Issue 24, 17 February 2005, http://www.bhamweekly.com.

45. Phil Smith, "Report from Birmingham: The Bride and Groom, Owens Takes the Stand," Scrushy-Report.com, 1 February 2005.

46. Kyle Whitmire, "A Short History of the Long Trial of Richard Scrushy," *The Birmingham Weekly,* Volume 8 Issue 38.

47. United States of America v Richard M. Scrushy, Court Transcripts, Opening Comments.

48. Whitmire, "When the Wheels Fell off the Wagon."

49. Carrie Johnson, "Jury Hears Tapes in Scrushy's Fraud Trial," *The Washington Post*, 10 February 2005, p. E01.

50. United States of America v Richard M. Scrushy, Court Transcripts, Day 16.

51. Michael Tomberlin, "Notebook Adds Twist to Trial," *The Birmingham News*, 20 February 2005.

52. Phil Smith, "The Defense and Leif Murphy's Cross-Examination," Scrushy-Report.com, 17 February 2005.

53. United States of America v Richard M. Scrushy, Court Transcripts, Day 18.

54. "Scrushy Watch: Zero Sum Game: Day 47," *The Birmingham Weekly*, 5–12 May 2005.

55. United States of America v Richard M. Scrushy, Court Transcripts, Day 20.

56. Kyle Whitmire, "Jumping 'Over the Wall," Scrushy Watch, Volume 8, Issue 27, *The Birmingham Weekly*, 10–17 March 2005.

57. Kyle Whitmire, "Spin Cycle: Killer Instinct," (Trial Days 25, 26 & 27), *The Birmingham Weekly*, 30 June 2005.

58. Jay Reeves, "HealthSouth Trial Reveals Redneck Tactics," The Associated Press, 27 March 2005.

59. Alex Stuart, "Keeping Secrets," *CFO Magazine*, 1 June 2005.

60. "Trial Days: March 15, 16, and 17," *The Birmingham News* (Extra Coverage), 19 March 2005.

61. Ibid.

62. "New Laws Triggered End to HealthSouth Fraud," The Associated Press, 4 February 2005, MSNBC.com.

63. "Smith: Bodyguards Part of Scrushy's Intimidation," *The Birmingham News*, 30 March 2005.

64. "Bowdre Chastises Prosecutors for Gun Comments," *The Birmingham News*, 30 March 2005.

65. United States of America v Richard M. Scrushy, CR-03-BE-530-S, Transcript, Closing Statements, Volume LVIII, 18 May 2005.

Chapter 9

1. Greg Farrell, "Scrushy Sticks to His Defense: They're All Lying," *USA Today*, 11 May 2003.

2. Capital Confirmation, Inc., Case Studies: Audit Confirmation Fraud: HealthSouth, (Tauzin), http://www.capitalconfirmation.com/ Confirmation_Frauds/ConfirmationFrauds.asp#Fraud2.

3. Michael Moss, "HealthSouth's CEO Exposes, Sues Online Critics," *The Wall Street Journal*, 7 July 1999.

4. Jamie Kizzire and Daniel Jackson, "23 Weeks, a Parade of Witnesses," *Birmingham Post-Herald*, 30 June 2005.

5. Carrick Mollenkamp, "Behind Scrushy's Courtroom Defenese: Shifting Teams and Feuding Lawyers," *The Wall Street Journal*, 2 February 2005.

6. Ibid.

7. Ibid.

8. Ibid.

9. Ed Welles, "The Player," *Fortune–Small Business,* June 2002.

10. Mollenkamp, "Behind Scrushy's Courtroom Defenese."

11. Ibid.

12. Dan Ackerman, "Richard Scrushy, Still Uncharged Is Unfrozen," *Forbes*, 8 May 2003.

13. Mollenkamp, "Behind Scrushy's Courtroom Defenese."

14. Stephen Taub, "Scrushy Lays the Blame on His CFOs," *CFO Magazine*, 15 October 2003.

15. Mollenkamp, "Behind Scrushy's Courtroom Defenese."

16. Lance Griffin, "A Hick with a Heart," *The Dothan Eagle*, 21 December 2004.

17. Ibid.

18. Kyle Whitmire, "Scrushy Watch: Third of Five HealthSouth CFOs Finishes Testimony," *The Birmingham Weekly*, Vol. 8, Issue 28, 17–24 March 2005.

19. Mollenkamp, "Behind Scrushy's Courtroom Defenese."

20. http://www.richardscrushy.com.

21. Greg Farrell, "Former HealthSouth CEO Scrushy Turns Televangelist," *USA Today*, 25 October 2004.

22. American Association of Community Colleges, Alumni Awards 2000: Richard Scrushy, http://www.aacc.nche.edu.

23. On his Web site, http://www.richardmscrushy.com, Scrushy claims Farrell's *USA Today* article of October 25, 2004, is wrong on several points, including when he joined the Guiding Light Church. Though Scrushy doesn't specify exactly when he began attending the Guiding Light church, he states on his Web site that it was "sev-

eral months" before his indictment. The Web site article doesn't dispute the contributions to either church.

24. Michael Tomberlin, "Scrushy Foundation Gave $1.05 million to Guiding Light," *The Birmingham News*, 24 February 2005.

25. Simon Romero (contr. Glynn Wilson), "Will the Real Richard Scrushy Please Step Forward; Race, Religion and the HealthSouth Founder's Trial," *The New York Times*, 17 February 2005.

26. Farrell, "Former HealthSouth CEO Scrushy Turns Televangelist."

27. Simon Romero, "Will the Real Richard Scrushy Please Step Forward; Race, Religion and the HealthSouth Founder's Trial."

28. United States of America v Richard M. Scrushy, CR-03-BE-530-S, Transcript, Opening Comments. Transcripts are also available for purchase from the court: Court Reporter Teresa Roberson, 1-205-492-2483, 1729 North 5th Avenue, Birmingham, Alabama 35203.

29. Kyle Whitmire, "Spin Cycle," *Birmingham Weekly*, 30 June 2005.

30. Verna Gates, "Testimony Focuses on Beam's Memory," *Birmingham Business Journal*, 27 January 2005.

31. "Scrushy Ordered 'Fix,' Says Ex-CFO Beam: Admits Certifying False Profit Figures," *The Birmingham News*, 27 January 2005.

32. United States of America v Richard M. Scrushy, Court Transcripts, Day 16, also described in Kyle Whitmire, "Week Four: Revenge of the Nerd," Scrushy Watch Week Four, *The Birmingham Weekly*, 24 February–3 March 2005.

33. Carrie Johnson, "Jury Hears Tapes in Scrushy's Fraud Trial," *The Washington Post*, 10 February 2005.

34. Ibid.

35. Ibid.

36. Phil Smith, "Week Seven Update," Scrushy-Report.com, 11 March 2005.

37. Kyle Whitmire, "Third of Five HealthSouth CFOs Finishes Testimony, Day 25," *The Birmingham Weekly*, 30 June 2005.

38. Yahoo! Finance HRC Message Board, Message #273949, 9 March 2005.

39. United States of America v Richard M. Scrushy, Court Transcripts, Day 27.

40. Ibid., Court Transcripts, Day 24.

41. Kyle Whitmire, "Untying Loose Ends," *The Birmingham Weekly*, Volume 8 Issue 37, 19–26 May 2005.

42. Ibid.

43. United States of America v Richard M. Scrushy, Transcript, Closing Arguments, Volume LVIII, 18 May 2005.

44. Jamie Kizzire, "Lawyers Use Theatrics in Closing," *Birmingham Post-Herald*, 3 June 2005.

45. Dan Morse and Evelina Shmukler, "Judge Tosses Out a Sarbanes Count in Scrushy Trial," *The Wall Street Journal*, 22 April 2005.

46. Note that Parkman's term chitlin' refers to chitterlings, a traditional Southern soul food, made from the well-cleaned small intestines of hogs. Traditionally, they are cooked out-of-doors because of their strong smell.

47. United States of America v Richard M. Scrushy, Transcript, Closing Arguments, Volume LVIII, 18 May 2005.

48. Ibid.

49. Ibid.

50. From the Web site of the National Park Service: Edmund Pettus Bridge (Landmark): On "Bloody Sunday," March 7, 1965, some 600 civil rights marchers headed east out of Selma on U.S. Route 80. They got only as far as the Edmund Pettus Bridge six blocks away, where state and local lawmen attacked them with billy clubs and tear gas and drove them back into Selma. http://www.cr.nps.gov/nr/travel/civilrights/al4.htm.

51. United States of America v Richard M. Scrushy, Transcript, Closing Day.

52. Ibid.

53. Ibid.

54. Ibid.

55. Carrie Johnson, "Judge Spurs Deadlocked Scrushy Jury," *The Washington Post*, Saturday, 4 June 2005.

56. Ibid.

57. Jay Reeves, "Scrushy Jury Ordered to Start Talks Anew," The Associated Press, 22 June 2005.

58. Val Walton, "Jurors Say They Doubted Government Witnesses," *The Birmingham News*, 28 June 2005.

59. Karen Jacobs (for Reuters), "Ex-HealthSouth CEO Scrushy Found Not Guilty," *The Washington Post*, 28 June 2005.

60. Daniel Jackson, "Tension Turns to Joy for Scrushy, His Lawyers," *Birmingham Post-Herald*, 29 June 2005.

61. "Scrushy 'Not Guilty' on All Counts," WFSA-TV, Montgomery, Alabama, http://www.wsfa.com/Global/story.asp?S=3530467.

62. Jacobs, "Ex-HealthSouth CEO Scrushy Found Not Guilty."

63. Dan Morse and Chad Terhune, "HealthSouth's Scrushy Is Acquitted," *The Wall Street Journal*, 29 June 2005.

Epilogue

1. Reed Abelson and Johathan Glater, "A Style That Connected with Hometown Jurors," *The New York Times*, 29 June 2005.

2. Russ Britt, "Scrushy Acquitted on All Charges," *MarketWatch*, 28 June 2005.

3. Krysten Crawford, "Ex-HealthSouth CEO Scrushy Walks," CNN/Money, 28 June 2005.

4. Abelson and Glater, "A Style That Connected with Hometown Jurors."

5. Greg Farrell, "Against the Odds, Scrushy Walks Out of Court a Free Man," 28 June 2005.

6. Daniel Jackson, "Inconsistencies," *Birmingham Post-Herald*, 29 June 2005.

7. Greg Farrell, "Juror Replaced by Alternate Thought Scrushy Guilty," *USA Today*, 29 June 2005.

8. Dana Hedgpeth and Dean Starkman, "From the Start, Acquittal Seemed Right," *The Washington Post*, 30 June 2005.

9. Dan Morse, Tad Cherhune, and Amy Carrns, "Clean Sweep: HealthSouth's Scrushy Is Acquitted," *The Wall Street Journal*, 29 June 2005.

10. Hedgpeth and Starkman, "From the Start, Aquittal Seemed Right."

11. Simon Romero and Kyle Whitmire, "Ex-Chief of Health-South Acquitted in Fraud Case," *The New York Times*, 29 June 2005.

12. Edward Iwata, "White-collar Crime Cases Prove Difficult to Prosecute," *USA Today*, 29 June 2005.

13. John Helyar, "CEOs on Trial," *Fortune*, 28 June 2003.

14. Farrell, "Against the Odds, Scrushy Walks Out of Court Free Man."

15. "Judge Defends Handling of Scrushy Case," The Associated Press, 30 June 2005, MSNBC.com.

16. Ann Marie Squeo, "Acquittal Casts Cloud Over the Sarbanes-Oxley Law," *The Wall Street Journal*, 29 June 2005.

17. James Brosnan, "Congress Weighs In on Verdict, Sarbanes-Oxley Law," *Birmingham Post-Herald*, 29 June 2005.

18. USDOJ/USAP/ALN, U.S. Attorney, Northern District of Alabama, Press Release, "Regarding Notice of Appeal on Perjury—Richard M. Scrushy," Statement of Alice H. Martin, 12 July 2005, http://www.usdoj.gov/usao/aln/Docs/July%202005/July%2012,%202005%20Scrushy%20Perjury.htm.

19. "Scrushy Trial, Judge Blocks Testimony, Drops Perjury Charges," *Birmingham Business Journal*, 12 April 2005.

20. "Judge Scuttles Scrushy Perjury Charges, Throws Out SEC Testimony," IT Compliance Institute, Editor, Cass Brewer, http://www.itcinstitute.com/display.aspx?ID=246.

21. Michael Tomberlin, "Scrushy Judge Bases Decision to Drop Perjury Charges on 'Overlap,'" *The Birmingham News*, 13 April 2005.

22. Peter Henning, "Back to Court for Scrushy," White Collar Crime Prof Blog, 29 June 2005, http://lawprofessors.typepad.com/whitecollarcrime_blog/2005/06/back_to_court_f.html.

23. "Prosecutors Drop Scrushy Appeal, Rule Out Second Trial," The Associated Press, 14 July 2005.

24. "Judge lets SEC file new suit over HealthSouth fraud," The Associated Press, 18 August 2000.

25. White Collar Crime Prof Blog, 29 June 2005.

26. Jay Reeves, "Legal Woes May Continue for Scrushy," ABC News, The Associated Press, 29 June 2005.

27. "HealthSouth: No Job Waiting for Scrushy," *Birmingham Business Journal*, 28 June 2005

28. Dean Foust and Brian Grow, "Scrushy Has a Score to Settle," *Businessweek*, 30 June 2005.

29. Carrie Johnson, "Jury Acquits HealthSouth Founder of All Charges," *The Washington Post*, 29 June 2005.

30. "Making Sure Crime Doesn't Pay," *The Birmingham News*, 30 August 2005.

31. You can learn more about SLAPP actions and anti-SLAPP laws at The First Amendment Project's Web site, http://www.thefirstamendment.org. The organization's anti-SLAPP Resource center offers a good overview of the legal issues surrounding this type of action, then recommends that you consult with an attorney for more detailed information and specific advice.

32. California anti-SLAPP project, http://www.casp.net/index.html.

33. Stan Morris, "The Limits of Free Speech on the Internet," attorney and member of the Editorial Board for Gigalaw.com.

34. Michael Tomberlin and Russell Hubbard, "Company Settles Suit with SEC on Fraud," *The Birmingham News*, 9 June 2005.

35. Matt Krantz, "Some Analysts See HealthSouth's Stock Poised for Comeback," *USA Today*, 29 June 2005

36. Some of those deficiencies are rapidly being repaired. HealthSouth filed its comprehensive Form 10-K for the years ended

December 31, 2000, through December 31, 2003, with the SEC (the filing can be found on the SEC's Web site at http://www.sec.gov). HealthSouth still faces the settlement of shareholder lawsuits pending during the trial.

37. All information gathered through personal communications (phone and e-mail) with the individuals referenced here.

References

Link to SEC Filings HLSH
http://finance.yahoo.com/q/sec?s=HLSH.PK

Historic Quotes HealthSouth (HLSH) from March 15, 2003
http://host.businessweek.com/businessweek/Historical
_Quotes.html?Symbol=HLSH&StartDate=3%2F15%2F03&End
Date=07%2F06%2F05&Type=1&Format=0&Button=Get+Quotes

Link to Message Board Investors stated share positions: **Instructmba**
http://finance.messages.yahoo.com/bbs?.mm=FN&board=
7076888&tid=hrc&sid=7076888&action=m&mid=72336

Link to **The_Dow_Bum**'s July 7, 2003, Gratitudes and Congratulations
to all http://finance.messages.yahoo.com/bbs?.mm=FN&board=
7076888&tid=hrc&sid=7076888&action=m&mid=80681

Link to **Corstrat**'s Perfect Storm, The Sequel
http://finance.messages.yahoo.com/bbs?.mm=FN&board=
7076888&tid=hrc&sid=7076888&action=m&mid=70872

Index